D1334604

TECHNOLOGICAL TRANSFORMATION IN THE THIRD WORLD
VOLUME III: LATIN AMERICA

The World Institute for Development Economics Research (UNU/WIDER) was established by the United Nations University as its first research and training centre and started work in Helsinki, Finland in 1985. The principal purpose of the Institute is to help identify and meet the need for policy-oriented socio-economic research on pressing global and development problems, as well as common domestic problems and their inter-relationships.

The Institute for New Technologies (UNU/INTECH) is the second research and training centre established by the United Nations University and started work in Maastricht, The Netherlands in 1990. The Institute's work is devoted to policy oriented-research and advanced training and advisory activities in the area of new technologies, with primary focus on the social and economic implications of these technologies for developing countries.

World Institute for Development Economics Research (UNU/WIDER)
Annankatu 42 C
00100 Helsinki, Finland

Institute for New Technologies (UNU/INTECH)
Kapoenstraat 23
6211 KV Maastricht, The Netherlands

Technological Transformation in the Third World

Volume III: Latin America

General Editor
SURENDRA J. PATEL
UNU/WIDER

A project of the
World Institute for Development Economics Research (UNU/WIDER)
Helsinki, Finland
and the
Institute for New Technologies (UNU/INTECH)
Maastricht, The Netherlands
of the
United Nations University

Avebury

Aldershot · Brookfield USA · Hong Kong · Singapore · Sydney

Published by
Avebury
Ashgate Publishing Limited
Gower House
Croft Road
Aldershot
Hants GU11 3HR
England

Ashgate Publishing Company
Old Post Road
Brookfield
Vermont 05036
USA

A CIP catalogue record for this book is available from the British Library

Typeset by
Anne Ruohonen and Liisa Roponen
UNU/WIDER

ISBN 1 85628 471 9
(Four-volume set ISBN 1 85628 473 5)

Printed and Bound in Great Britain by
Athenaeum Press Ltd., Newcastle upon Tyne.

Contents

Contents   v
List of tables and figures   vii

Foreword   xii
Lal Jayawardena and Charles Cooper

Preface   xiv
Surendra J. Patel
  I   The golden age of south's development   xiv
  II   The framework of approach   xvi
  III Technological transformation: Volume III - Latin
      America   xix
  IV Acknowledgements   xx
      Appendix   xxi
      Notes   xxv

Mexico   1
Miguel S. Wionczek and Miguel H. Márquez
  I   Introduction   3
  II   The start of the industrialization process   9
  III Growth without structural change   16
  IV The technological development process   25

V   Technological development policies   44
VI   Concluding assessment   50
VII Annex - Domestic technological capability: the
     contribution of the Instituto Mexicano del Petróleo
     (IMP) (Mexican Petroleum Institute)   54
VIII Appendix   63
     Notes   90
     References   96

Puerto Rico   101
Sandor Boyson
     Preface   103
I   Introduction and aims of the study   105
II   The Puerto Rico case study: overview of the
     transformation process   108
III Overcoming technological stagnation: Operation
     Bootstrap and the rise of the industrialization strategy 129
IV   Part one: The rise of high-tech manufacturing   146
IV   Part two: The pharmaceutical industry: a driving force
     in the rise of high-tech manufacturing   153
V   The rise of the information sector   168
VI   Conclusions   197
VII Appendix   221
     Notes and references   232

Venezuela   237
Alfonso Cordido J. and Luis Matos A.
I   Introduction   239
II   Socio-economic change and technological transformation 241
III Structural changes   245
IV   Procurement of technological capacity   251
V   Management of the technological transformation process 260
VI   Conclusion   264
VII Tables and figures   266
     Notes   312
     References   314

List of tables and figures

Mexico

Tables

2.1	Structure and characteristics of the manufacturing industry by branches: 1950	12
2.2	Investment and GDP growth: 1939-69	15
3.1	GDP growth rates: 1960-85	17
3.2	GDP structure and growth rates by sector: 1960-85	18
3.3	Percentage structure and growth rates for the manufacturing industry: 1960-85	19
4.1	Growth of technical education: 1970-78	33
8.1	Installed electric energy capacity	63
8.2	Electric energy production	63
8.3	Electric energy supply and consumption	63
8.4	Railway services: 1937-55	64
8.5	Road network: 1937-55	64
8.6	Motor vehicles in circulation: 1937-55	64
8.7	Evolution of the manufacturing industry: 1950-70	65
8.8	Price indexes: 1960-85	66
8.9	Gross domestic product: 1960-65	67
8.10	Per capita GDP: 1960-65	67
8.11	Manufacturing output by industrial branches: 1960-85	68
8.12	Labour force by sectors: 1960-85	69

8.13 Changes in the GDP structure and foreign trade: 1960-85   70
8.14 Merchandise exports by sectors of origin: 1960-85   71
8.15 Merchandise imports by major categories: 1960-85   72
8.16 Trade balance: 1960-85   72
8.17 Gross fixed capital formation: 1960-85   73
8.18 Sectorial distribution of gross fixed investment: 1953-67   74
8.19 Public and private investment   74
8.20 Direct foreign investment   75
8.21 Sectorial destination of the gross fixed investment   75
8.22 Investment financing   75
8.23 Gross domestic production of capital goods: 1960-85   76
8.24 Average annual growth rates of the capital goods
     production: 1960-85   77
8.25 Structure of the production of capital goods: 1970-85   78
8.26 Imports/demand ratio in final capital goods: 1970-83   78
8.27 Dynamics of labour productivity in manufacturing industry   79
8.28 Labour productivity   79
8.29 Federal expenditure for education: 1960-84   80
8.30 Expansion of the enrolment and the termination of
     studies in the Mexican educational system   81
8.31 Technology transfer payments and other foreign exchange
     transfers abroad by direct foreign investments: 1950-78   82
8.32 Gross product and technological expenditure of
     foreign-owned and domestic enterprises: 1975   82
8.33 Technological expenditure of foreign-owned enterprises
     in technology intensive sectors: 1975   83
8.34 Technological expenditure of domestic firms in
     technology intensive sectors: 1975   84
8.35 Number of registered technology transfer contracts: 1979   85
8.36 Frequency of technological elements in the contracts of
     each enterprise in four industrial goods groups: 1979   85
8.37 Major indicators of domestic expenditure in scientific
     technological activities: 1970-85   86
8.38 National science and technology council expenditures   87
8.39 Federal expenditure in science and technology   87
8.40 Functional distribution of the public sector in science
     and technology   88
8.41 Scientific and technological centres and their personnel:
     1982-83   88
8.42 Scientific publications in Mexico: 1984   89
8.43 Applications for registration of patents to the end of 1980   89

Puerto Rico
Tables
2.1 Changes in real GDP: 1950-87   109
2.2 GDP by economic sectors - selected years   113

2.3	Changes in branch shares of manufacturing value added: 1950-87	114
2.4	Sectoral distribution of labour	115
2.5	Changes in branch shares of employment in manufacturing industry: 1961-87	117
2.6	Changes in trade and its structure: 1950-86	119
2.7	The socio-economic infrastructure: selected indicators	121
2.8	Income share of poorest 40% of families, selected Latin American countries	121
2.9	A comparison of US annual direct investment in manufacturing in Puerto Rico, Latin America and all developing countries: 1953-69	123
2.10	A comparison of US accumulated direct investment in manufacturing in Puerto Rico, Latin America and all developing countries: 1953-69	124
4.1	Tax savings for sixteen companies resulting from 936 operations	151
4.2	Distribution of Fomento plants operating by municipality and tax exemption period	158
4.3	Manufacturing strategic alternatives - financial comparisons	161
5.1	Expenditures on education and training: 1972-87	173
5.2	Research and Development in industry: 1982-87	175
5.3	Total university research expenditures: 1979-87	176
5.4	The rise of the communications services sector: 1972-87	178
5.5	The communications sector: indices of market penetration: 1988	179
5.6	The growth of the electronics sector - SIC major group 36	181
5.7	Import/export profile of the telematics industry	183
5.8	The growth of selected 'knowledge intensive' services: 1972-87	186
5.9	The growth of the computing services industry: 1977-87	186
5.10	Knowledge production	188
5.11	The relative growth of the information sector viz-a-viz the rest of the economy	191
7.1	Changes in value added per employee in manufacturing industry: 1952-87	222
7.2	Changes in value added per employee in services industry: 1952-87	225

Figures

2.1	World economies showing the fastest rates of growth: 1965-80	111
2.2	Comparison between gross domestic product and investment: 1980-85	126

5.1	University enrolment as a percentage of the 18-22 age bracket	171
5.2	Public investment in education as a per cent of total expenditures by the central government: 1985	172
5.3	Fortune 500 companies - manufacturing in Puerto Rico (map)	182
7.1	Importance of section 936 at the international level	227
7.2	Employment of production workers: 1971-86	229
7.3	Employment distribution in manufacturing: high-tech and other industries	230
7.4	Export distribution per industrial group	230
7.5	Relative importance of high-tech industries in national income: Puerto Rico and United States	231

Venezuela

Tables

7.1	Main agricultural exports: 1903/04-1927/28	267
7.2	Oil export, volume and value: 1920/21-1929/30	267
7.3	Venezuela's imports and exports: 1920-42	268
7.4	Dutch-British and US capital investment in Venezuela: 1912 and 1929	268
7.5	Oil income and its share in the regular income totals	269
7.6	Composition of imports: 1913 and 1926	270
7.7	Share of national production and imports in the total private goods consumption	271
7.8	Investment structure: 1945-56	272
7.9	Gross fixed investment per capital stock type	273
7.10	Sectorial share of GNP: 1950-76	274
7.11	Sectorial share of the industrial product	275
7.12A	Public and private gross fixed investment	276
7.12B	Fixed gross investment	276
7.13	Import of capital goods: 1973-75	277
7.14	Investment in concrete projects by developing agencies	278
7.15	Total gross fixed investment: 1970-80	280
7.16	Public investment: 1976-80	281
7.17	Balance of payments in current account	283
7.18	Real gross fixed investment	284
7.19	Balance of payments, general summary	285
7.20A	Accumulated flows of international transactions, nominal flows	286
7.20B	Accumulated flows of international transactions, real flows	286
7.21	Manufacturing enterprises of the public sector, non-traditional products; production, domestic sales and exports	287
7.22	Exports per sectors and products	287

7.23	Gross fixed investment per sectors	288
7.24	Share of financial resources assigned to science and technology activities within GDP: 1978-85	289
7.25	Expenditure on research and development as a percentage share of world GNP	290
7.26	Students enrolled according to educational levels: 1948-76	291
7.27	Students enrolled in secondary education according to branches: 1948-76	292
7.28	Sectors having state participation	293
7.29	Demographic indicators given in five year periods: 1960/65-1975/80	295
7.30	Structure of industrial production: 1970-79	295
7.31	Evolution of the ratio of investment and investment composition and financing	296
7.32	Ratio evolution of the import, export and purchasing power of services and goods exports	296
7.33	GNP per person employed in each sector: 1978 and 1983	297
7.34	Volume of agricultural production: 1978 and 1983	297
7.35	Behaviour of GNP: 1957 and 1973	298
7.36	Behaviour of GNP per sector: 1957 and 1973	299
7.37	Sectorial share of GNP: 1957 and 1973	299
7.38	GNP per person employed in each sector: 1957 and 1973	300
7.39	Behaviour of GNP: 1973 and 1978	300
7.40	External sector indicators	301
7.41	Volume of agricultural production: 1957 and 1973	301
7.42	Volume of industrial production: 1957 and 1973	302
7.43	GNP composition at market prices	302

Figures
7.1	Behaviour of GNP: 1957 and 1973	303
7.2	Sectorial share of GNP: 1957 and 1973	304
7.3	Sectorial behaviour of GNP: 1957 and 1973	305
7.4	GNP per person employed in each sector: 1957 and 1973	306
7.5	Volume of agricultural production: 1957 and 1973	307
7.6	Volume of industrial production: 1957 and 1973	308
7.7	Behaviour of GNP: 1973 and 1978	309
7.8	GNP per person employed in each sector: 1978 and 1983	310
7.9	Volume of agricultural production: 1978 and 1983	311

Foreword

Lal Jayawardena and Charles Cooper

The papers which are presented in this series of volumes, result from a major research project carried out, under the leadership of Dr. Surendra J. Patel, at the World Institute for Development Economics Research of the United Nations University (UNU/WIDER) in Helsinki. Dr. Surendra J. Patel had been for many years Head of the Technology Division at UNCTAD.

Whilst Dr. Patel's project was in progress, the United Nations University and the Government of the Netherlands reached an agreement to set up a new institute at Maastricht in the Netherlands, to carry out policy research on the economic and social impacts and implications of new technologies, especially in the developing countries. The new institute is the UNU Institute for New Technologies (UNU/INTECH). It is a sister institute to UNU/WIDER, within the UNU system.

Given the mandate of UNU/INTECH, it was obvious to us, as Directors of the Institutes, that Dr. Patel's project should become a joint undertaking. That is why the books in this series are published under the names of both UNU/WIDER and UNU/INTECH. We expect that there will be further joint undertakings in the future.

Dr. Patel focused the country studies, on which the project is based, towards 'technological transformation' within national economies. This reflected his own perceptions, formed by his experience at UNCTAD, that technological change (and policies to promote it) are given too little attention by policy makers concerned with economic development. Experience in some of the Newly Industrializing Countries (NICs) strongly suggested to some that technological policies played an important part in their success, especially in the rapid and sustained increase in factor productivities on which that success was based. Others, who accept that factor productivity growth has made significant contributions to economic growth, both directly and through sustaining international competitivenes, are more doubtful about the role of policy in the process. Dr. Patel's project seeks to illuminate these issues. From the beginning it was obvious that the studies had to extend beyond the NICs to include other countries where the emphasis on technology policy was either less marked or different in orientation.

It is inherently very difficult to conclude the arguments between those who see technology policy as instrumental in technological change, and those who are sceptical about state intervention in this field. At the centre of the debate is the claim that, in the countries where productivity growth has been important in economic development, technological change would have been as, or even more rapid if there had been no policy interventions. The difficulty is, of course, that this is a counterfactual claim, which is by its nature impossible to prove or to disprove in any particular case. Nevertheless, it is possible that comparative studies can help to inform our judgements on this important matter, even though they do not completely resolve the basic methodological difficulty. The strength and interest of Dr. Patel's project is that it has this internationally comparative orientation. It will be for his readers to judge the evidence, which he and his distinguished colleagues have assembled.

Lal Jayawardena
Director
UNU/WIDER

Charles Cooper
Director
UNU/INTECH

Preface

Surendra J. Patel

The thirty years since the end of the World War II have been the golden age of political liberation, economic growth and technological progress. Tidal waves of independence movements swept the colonies and dependencies. Empires much larger than any that existed in the past, crumbled like sandcastles in a matter of only a few short years. New and independent nation states were born. The world political map, altered beyond recognition, was completely redrawn.

Meanwhile, the global economy grew at an unprecedented pace. Its total output more than quadrupled. Scientific discoveries piled on one another. The process of technological transformation was swift. New nations adopted processes and techniques that had only recently been invented. Hope spread like wild fire - in the spirit of Shelly's immortal lyric 'Prometheus Unbound' - where man: 'tortured to his will iron and gold, the slaves and signs of power...' But the extravagant visions and promises of that era were smothered in a series of crises beginning in the mid-1970s.[1]

I The golden age of south's development

Concern with contemporary crises has completely overshadowed the real advances achieved in the 35 years since 1950.[2] The overall GDP of the third world has increased some six times, and per capita GDP 2.5 times, since 1950. Its industrial output is now 11 times higher than in the 1950s.

Technology embodying inputs in these countries have expanded even more impressively. For instance, annual real gross capital formation is now 15 times higher. Enrolment in the third level of learning at universities and institutes of higher education, have simply exploded - rising nearly 25 fold. Educational infrastructure, the foundation for sustained development in the future, has been laid with great effort and sacrifice.

Social advance, particularly in health, was simply spectacular. Infant mortality rates fell from 200 per thousand to between 30 to 70. Death rates declined from 25-30 to only 10-15. And life expectancy rose from below 40 years to about 65. With a spectacular sprint, the south had within less than 40 years caught up with the north of the 1960s.

The average annual rates of growth in these strategic areas, sustained for 35 years since 1950, were impressive - some 5.5 per cent for GDP, 7.5 per cent for industrial output, 8.4 per cent for capital formation, and 10 per cent for third level education. They were much higher than during comparable periods in the technological transformation of the north. Moreover, they were sustained long enough to create a highly visible effect.[3]

Consequent structural changes in the third world were profound. The share of agricultural output in GDP has fallen from about one third to one sixth. Conversely, that of industry has risen from about one sixth to about one third. Industry related services have expanded their share parallel to that of industry.

Shares of the technology embodying inputs have risen much more. Capital formation has increased from 7 per cent of GDP to over 25 per cent in 1980 - generally above that in most countries of the north. Structures of exports and imports have also witnessed similar movements. The share of primary exports has fallen. The shares of producer goods in imports, and of manufactured goods in exports, have risen significantly. Output of capital and intermediate producer goods has expanded sharply.

In consequence, the structure of industrial output in the third world is beginning to resemble that of most developed countries in the inter-war period. The actual volume, however, is of course much lower. Half a dozen developing countries now supply over two thirds of all their capital goods requirements (physical technology) from domestic sources. Another dozen countries supply over two fifths. Availability of skilled manpower, and its quality, have risen very sharply.

Professor Kuznets, reflecting on the 22-year period between 1950 and 1972, was deeply impressed by the high per capita growth rates already achieved by the third world. He considered these growth rates 'quite high in the long term perspective of both less developed countries and the developed countries.'[4] With a touch of bewilderment, he then added in 1975:

If growth rates in the per capita product of the LDCs over almost a quarter of a century were impressively high, one may ask why the reaction to them in the general flow of news about those countries, in the persistent concern about critical conditions with respect to supplies of economic goods, seems to ignore these growth achievements.

He wondered 'why no litanies of praise' were sung 'for these economic miracles'! Instead, there were only references to 'dangers of collapse in the third world.'

II The framework of approach

These vast changes have not been captured in the narrow confines of contemporary technology studies.[5] At least two reasons may have been instrumental for this. One, concern with technology issues is relatively recent in origin. Second, the literature on technology which has mushroomed over the last 15 years concentrated mainly on several micro facets. The issues covered by these studies were of course very important. They have helped advance our understanding of technological processes. But they overlooked the overall structural changes in a long term historical context.

In order to overcome this weakness, WIDER invited a group of experts to Helsinki in November 1985 to discuss the broad approach to be used in the study of technological transformation in the third world.[6] They discussed the proposals made by WIDER on a comprehensive long term programme of work of WIDER. This also included a detailed outline which was to serve as a guideline for the preparation of the individual country studies.[7] The outline was intended to assure a degree of uniformity in the preparation of the country studies, thereby facilitating a broad comparative assessment of the country experiences. A more detailed framework of our approach is given in the opening chapter of Volume V - *The Overview* of this series. Only a brief summary is therefore given here to facilitate an easier comprehension of the contents of individual country studies.

Following the expert meeting, WIDER initiated in 1985 in-depth studies of long term changes in the following 16 third world countries:

Asia:	Latin America:	Africa:	Europe:
Bangladesh	Brazil	Algeria	Yugoslavia
China (including	Island of Puerto Rico	Angola	
Province of Taiwan)	Mexico	Nigeria	
India	Peru	Tanzania	
Republic of Korea	Venezuela	Zimbabwe	
Sri Lanka			

In addition, four developed countries, Finland, Greece, Japan and the USSR were also included in the WIDER project since their technological transformation spanned the twentieth century.

It needs no emphasis that the 16 third world countries differ from one another in so many ways: for instance, in their resource endowment, climatic and soil conditions, degree of external vulnerability, size of their population, the level of development achieved, the rates of growth realized, the structure of their economies and in the policies, plans and priorities pursued by them. They are located in all the major continents.

In terms of countries, these 16 represent only a small minority of the 130 countries constituting the third world as a whole. But the small number of units is potentially misleading. In terms of their population and output, these 16 represent over 70 per cent of the third world total.

An analysis of such widely varying experiences could, it was hoped, help identify the main patterns of technological transformation which have emerged over the last 35 years. It could point to both the strengths and the weaknesses exhibited over this period. Such an effort could, it was hoped, help assess differences in the patterns of technological inputs and in the decision making process governing the acquisition, use, adaptation, diffusion, improvement and innovation of technologies. It could also improve our understanding of both the quantitative and qualitative implications of changes in several parameters which, as an ensemble, could be considered to constitute the process of technological transformation.

The full realization of the technological possibilities open to a country is governed by a number of factors. They are at once economic, social, political and cultural in character. Some are internal to the country while others are external in origin. In combination, they govern the pace of technological transformation and period over which this happens.

The WIDER project, it is hoped, would at least begin charting the trajectories along which the technological transformation in the third world might have proceeded. This is not to imply that such a dynamic process can be imprisoned in the strait-jacket of a rigid structure.[8] Freezing this process into the mould of a rigid definition would not therefore be very meaningful.

It should also be underlined that technological transformation is a process that is much wider in scope than is industrial development. It does include industrial development, but also includes many aspects of agricultural production, as well as development of infrastructure and services. Indeed, the entire economic system is involved in the process of transformation.

Its scope is also wider than that of economic growth,[9] or economic development - a term which has more recently begun to become the current coin.[10] Beyond the simple rate of economic growth, and beyond the rate of capital formation which is conventionally invoked for economic growth, technological transformation includes in particular the influence on growth of human capital formation and associated productivity increases, as well as the impact of major institutional, political, and social innovations on the productive system in general. These differences should not, however, be pushed too far. Economic growth looks at the outputs, and technological transformation at the inputs: these are after all two sides of the same coin, the process of production.

It is only possible to chart aspects on which data are more readily available. They include a number of crucial points and widely recognized essential profiles. A list of these would certainly include:

- The rate of growth of GDP and per capita GDP
- Changes in the structure of production
- Changes in the structure of trade
- Domestic production of machinery and equipment
- Availability of advanced education
- Infant mortality rate
- Literacy rate
- Consumption of energy per capita

None of these indicators yield absolute targets to be aimed at. Technological transformation is a process - not as a finite objective which, once attained, loses its validity. Several elements of this process may be identified as landmarks, marking the changing terrain of the journey. Like any process, or passage through time, technological transformation too traverses several phases and sub-phases with overlapping interludes. Economic historians have always been fascinated by these. They have attempted to divide the process into its major components. These categorical classifications have too often provoked lively but diversionary controversies among contemporary scholars. Often the heat of this debate has had little relationship to its usefulness. Most schemes later proved too rigid for predictive purposes or policy formation.

Technological transformation is a process so recent in its arrival, so short in its duration, so meteoric in its pace; almost contagious in its spread to so many countries and continents. These countries each have their own specific domestic features. They have faced widely varying external environments, including the historical stock of technological innovations they could draw upon, and their ease of access to that stock. They have varied in the development of their own technological capabilities.

The experience of the 20 countries analysed under the WIDER project was reviewed at the WIDER Conference on Technological Transformation in the Third World, held in Helsinki from August 19 to 23, 1988.[11] A review of the drafts of the studies suggested that 13 of them together with an Overview should be published as a joint project of the two Institutes of the United Nations University: the World Institute for Development Economics Research (UNU/WIDER, Helsinki, Finland) and the newly established Institute for New Technologies (UNU/INTECH, Maastricht, The Netherlands). The studies were grouped into four volumes as follows:

I   Asia
II   Africa
III   Latin America
IV   Developed countries

A fifth volume, an Overview by Surendra J. Patel, will also be added to the series as a concluding contribution to the WIDER project.

These volumes owe a heavy debt to past contributions on the subject. This applies particularly to Volume V - the Overview. We have drawn freely upon the vast research effort which has gone into development economics, economic history, technology studies in general, and country studies in particular. The intellectual debt we owe to these contributions is simply enormous. If many of them are missing in the list of references, it is in no way meant to detract from our debt to them.

III Technological transformation: Volume III - Latin America

The third volume in this series contains three studies from Latin America: Mexico, Puerto Rico, and Venezuela. The study on Mexico was prepared by Professors Miguel S. Wionczek and Miguel H. Márquez from El Colegio de Mexico. Dr Sandor Boyson, Science and Technology Coordinator of the Governor's Economic Advisory Council in San Juan, has prepared the study on the island of Puerto Rico. The third study on Venezuela was prepared by Drs Alfonso Cordido J. and Luis Matos A., Caracas; since the study was originally written in Spanish, it has been translated into English by Mr Juan M. Mallea.

I am indebted to the authors of these three studies and their collaborators, who have attempted to capture the moving image of a complex, dynamic process into a readable story. These studies bring out sharply the processes at work in Latin America between 1950 and 1980, which were responsible for the crisis that the continent faced in the 1980s. In each case there was a striking failure in building up national technological capability so that the country could grapple with the grave problems it faced in the 1980s. In a certain sense, the three countries portray a mirror image of the crises faced by the rest of the continent during the *lost decade* of the 1980s.

The countries covered here of course differ significantly from one another. It is therefore hazardous to draw close parallels. Too often, both the causes and the consequences for each country differ by several degrees from those for other countries. In that sense, these three countries also differ significantly from one another.

Mexico is perhaps the most advanced country in Latin America. It has common border with the United States in the north; and it had followed in general policies of close cooperation with the enterprises from the United States. Despite its suddenly found oil wealth, it failed during the 1980s to handle its debt and development crisis. The imprint of that crisis still lingers on in its real per capita remaining practically at the 1980 level.

In contrast to Mexico, Puerto Rico is a tiny island which, owing to its special status with the United States, can hardly be described as a country. Its experience underlines the striking structural transformation which it had achieved in part by this very special relationship with the United States and in part by major emphasis given by the island on training its workforce. Despite the fast growth upto late 1970s, Puerto Rico too, like other Latin American countries, continues to be severely affected by the recession and slow growth in the United States in the 1980s.

Venezuela sits somewhere between the two extreme cases cited above. A dominant proportion of its national output was derived from exports of crude petroleum. Several attempts were made to spread the benefits from oil revenues to the rest of the population, and to build up a degree of self-reliant industrial development, particularly in oil. As the authors show in detail, these attempts did not succeed due to many reasons; but perhaps the most important ones among them were the inability to foster domestic research and development facilities and strengthen national technological capability.

IV Acknowledgements

A project like this is necessarily a collective venture. It is impossible to list all those who helped the process. But there are some who merit special mention for without their cooperation the project would have been neither initiated, nor completed.

I wish to thank Dr Lal Jayawardena, the Director of UNU/WIDER who encouraged me to initiate this project and helped towards the completion of the country studies. I am indebted to Professor Charles Cooper, the Director of the newly established Institute of New Technologies (UNU/INTECH), who assisted me in selecting the studies for publication.

It has been a pleasure to have the help of Ms Anne Ruohonen, who from the very outset of the project in 1985 has worked very closely with me to ensure the completion of this project. She has gone through several drafts of the country studies as they came in, and meticulously prepared the final print-ready manuscript. I owe special thanks to Ms Liisa Roponen who has with remarkable patience prepared and checked all the tables and charts in the text. In addition I wish to thank Ms Ann Halme and Ms Abby Johnson for their substantial contribution to the typing of the country studies.

Surendra J. Patel
General Editor
UNU/WIDER

Appendix

Lists of participants in UNU/WIDER meetings on Development and
Technological Transformation in the Third World: Progress Achieved
and Problems Faced

Planning Meeting, Helsinki 23-25 November 1985

Participants

Abu A. Abdullah
BIDS
Dhaka, Bangladesh

Ojetunji Aboyade
PAI Associates International
Ibadan, Nigeria

M.R. Bhagavan
The Beijer Institute, The Royal
  Swedish Academy of Sciences
Stockholm, Sweden

Ajit S. Bhalla
Technology & Employm. Branch
ILO
Geneva, Switzerland

Charles Cooper
UNU/INTECH
Maastricht, The Netherlands

Eduardo A.A. Guimaraes
Brazilian Institute of Geography
  and Statistics (IBGE)
Rio de Janeiro, Brazil

Jeffrey James
World Development Institute
Boston University
Boston, MA, USA

Linsu Kim
School of Business Administrat.
Korea University
Seoul, Republic of Korea

Felipe M. Medalla
School of Economics
University of the Philippines
Quezon City, the Philippines

Wilfred S. Nanayakkara
International Economic Co-operation
  Division
Ministry of Finance and Planning
Colombo, Sri Lanka

Prafulla Sanghvi
National Council of Applied
  Economic Research
New Delhi, India

Paul Streeten
Economic Development Institute
World Bank
Washington, DC, USA

Pentti Vartia
Research Institute of the Finnish
  Economy (ETLA)
Helsinki, Finland

Zhang Wei
Tsinghua University
Beijing, China

Masafumi Nagao
Sasakawa Peace Foundation
Tokyo, Japan

Geoff Oldham
Science Policy Research Unit
University of Sussex
Brighton, UK

Jon Sigurdson
Research Policy Institute
University of Lund
Lund, Sweden

Mikoto Usui
Institute of Socio-Economic
  Planning, University of Tsukuba
Tokyo, Japan

Aurelie von Wartensleben
Advisory Service on Transfer of
  Technology (ASTT), UNCTAD
Geneva, Switzerland

Research Adviser

Surendra J. Patel
UNU/WIDER
Helsinki, Finland

Conference Secretary

Anne Ruohonen
UNU/WIDER
Helsinki, Finland

Research Conference, Helsinki 19-23 August 1988

<u>Participants</u>

Abu A. Abdullah
Bangladesh Institute of Development
  Studies
Dhaka, Bangladesh

Abdellatif Benachenhou
Division of Development Studies
UNESCO
Paris, France

M.R. Bhagavan
The Beijer Institute, The Royal
  Swedish Academy of Sciences
Stockholm, Sweden

Carsten Blennow
Research Policy Institute
University of Lund
Lund, Sweden

Sandor Boyson
Governor's Economic Advisory Council
San Juan, Puerto Rico

Mohamed B.E. Fayez
National Research Centre
Cairo, Egypt

Tassos Giannitsis
University of Athens
Athens, Greece

Eduardo A.A. Guimaraes
Brazilian Institute of Geography
  and Statistics (IBGE)
Rio de Janeiro, Brazil

Linsu Kim
School of Business Administration
Korea University
Seoul, Republic of Korea

Miguel H. Márquez
El Colegio de Mexico
Mexico City, Mexico

Luis Matos A.
Caracas, Venezuela

Wilfred S. Nanayakkara
UNDP
Lalitpur, Nepal

Iz. Osayimwese
Dept. of Economics and Statistics
University of Benin
Benin City, Nigeria

Francisco R. Sagasti
Strategic Planning Division
The World Bank
Washington, DC, USA

Georgy Skorov
Institute of the USA and Canada
Moscow, USSR

K.K. Subrahmanian
Centre for Development Studies
Trivandrum, Kerala, India

Marjan Svetlicic
Research Centre for Co-operation
  with Developing Countries
Ljubljana, Yugoslavia

Mikoto Usui
UNIDO
Vienna, Austria

Constantine V. Vaitsos
University of Athens
Athens, Greece

Samuel M. Wangwe
UNU/INTECH
Maastricht, The Netherlands

Pentti Vartia
Research Institute of the Finnish
 Economy (ETLA)
Helsinki, Finland

Zhang Wei
Tsinghua University
Beijing, China

Special invitees

Amir Jamal
Embassy of the United Republic of
 Tanzania
Geneva, Switzerland

Masafumi Nagao
Sasakawa Peace Foundation
Tokyo, Japan

Ashok Parthasarathi
Ministry of Science and Technology
New Delhi, India

Manmohan Singh
The South Commission
Geneva, Switzerland

Paul Streeten
Economic Development Institute
World Bank
Washington, DC, USA

Synnöve Vuori
Research Institute of the Finnish
 Economy (ETLA)
Helsinki, Finland

Saara Kehusmaa-Pekonen
PRODEC
Helsinki School of Economics
Helsinki, Finland

Massimo Ricottilli
Universitá degli Studi di Bologna
Bologna, Italy

Pu Shan
Institute of World Economics
 and Politics
Beijing, China

Ivan Sronek
Praha, Czechoslovakia

Fedi Vaivio
Helsinki School of Economics
Helsinki, Finland

Research Adviser

Surendra J. Patel
UNU/WIDER
Helsinki, Finland

Conference Secretary

Anne Ruohonen
UNU/WIDER
Helsinki, Finland

Notes

1. See Annual Reports by UNCTAD, United Nations and its Regional Commissions, and specialized agencies, the World Bank.
2. For details see Patel, Surendra J., 'In Tribute to the Golden Age of South's Development', in *World Development*, June-July 1992; 'The South Commission: Main Lines of its Action', Paper presented to the Commission in March 1988. See also the author's 'Age of the Third World', in *The Third World Quarterly*, January 1983, vol. 5, no. 3; 'L'age du Tiers Monde est Proche' in *Le Temps Strategique*, Geneva, no. 2, Automne 1982; and in Spanish in *Comercio Exterior*, Mexico, June 1983.
3. Paul Streeten called the post-war development process 'a spectacular, unprecedented, an unexpected success'. p. 11. The word 'unexpected' (Streeten) gives an insight into how development economists had rated the growth prospects for the third world - not very highly at all. The tone of the discussion was set as early as the 1951 Report of the first United Nations Expert Group (1951), *Measures for the Economic Development of Under-Developed Countries*, New York. In that report, the experts, including Prof. Arthur W. Lewis among them, had called for a minimum net investment equalling 20 per cent of the national income of these countries (one half of it to be financed mainly by the United States). Such huge investments, they concluded, might raise their national income by about '2.5 per cent'. The per capita

figure would have been only 1.25 per cent, since they had estimated population to grow at 1.25 per annum (p. 78). But in order to avoid giving too low a figure, and to add a touch of optimism, they simply rounded it upwards to 2 per cent!
The implicit incremental capital output ratio was 8 on a net basis, and possibly as high as 11 or 12 on a gross basis.

4.   Kuznets, Simon (1975), *Aspects of Post-World War II Growth in Less Developed Countries*, Economic Growth Center, Yale University, Discussion Paper no. 234. See footnote 9 below for some details on the background to this query. See also Morawetz, David (1977), *Twenty-five Years of Economic Development, 1950 to 1975*, Baltimore, Md., Johns Hopkins University Press. Streeten, Paul and Associates (1981), *First Things First: Meeting Basic Human Needs in Developing Countries*, Oxford University Press, Maddison, Angus; (1982), *Phases of Capitalist Development*, Oxford University Press, New York.

Professor Lewis, for example, had been earlier very sceptical about the capacity of the developing countries to grow at even 4 per cent, which he considered to be 'so difficult to obtain that it is really quite an ambitious target'. See Institute of Development Economics, *Economic Digest*, vol. 3, no. 4, Winter 1960, p. 3. But while receiving the Nobel prize in Economics in Stockholm in December 1979, he drew attention to the much higher growth rates which these countries had achieved. His tone changed. He concluded:

> Some people were even more surprised by the performance of the LDCs. In 1950 these people were sceptical of the capacity of the LDCs to grow rapidly because of inappropriate attitudes, institutions or climates. The sun was thought to be too hot for hard work, or the people too spendthrift, the government too corrupt, the fertility rate too high, the religion too otherworldly, and so on. This kind of analysis has now almost completely disappeared from the literature... I think the LDCs have demonstrated beyond doubt their ability to use physical and human resources productively.

See Lewis (1980), 'The slowing down of the Engine of Growth' (revised version) in the *American Economic Review*, vol. 70, no. 4, Sept. 1980, pp. 555-64.

5.   WIDER (1985), 'Technological Transformation of the Third World: Progress Achieved and Problems Faced', WIDER/TT/1.2, pp. 1-3, unpublished project outline.

6.   See Appendix for a list of the participants.

7.   Op. cit. footnote 5, pp. 3-7, and Annex II 'An Indicative Outline for the Country Studies', pp. 9-22, including 9 table formats.

8.   Like science, technology has many facets. In his extensive review in *Science and Progress* (no. 146, 1949) of Bernal's *The Social Function of Science*, Professor Dingle listed ten different ways in which Bernal

used the word *science*, or *scientific*, and demanded that Bernal define precisely what he meant by science. In response, Bernal cited Einstein and Black in support of his position, and stated that: 'With any concept so wide-ranging in time, connection and category, multiplicity of aspect and reference must be the rule. The words science and scientific have a number of different meanings according to the context in which they are used.' Bernal, J.D. (1965), *Science in History*, Penguin Books, p. 31. He had earlier already stated in his preface that 'Science throughout is taken in a very broad sense and nowhere do I attempt to cramp it into a definition... Science, in one aspect, is ordered technique; in another, it is rationalized mythology' (p. 3). He also noted that '...the real source of wealth lies no longer in raw materials, the labour force or machines, but in having a scientific, educated, technological manpower base. Education has become the real wealth of the new age.' (p. 17).

9. Kuznets, S.S. (1966), *Modern Economic Growth: Rate, Structure and Spread*, New Haven, Yale University Press. He defines modern economic growth as an *economic epoch*, a relatively longer period extending well over a century. It is characterized by the epochal innovation of 'the extended application of science to the problems of economic production' (p. 9). Some epochal innovations 'may be largely technological', he stated, but 'the exploitation of the potential of growth provided by them usually requires much social invention - changes in arrangements by which people are induced to co-operate and participate in economic activity.' (p. 5) What Kuznets calls 'social invention' may be more appropriately termed social inventions and innovations, or simply 'social technology' as has been done in our study. In this connection see also the end of footnote 7 above.

10. Following the works of Lewis, W.A. in 1950 and Kuznets, S.S. in 1960s, the early emphasis in development economics was on growth of output or GNP, which was not expected to be particularly high. In reality, there was indeed an impressive growth of GNP in the developing countries since 1950. But as this did not succeed in eradicating poverty and meeting basic needs of the vast majority of the population. Some scholars, mostly untrained in the intricacies of economic measurement, intensely unhappy at this outcome even argued for *dethroning* GNP, and called for a substitution of the phrase *economic growth* by *economic development*. In reality, however, all development was predicated upon accelerating *economic growth*, see Lewis, W.A. (May 1954), 'Economic Development with Unlimited Supplies of Labour', Manchester School of Economic and Social Studies, vol. 22, no. 2, pp. 139-91; Kuznets, S.S. *Modern Economic Growth*, op. cit.; Streeten, Paul and Associates *First Things First*, op. cit., pp. 8-22.

11. See Appendix for a list of the participants.

Mexico

Miguel S. Wionczek
Miguel H. Márquez

I   Introduction

The test of a successful self-reliant strategy of industrialization is the extent to which it reduces the gap between the high income in the high-productivity, high-technology sector and the low incomes in the low-productivity, low-technology sector, by raising the performance of the latter, without impeding progress in the former.

Paul Streeten[1]

During the past 50 years, Mexico has experienced or suffered - depending on the observer's viewpoint - the consequences of the subsequent implementation of several development models which provided the country until the early 1980s with a certain degree of welfare and social peace resulting from high economic growth rates. (At present Mexico is classified internationally as one of the newly industrialized countries, NICs.)

These development models had their historical roots in a complex mixture of the colonial development style, the demonstration effect of the 19th century industrial revolution in western Europe, Mexico's unique geo-political situation in terms of its proximity to the United States, and last but not least, the production factors endowment.

In the country's development following the world crisis of the 1930s a distinction among three subsequent broad industrialization models is

3

usually made. According to conventional terminology used in Mexico they were the 'industrializing', 'stabilizing' and 'shared' development periods covering respectively 1930-68, 1968-74 and the most recent decade. It is quite difficult to define with some rigour the difference among these three stages for various reasons: the first is that their usage has important political and social rather than economic connotations; the second because they imply a successful application of a sort of the unique and coherent overall development strategy over a long period; and the third because for a reasonably objective observer they look rather as more of the same with only accidental and marginal changes. Moreover, considering periodical adjustments in response to changing external and internal conditions, the evidence available from modern Latin American economic history, including that of Mexico, strongly suggests that while socio-political language used by the economic policy makers has a considerable rhetorical content, none of the Latin American countries followed during the past half a century or so one single economic development strategy pattern.[2]

The first period extending from the mid-1930s to the early 1960s, marked the start of an inward-oriented industrialization process based on import substitution, accompanied by reasonable financial stability. The second period, which covered the late 1960s to the mid-1970s corresponded to the final stage of a relatively easy import substitution process, with largely unsuccessful efforts to extend it to intermediate goods and, in some cases, to capital goods as well. In this period, while GDP growth rate declined, price stability continued. The third period, from the mid-1970s until the present started with the acceleration of overall economic growth largely as a result of massive oil discoveries. The social and economic consequences of this short-lasting oil-fed expansion proved to be very negative. When at the beginning of the present decade the oil boom started fading away, the country faced simultaneously increased financial dependence from abroad, accelerated inflation, further deterioration in income distribution and an unemployment explosion.

By mid-1982, the difficulties faced by Mexico's development process assumed alarming proportions, paving the way for the eruption shortly afterwards of a serious financial and economic crisis of which no end is in sight. Although Mexico's plight has not been unique in the region deeply affected as a whole by acute crises of all sorts, two questions arise: first, why did the crisis assume such large dimensions in Mexico - as evidenced, for example, by the magnitude of external indebtedness and the continuous decline in productivity and efficiency of the whole economy; and second, which factors are particularly responsible for the specific characteristics of the Mexican crisis.

These important questions cannot be answered by pointing towards the alleged scarcity of natural resources, because Mexico possesses them in abundance in most cases with the possible exception of water.[3] The country counts not only on vast coastal farmlands, plentiful mineral resources and massive oil fields but also on a reasonably large and modern infrastructure.

Under such conditions one may accept a hypothesis that the basic factors which explain the country's relative lack of economic progress as compared even with other newly industrialized countries (NICs) may be, first, its managerial and technological underdevelopment in face of the rapidly growing needs of the population which, over the four post-war decades, more than tripled, and second, the malfunctioning of a mixed economy managed by a *sui generis* political system. Since this paper is supposed to focus on the 'technological transformation of modern Mexico' we shall not dedicate much time to the second problem since it clearly belongs to the realm of comparative political science studies.

Technological backwardness can be defined as the insufficient development of the set of social practices through which information is expected to become knowledge applied to production. The analysis of the behaviour of the *technological factors* as well as the identification of both dynamic factors and obstacles which defined the country's development process calls for at least a superficial examination of three essential features which explain the context in which those *technological factors* operate in Mexico.

The first of these features is political in nature and accounts for the persistence of deep-rooted and long-standing conflicts in Mexican society. In effect, the idea of modernizing politically, socially and in economic terms the ex-Spanish mining colony through industrialization, appeared in Mexican thought shortly following independence. When the United States was still an extremely underdeveloped country by European standards, especially in the regions adjacent to its border with Mexico drawn after the 1847-48 war, Mexican elites were embroiled in endless debates and fights covering three issues: centralism vs. federalism, conservatism vs. liberalism and free trade vs. protectionism. The fact that during the 150 years which have elapsed since the date of Mexico's political independence, none of these issues has been settled definitively makes it difficult for an outsider to understand the country's recent political, social and economic policy patterns.

As a reflection of these unresolved conflicts, Mexico's economic history has been shaped by political and economic cycles of varying length and fluctuations of varying depth within the general framework of underdevelopment until 1910 and of a dependent and highly unbalanced development in modern times. The persistence of those cycles and fluctuations has not been conducive either to designing and implementing effective economic policy or building consistent long term economic strategy models. Perhaps more than any other factor, the frequent policy changes resulting from largely political circumstances are responsible for both the 'mixed' economic model adopted finally in the 1930s and the Mexican 'pragmatism' practiced for the last 50 years. An important caveat must be introduced at this point. A model which is supposed to be both 'mixed' and 'pragmatic' may become, in the long term, chaotic and contradictory more through error and omission than by design. There is the very substantive evidence to the effect that this has occurred in Mexico in the recent decades preparing the ground for the deep-seated political and economic crisis that the country has been facing since the beginning of the 1980s in spite of or perhaps because of the presence of a highly centralized state, practically unlimited powers of the subsequent presidents and a one-party political system.

The second issue is that of the persistence of Mexico's technological backwardness and its reasons. In general, both science and technology have followed the overall course of external dependence which characterizes the Mexican economy and the society. The impetus given to economic development via import substitution in the 1930s coincided with the emergence of incipient scientific and technological activities. They have not received, however deserved, support either from the state or from the productive sectors. While measures to promote industrialization were accompanied by increased spending on higher education, which contributed to the advancement of certain areas of scientific research, no similar effort took place in the field of technology with the sole exception of civil engineering, a field in which the combination of accumulated experiences, adequate training of engineers and technicians and various legal incentives, in particular credit policies, permitted considerable domestic technological development. This general lack of interest in technological development must have been related to the fact that technology could be acquired from the outside, mostly the United States, at costs easily transferable to the final consumer in a heavily protected economy and, moreover, not much technical know-how was needed in the initial import substitution stages. Consequently, foreign capital goods, know-how and technical assistance were imported *en masse*. As the highly skewed income distribution and patterns of consumption, affected by the vicinity of the United States, shaped the technological profile of Mexican industry and the agricultural commercial sector, technological dependence on the outside world went on increasing progressively.

Such dependence was considered inevitable by the country's economic policy makers and highly profitable both by the foreign technology sellers and its local buyers and users. The issue of choosing technologies appropriate to the local endowment of other production factors was not yet perceived, while at the enterprise level no risks of importing proven technology seem to exist. The result was that as late as in the early 1970s no Mexican technological policies existed, little if any technology was created at home, and the meaningful absorption of imported technology including management capacity into the economy and the society was hampered by the absence of local technological capability. Accepting the partial or sectoral guidelines (support offered to industrial development, indicative sectoral plans, etc.) and mechanisms adopted for the purpose of regulating the transfer of technology processes represented praiseworthy efforts favouring some technological development, their impact was limited and reduced to some areas and enterprises only mostly in the public sector.

6

Only in the early 1970s did the state start thinking about the need for R and D policies. Some ambitious efforts were made to establish policy guidelines for science and technology, to provide more financing for R and D at university and polytechnical levels and to link local scientific and technological output with the needs of productive sectors through supporting legislation in respect to technology transfer from abroad and the country's access to the international patent system. But given the advanced degree of the overall technological dependence and the omnipresence of transnationals in Mexico, except in the case of upgrading the skills of the higher level human resources by sending large numbers of promising university graduates abroad, not much has been achieved in all these fields. What was absent was the understanding at the highest political level that no self-reliant economic and social development was possible in face of the persistent weakness of scientific and technological efforts largely divorced from the productive sector.

Thus, despite rather impressive overall industrial growth and the rapid modernization of commercial agriculture, Mexico has lagged scientifically and technologically even behind other large or small countries which have entered after the end of World War II into the industrialization *cum* modernization process, and the country condemned itself to the dependent development patterns. It could not be otherwise as long as overall policies were largely improvised and industrial, fiscal and monetary policies continued disconnected from science and technology support policy proposals.[4]

The third factor, closely related to the preceding one, concerns Mexico's educational system high level manpower training capacity. The priority given for political reasons in the past decades to a quantitative expansion of higher education in Mexico to forestall the entrance of young people into the labour force has resulted in a deterioration in the schooling quality at lower levels. This phenomenon created additional bottlenecks in the satisfactory relationship among the educational system, R and D activities and the productive sector. Consequently, neither has knowledge and know-how generated within the country been effectively applied to improve educational standards nor have they been efficiently used to provide technological inputs to advance production of new goods and services. As should have been expected, the limited local supply of scientific and technological knowledge has not created a sufficient demand for such knowledge. With few exceptions the demand continued to be covered by imported technology in the case both of domestically owned manufacturing facilities, whether privately or publicly owned, and of foreign investors. From the viewpoint of domestic buyers of technology it was a risk-averting operation; from that of foreign investors, particularly transnationals, it was just an excellent business proposition.

The persistent weakness of close permanent links among the educational system, R and D and its users made itself strongly felt during the Mexican oil boom started in the mid-1970s. The discovery of vast hydrocarbon

7

reserves together with the first large international oil price increases of 1973-74 prompted the federal government to design and start implementing investment programmes of unprecedented magnitude. The first of them, the National Development Plan for 1977-82, allocated about US$20 billion to the oil and petrochemical sectors, slightly more than one quarter of total public investment for the period.

The successful fulfilment of the plan's targets depended to a considerable extent on external financing, large capital goods imports and the availability of advanced technology. Serious shortcomings in this over-ambitious forced industrialization strategy became apparent shortly after it started being implemented. Public investment largely exceeded original estimates, the import bill shot up, delivery dates of large industrial projects in the oil sector and elsewhere suffered long and costly delays, and inflationary pressures accelerated across the board. On the other hand, despite a beneficial second oil shock of 1979-80 not only the capital accumulation rate slowed down but capital formation dropped by about five per cent.

At the height of the oil boom this recessive picture hardly perceived the important fact: the Mexican economy has not been ready for a process of accelerated expansion due to malfunctioning of the productive apparatus which resulted in the most serious bottlenecks in the industrial sector and particularly in capital goods and technology supply. Thus, while the oil boom bought about considerable growth in the country's overall productive capacity, it paved the way at the same time for a major financial and economic crisis in mid-1982. Although the situation preceding that crisis was serious enough in itself, the fact that urgently needed equipment and technology, as well as high level technicians, had to be brought from abroad because the local productive apparatus failed to respond to growing demand is perhaps even more critical. The effect was doubly negative: while investment costs went up resulting in the explosion of foreign indebtedness, technological policies which, if pursued consistently from their inception ten years earlier might somehow help self-reliant and sustained development, were completely forgotten.

II   The start of the industrialization process

Like many other Latin American countries in the early 1950s Mexico could still be considered a predominantly rural society with certain modern traits attributable to the role played by its growing urbanization and its sustained, albeit limited, industrial development.

Mexico's population rose from 16.5 million in 1940 to just under 25.8 million in 1950. In that year the urban population accounted for 42.5 per cent of the total (35 per cent in 1940) and the remaining 57.4 per cent were living in rural areas (64.9 per cent in 1940). The economically active population amounted to 8.2 million persons. Slightly more than 50 per cent were employed in the primary sector; 15.9 per cent in the secondary sector, which included the oil industry; and 25.6 per cent in services.[5]

Gross National Product stood in 1950 at 86,973 million pesos (at 1960 prices)[6] reflecting seven per cent annual percentage GNP increase over the 1940-50 period. The GNP growth rate was above that of demographic growth (an average of 2.8 per cent) and remained so for the next two decades. The primary sector's mainly mining and agricultural contribution to GNP was of the order of 20 per cent, the share of these two subsectors being 58.8 per cent of the primary sector's total and 11.7 per cent of GNP. The participation of the industrial sector including oil and coal mining in the GNP was about 24.1 per cent and that of the services sector - 55.9 per cent.

9

The share of mining and agriculture shows their relative importance to the Mexican economy as the pillars upon which the industrialization process started in those years. In fact, the sustained economic growth registered between the early 1940s and the early 1980s (GNP average annual growth rate of 6 per cent) could not have been achieved without the dynamism of these two sectors from 1930 to the mid-1960s. In the 1940s and 1950s both mining and agriculture produced significant export surpluses. The same trend continued still in the 1960s as a result of the policy providing guaranteed domestic agricultural prices above those of the world market.[7]

The existence of an agricultural sector with the characteristics described does not in itself explain, however, the constant and sustained growth of the economy accelerated in the 1940s. Other equally or perhaps more important factors, such as increased domestic demand, higher commodity exports and the import substitution process must be taken into account. According to research available upon the role of import substitution in Mexico as an engine of growth, this factor contributed most significantly to the expansion of production in general and manufacturing in particular from 1940 to 1950. In the following decades its role declined progressively.[8]

Brief comments on this point are in order. First, because it is generally accepted that 'the explicit and implicit objective of the resources allocation in Mexico over the last 50 years has been to transform a predominantly rural nation into a medium-sized industrial power...'[9] Second, because the characteristics of the industrial import substitution process considered jointly with the factors directly responsible for sustained economic growth, defined the technological profile of the early 1950s, its subsequent evolution, as well as the level and degree of skills incorporated in one of the major production factors - the labour force, affected negatively Mexico's economic growth.

Strong incentives for industrial expansion - understood as the kernel of the import substitution process - were provided by the government mostly through growing credit allocation, building up the physical infrastructure and fiscal and foreign trade policies. Credits whether from domestic savings or foreign credits were preferentially channelled to industry. For example, in 1950 almost three quarters of the financial resources handled by *Nacional Financiera*, the official industrial development bank, were devoted to industrial development projects.[10] Assigning resources to the industrial sector on a priority basis went hand in hand with increased public investment in infrastructure. In the same year of 1950, the installed capacity for generating electric power was 1,235,000 Kw. as compared with 681,000 Kw. in 1940 (Appendix - Table 8.1). Production and consumption of electrical power more than doubled during the 1940s (Appendix - Tables 8.2 and 8.3) as did the volume of surface transportation services. By 1950, rail-roads tripled the number of passengers carried per kilometre and moved one third more of freight (Appendix - Table 8.4), which meant an increase of slightly over 23,000 km in the railroad network. That same year, the highway network was extended from the 929 km available in 1940 to 21,422 km with 13,600 km of new paved roads (Appendix - Table 8.5). The number of motor vehicles (including freight trucks and buses) more than doubled from 145,708 units in 1940 to 302,978 in 1950 (Appendix - Table 8.6). Increases in air and maritime transportation were equally impressive.[11]

On the fiscal policy front generous exemptions from personal income, sales, import and export taxes were given to practically all new industries for periods of between 5 and 10 years depending on the type of manufactured goods involved. If these incentives were not enough, foreign trade policy was also revised to promote the import substitution process: tariff levels were increased for consumer goods and decreased, in some cases to the point of elimination, on all sorts of manufacturing input and especially on capital goods.

It is relevant at this point to describe briefly the structure of the Mexican industrial sector along with its relations with the outside world in 1950, after the first two decades of the industrialization process. For this purpose the distinction must be made among three major groups of industrial activities: the so-called mature industries, the intermediate industries and the 'new' industries (see Table 2.1). The first group consisted almost exclusively of the branches producing consumer non-durables and processing specific local inputs for them; the second group covered intermediate goods and certain relatively simple consumer durables (chemicals, basic metals, processed minerals, paper and rubber); the third, mostly more complicated consumer durables and marginally capital goods (non-electric machinery, transport equipment, metal products and machinery and electric equipment.

In 1950, consumer non-durables accounted for 72 per cent of total manufacturing output, intermediate goods for 18 per cent and 'new' industries for 10 per cent. The first manufacturing sub-sector achieved a high degree of integration: not only did it cover over 60 per cent of domestic demand but its imports amounted to only 8 per cent of total manufacturing imports while at the same time it accounted for almost 80 per cent of the total, still incipient, manufacturing exports of Mexico. The situation of the two other sub-sectors - intermediate and 'new' industries respectively - was quite different. While in the case of intermediate goods their share in the total manufacturing output, the coverage of the domestic demand and exports was almost equal - slightly below 20 per cent, their dependence upon imports was considerably larger - over 30 per cent of total manufactured goods brought from abroad. To the 'new' industries corresponded 10 per cent of total industrial output, their share in supplying the domestic market was 20 per cent, their exports were practically nil but their imports accounted for 60 per cent of the total manufacturing goods import bill.[12] This simple presentation strongly suggests *ex-post* that unless the industrial policy would be designed with the aim of 1) developing the capital goods sector; 2) strengthening intra-industrial links between

TABLE 2.1

STRUCTURE AND CHARACTERISTICS OF THE MANUFACTURING
INDUSTRY BY BRANCHES: 1950
(PERCENTAGES OF THE MANUFACTURING SECTOR)

	Production	Domestic demand	Imports	Exports
'Mature' industries	71.9	60.6	8.8	79.4
Foodstuffs	36.7	30.0	2.3	41.0
Textiles	10.9	9.1	3.3	27.0
Footwear and clothing	9.0	7.8	0.6	2.0
Wood and cork	3.6	3.0	0.9	6.3
Leather	2.2	1.8	0.2	1.6
Printing and publishing	2.2	1.9	0.4	1.3
Tobacco	2.0	1.7	0.0	0.0
Beverages	5.3	4.7	1.1	0.2
Intermediate industries	18.1	19.9	31.2	19.0
Chemicals	6.8	7.8	15.4	10.5
Basic metals	3.9	4.3	6.3	7.8
Non-metallic minerals	3.0	2.8	1.5	0.7
Paper	3.0	3.3	4.8	0.0
Rubber	1.4	1.7	3.2	0.0
'New' industries	10.2	19.6	60.0	1.5
Transportation	4.7	8.2	23.5	0.3
Metal products	2.7	3.9	8.4	0.6
Machinery and electrical appliances	1.8	2.3	4.3	0.3
Non-electrical machinery	1.0	5.2	23.9	0.3
Total	100.0	100.0	100.0	100.0

Source: Ros, Jaime and Vásquez, Alejandro, 'Industrialización y comercio exterior
1950-1977', op. cit.

12

production of consumer, intermediate and capital goods; 3) modernizing the consumer goods sector for the purpose of entering new external markets; and 4) providing agriculture with necessary capital investment and technology for steady growth, the import substitution model in force would shortly run into trouble on the country's balance of payment current account front.

Despite the optimism prevailing in official circles at that time, an ECLA study of the Mexican economy's past experiences and prospects, published in 1952, arrived at similar conclusions.[13] Its main thesis was that the serious problems of external disequilibrium had already faced the Mexican economy between 1940 and 1950 because of the persistent balance of payments deficit

This disequilibrium could not be explained by prices and costs overvaluation or an excess of investments over savings. Since it resulted from the increased imports of goods and services, it had to be traced to structural transformations induced by the development style adopted. Under such circumstances, according to the ECLA study, the continuation of monetary, financial, fiscal and trade policies in force with periodical exchange rate adjustments were neither sufficient nor capable of working definitely. New policies would have to be designed and implemented, addressing themselves to the consequences of the kind of growth without development: income concentration, rapidly growing demand coming from middle and upper-income groups for imported final consumer goods, increased the need for intermediate goods reflecting the first stages of industrialization, and the disproportionate demand for capital goods in terms of GDP growth rates.

All of these problems could be taken care of only by a consistent and integrated industrial and agricultural policy as a key factor in a global planning scheme. In addition to protectionist measures and incentives, such a new policy would have to adjust and correct the malfunctioning of the development model itself. This sort of overall and coherent economic planning, however, so vitally needed already in the early 1950s, has not been possible at any point in time in the modern Mexico for many political, technical and other reasons.[14] The exercises in unplanned, 'mixed' and 'pragmatic' short term policies continued leading many domestic and external observers to the conclusion that Mexico has become one of the least successful examples of the combination of centralized formal over-planning in the framework of a largely free-market economy.

The other factor that explains the characteristics of the production process between 1940 and the mid-1950s and its relationship to the low labour skills might be mentioned briefly again. During the period under consideration, economic growth was largely due to the primary sector's significant growth rate of 7.4 per cent, which surpassed the 6 per cent overall GNP increase and even the 6.7 per cent increase in the manufacturing sector, including the petroleum industry. The industrialization model based on import substitution assigned important tasks to the primary sector itself and of wage-goods for the labour force employed in the rest of the economy; production of inputs needed for intermediate industries and generation of export surpluses to cover the foreign exchange costs of most of the goods and services imports, especially for the industrial sector. Moreover, the agricultural sector was to contribute also to the growth of other sectors providing labour and investment funds via taxes or deteriorating terms of trade. The fulfilment of these tasks by agriculture proved impossible because of the increasing productivity gap between the commercial and subsistence agricultural sectors.

Under such conditions, the growth model adopted in the 1930s and continued for several decades, resulted in large migrations from the backward interior to large urban concentrations. While it provided cheap industrial labour, the availability of a low-skilled labour force strengthened the model itself. Between 1940 and 1960 the growth of the industrial labour force, impressive by any standards but accompanied by deepening income inequality brought serious limitations to the expansion of the domestic market. Labour employed in the industrial sector expanded in this period at an average annual rate of 5.4 per cent, higher than that of the total labour force (3.3 per cent) and more than double that of its increase in agriculture (2.3 per cent). These data indicate that over the same period the economic growth of Mexico was extensive rather than intensive. It was primarily reflected in larger employment (Appendix - Table 8.7) and not in productivity increase, contrary to the experiences of the industrialized countries at their early growth stages.

There would be no reason for criticisms in this respect if the originally labour-extensive growth had produced eventually substantial productivity increases. This was not the case, however, for the Mexican economy of the period.[15] Most probably, the country faced a structural problem, difficult to modify in the short term. But it is precisely in the field of productivity where at a certain stage of social modernization and industrial advancement the notion of efficiency in the utilization of the resources mix available becomes crucial. The historical series of production function tells us that a large portion of output growth cannot be attributed exclusively to the absolute availability of labour and capital. Other factors, equally or more important in a given moment, are the educational or skilling level of the labour force and domestic technological and managerial capacity, intimately related to the former.

If one accepts that during the period 1930-50 Mexico registered sustained investment growth (Table 2.2) and increased capital density on the one hand, while technical progress was incorporated in new equipment and machinery acquired mainly from abroad on the other, stagnant production efficiency would seem to be explained to a large extent, if not completely, by the difficulty in quantifying social and other factors. In brief, the development model adopted in Mexico, i.e. the industrialization process based on import substitution had run into serious obstacles in the fields of education and technological capability, which resulted in persistent low productivity both of capital and labour.

The above data indicate that the government's efforts in the field of education brought poor results with regard to increased efficiency in qualitative terms. This failure was due basically to the assumption underlying educational policies that the economic growth process by itself would promote and develop both higher education and upgrading skills through training at the workplace as well.[16] Unfortunately, this did not occur. As a result, an acute shortage of medium level technicians and high level professionals appeared. In the words of one observer: '...it proved to have been easier to import and install modern industrial machinery than to train and supervise the labour force engaged in its efficient operation'.[17] The shortages of adequately skilled labour were apparently largely filled by personnel who took jobs with less *educational* training than actually necessary.

To summarize, the problems which emerged relatively early in the Mexican industrialization process had their roots in a lack of efficiency in handling physical resources and technology in the productive process traceable to serious deficiencies in education and manpower training, rather than the scarcities of other production factors.

TABLE 2.2

INVESTMENT AND GDP GROWTH: 1939-69
(AVERAGE ANNUAL PERCENTAGE RATES)

	Gross fixed investment a)	GDP b)	a/b
1939-49	12.5	5.1	2.45
1950-59	7.4	6.3	1.17
1960-69	9.9	7.1	1.39

Source: Banco de México.

III   Growth without structural change

As the Mexican economy evolved after the beginning of the 1960s, factors and conditions which had sustained the development style followed between the 1930s and the 1950s lost their strength, giving rise to a new stage in the country's development process.

The most important change registered in the 1960s was that the growth process essentially based on industrialization was concentrated now on the production of consumer durables rather than consumer non-durable goods. This new phase took place within the context of a set of positive international factors: accelerated world economic growth, the expanded flow of investment and technology from industrial countries to the developing regions and the extensive development of international capital markets, particularly of private bank credit.

An overview of the Mexican development process from the early 1960s on reveals that the Mexican GDP grew steadily until late 1973 with the exception of a decline in 1971 due mainly to political factors. The GDP rose from 212,586 in 1960 to 444,271 million in 1970, at 1970 pesos[18] (Appendix - Table 8.9). The average annual GDP growth rate of 7 per cent between 1960 and 1969 (Table 3.1) exceeded that of the 6 per cent for the whole 1960-85 period. GDP per capita also rose from 6,081 in 1960 to 8,681 pesos in 1970 (Appendix - Table 8.10).

TABLE 3.1

GDP GROWTH RATES: 1960-85
(PERCENTAGES)

	Period	Growth rate
GDP at current prices	1960-69	10.7
	1970-75	19.9
	1976-80	32.9
	1981-85	66.9
	1960-85	25.7
GDP at 1970 prices	1960-69	7.0
	1970-75	6.5
	1976-80	7.3
	1981-85	0.1
	1960-85	6.0

Source: NAFINSA, op. cit.

As can be seen in Table 3.2, the relative GDP share of each sector changed slowly but steadily in favour of the industrial sector (29.2 per cent in 1960, 31.1 per cent in 1965 and 32.5 per cent in 1970) over the agriculture in particular (15.9 per cent, 14.4 per cent, 12.2 per cent) with the share of the services sector being left intact (55.9 per cent, 55.4 per cent, 56.3 per cent).

While the important qualitative change took place in the Mexican economy in the 1960s, its most interesting facet was the transformation which took place within the manufacturing industry.

The industrialization process was no longer governed now by the massive expansion and standardization of wage goods. Instead, it was supported by the production of consumer durables and to some extent that of machinery and equipment. By their very nature these goods required more sophisticated inputs, which could only be obtained by a considerable increase in local production and growing imports.

According to Table 3.3 (see Appendix - Table 8.11) which gives the structure of the manufacturing industry and growth rates for five-year periods, the 'new' industries' share in manufacturing output went from 18.8 per cent in 1960 to 23.3 per cent in 1965 and 22.5 per cent in 1970. Between 1960 and 1969 the growth rate for these 'new' industries, which averaged 11.6 per cent, is particularly high, considering that of other industries for the same period, or even the same industries during any other period appearing in the same table. The share of 'intermediate' industries also rose: 20.4 per cent in 1960, 21.2 per cent in 1965, 28.5 in 1970. The

17

TABLE 3.2
GDP STRUCTURE AND GROWTH RATES BY SECTOR: 1960-85
(PERCENTAGE AT 1970 PESOS)

	Structure							Growth rates				
	1960	1965	1970	1975	1980	1985		1960-69	1970-77	1978-81	1982-85
Gross domestic product a)	100.0	100.0	100.0	100.0	100.0	100.0		7.6	5.8	8.5	0.3
Primary sector	15.9	14.4	12.2	10.3	9.0	9.4		3.2	3.3	3.6	2.5
Agriculture, livestock and fishing	15.9	14.4	12.2	10.3	9.0	9.4		3.2	3.3	3.6	2.5
Industries	29.2	31.1	32.4	33.4	35.1	34.9		8.7	6.2	9.7	1.0
Mining	4.9	4.7	2.5	2.4	3.2	3.8		5.5	6.2	17.4	-0.0
Manufacturing industry	19.2	21.0	32.4	24.3	24.9	24.6		9.0	6.3	8.2	0.9
Construction	4.1	4.0	5.3	5.4	5.5	4.7		9.7	4.7	12.4	-4.6
Electric	1.0	1.4	1.2	1.3	1.5	1.8		9.7	5.3	8.4	5.0
Services	55.9	55.4	56.3	57.5	57.2	57.1		7.1	6.0	8.7	2.2
Restaurants and hotel business	33.6	32.6	25.9	26.0	25.7	23.8		6.5	5.3	9.4	-1.9
Transportation, storage and communications	3.3	2.9	4.8	6.2	7.5	7.6		4.6	9.3	13.4	1.3
Financial services, insurance and real estate	9.2	9.1	11.3	10.8	9.8	10.5		7.2	5.2	4.9	2.5
Community, social, and personal services	9.8	10.8	14.3	14.5	14.2	15.2		9.2	6.1	7.7	10.4
Chargeable banking services	-1.0	-1.0	-1.2	-1.2	-1.3	-1.5		11.6	5.0	12.8	3.2

Source: Elaborated by the authors with information available in NAFINSA, op. cit.; and the Planning and Budget Secretariat, National Accounts System, 'Preliminary Estimates 1985', February 1986.

Note: a) According to the classification of Mexico's National Accounts System prepared by the Planning and Budget Secretariat.

18

TABLE 3.3

PERCENTAGE STRUCTURE AND GROWTH RATES FOR THE MANUFACTURING INDUSTRY: 1960-85
(IN MILLIONS OF 1970 PESOS)

	1960	1965	1970	1975	1980	1985	Growth rates (per cent)			
							1960-69	1970-77	1978-81	1982-85
Total manufacturing industry	100.0	100.0	100.0	100.0	100.0	100.0	9.0	6.3	8.3	0.9
'Mature' industries										
Foodstuffs, beverages and tobacco	36.7	31.3	27.9	25.5	23.6	25.4	5.5	4.7	6.3	1.7
Textiles, clothing and leather goods	18.8	19.6	14.7	13.6	12.4	11.6	11.7	4.9	6.5	0.0
Wood and wood products industry	3.1	2.3	3.4	3.1	3.3	2.8	2.8	6.0	7.0	-4.1
Intermediate industries										
Paper, paper products, printing and publishing	5.0	6.1	5.4	4.8	5.2	5.3	10.1	5.5	8.5	1.3
Chemicals, petroleum by-products, rubber products and plastics	11.3	10.7	17.5	20.0	21.6	24.7	8.6	9.3	9.5	3.4
Non-metallic mineral products, except for petroleum and coal	4.1	4.4	5.8	5.9	5.6	5.6	11.8	5.7	8.0	1.6
New industries										
Basic metal industries	9.7	9.6	5.6	5.5	5.6	5.1	8.7	6.1	5.0	1.0
Metal products, machinery and equipment	9.1	13.7	17.9	19.9	21.2	18.0	14.4	6.9	12.4	-2.1
Other manufacturing industries	2.2	2.2	1.7	1.6	1.4	1.4	8.8	5.2	5.5	0.6

Source: Prepared by the authors with data from Table 8.11.

largest share in this category corresponded to manufacturing of chemicals and petroleum derivatives.

Finally the relative share of the 'mature' branches of the manufacturing industry declined steadily between 1960-69, from 58.6 per cent in 1960 to 53.2 per cent in 1965 and 46.0 per cent in 1970.

The direct and indirect effects felt by the Mexican economy and reflecting at the same time the qualitative changes were as follows:

First of all, there was a change in the employment share by sector. The number of people employed in the industrial sector increased significantly as did the personnel working in the manufacturing subsector (Appendix - Table 8.12).

Second, important changes took place in the foreign trade structure (Appendix - Table 8.13) not only in respect of shifts in the distribution of exports between primary and manufactured goods in favour of the latter, (Appendix - Table 8.14) but also in the imports of manufactures (Appendix - Table 8.15).

Third, during the 1960s, monetary, credit and banking policies promoted the expansion of the national banking system and the credit boom was accompanied by the growth of the public enterprises which became the cornerstone of the governments intervention in the economy. Both proved to be very important. In the early 1960s, some government enterprises underwent completely thorough reorganization. The strategic electric power sector was nationalized. A state-owned fertilizer industry was established along with a heavy petrochemical industry and other productive units under the umbrella of the state oil monopoly. However, the transition to this new industrialization phase was not problem free. The domestic market not only continued very limited but registered gradual contraction as a result of the deterioration of income distribution. Although conditions and opportunities for new industries had emerged, constraints and contradictions inherited from the preceding period persisted.

Other problems arose because of the type of relationship established in this period between the newly created large and small enterprises in respect to management performance. While large firms modernized rather rapidly, small ones remained stagnant making difficult the appearance of backward and forward linkages in manufacturing.

Another important outcome of the industrialization dynamics in the 1960s was unequal regional development. Certain regions continued to stagnate (the southeast), economic performance of some declined (the Gulf), and others became very poor agriculturally as a result of over exploitation of land (the central plateau). The development inequality by regions was compounded by the accelerated growth and modernization of major urban centres such as the Federal District, Guadalajara and Monterrey.

Finally, the policy of 'stabilizing development', seriously undermined by huge tax concessions for industrial activities and excessively generous subsidies to state enterprises was, perhaps, one of the major sources of

20

contradictions of that particular model and its negative impact on the overall development process during the 1960s. As a result, the federal government deficit in constant pesos grew steadily (from 14,000 million pesos in 1964 to 52,990 million in 1968 and 93,000 millions in 1969), aggravating the struggles for bank credit between the state and the private sector.

In addition, the trade deficit worsened (Appendix - Table 8.16) mainly as a result of a rapid increase in intermediate and capital goods imports. Both the lags in manufacturing goods exports and the stagnation of traditional primary exports were also responsible for the size of this deficit. The deterioration of the situation, in the early 1970s, accentuated by higher fiscal deficits and the growing opening of the economy to the outside world, foreshadowed the decline of the economic growth rates obviously related also to the similar trends observed throughout the world economy.

The magnitude and characteristics of the problems to be solved called for a government's response at all levels - economic, social and political. Its response came soon. In 1972, the Mexican government adopted a strategy of state intervention greater than ever before.[19] This strategy based on the Keynesian use of fiscal deficits put emphasis on alleviating some accumulated serious problems, such as unemployment and income concentration, for the purpose of creating the conditions that would assure longer term economic growth with some degree of stability. More active state intervention was one of the pillars of this strategy. Another was to be the increase of the share of wages in national income, that would - it was hoped - expand the domestic market and stimulate the better use of the available productive capacity.

Brief comments on the results and implications of this strategy are in order. First of all, the new wage policy brought about price increases and depressed private investment. Larger public spending, financed with the expanded money supply and the high level of banking deposits retention by the central bank, produced tensions in the economy by accelerating inflationary pressures. At the same time, the subsidies policy turned into a means of compensation for the weakening financial position of public and private enterprises rather than a tool for stimulating and strengthening productive activities. According to available estimates, direct subsidies to capital accumulation accounted for 5.6 per cent of national income in 1977. The impact of subsidies which went beyond the question of their magnitude became without any doubt an obstacle to the elimination of inefficient enterprises in industry and obsolete and technologically disfunctional production systems.

Nevertheless, this economic model had some positive effects. GDP grew in 1972 and 1973 causing a recovery process which extended to the rest of the economy. However, this recovery was short lived. A considerable reduction in public expenditure in 1974 brought at once a decline in growth rates as the Mexican economy marched inexorably towards what looked like a new crisis.

The brief and artificially induced boom in the early 1970s took place within the context of numerous bottlenecks, such as the shortages in the production of basic industrial inputs and the stagnation of agricultural production. This last phenomenon is an extremely important element in the Mexican development process. It resulted from several concurrent factors: the forced transfer of savings from non-commercial agriculture to the industry and services sectors, the pressure of the rural population on the land and the political decision to abandon subsistence agriculture to its own precarious fate.

The impact of this departure from the reasonably balanced economic development patterns was felt strongly in the early 1970s when Mexico went from the position of an important net exporter of agricultural products to that of an importer of large quantities of basic grains, mostly from the United States. This change gave rise to one of the structural balances-of-payments blockages which still persist in the Mexican economy.

Several macroeconomic indicators confirm that by the mid-1970s the country once again faced a distressing recessive situation. The first policy measures enacted at the beginning of the new presidential term (1977-82) only served to worsen the recession. They included: reduction of imports (by substituting tariffs for import permits), restricting money supply, introduction of controls on wages and prices of few mass-consumption goods, and lastly, the administrative reform.[20]

However, the picture was to change completely with the confirmation of the discovery in Mexico of huge oil and natural gas deposits, known already in 1974, which led to the design of tremendously ambitious investment plans and programmes. The most important of these was the National Development Plan for 1976-82, the heart of which was the petroleum sector development programme. The confirmed presence of vast hydrocarbons wealth together with increasing international oil prices prompted the new administration to switch almost overnight to a strategy which called this time for an industrialization process devoid of financial restrictions, thanks to greatly increased availability of foreign exchange on current account and the practically unlimited supply of external credits

Within this strategy and in answer to the dissenting voices which expressed concern about the highly probable negative repercussions of an excessively ambitious development process based on petroleum the foreign trade liberalization was considered an easy option. It was expected to take care of excessive demand for goods and services which the relatively weak domestic productive system was unable to supply. Costs of increased imports were to be covered by expanding oil exports in a limitless international oil market.

As a result of the powerful incentives contained in the National Development Plan, the Mexican economy experienced between 1977 and 1980 the most extraordinary albeit again short-lived boom in its entire history. At some points of this boom the highest government officials started comparing Mexico's growth performance with that of Japan.

Nevertheless, at the height of the boom and oil euphoria in 1980, intensified by the second oil shock, some threatening recessive signs became apparent. The capital accumulation rate decreased, capital formation dropped from 20 per cent to slightly under 15 per cent, annual inflation rose from 20 per cent to 30 per cent and GDP growth declined one point below that registered in 1979. The slowdown in economic growth was traceable to the increased costs of a skilled labour force and, no matter how contradictory it might seem, to the credit shortage,[21] translating itself in the high dollar debts of many enterprises on one hand, and the capital outflow, on the other. Both were due in part to the overvaluation of the peso and large windfall profits of the private sector. This situation can be explained in broad terms, by the inconsistency between unrealistic growth targets based on the expected oil revenue which was to support the development process, and the serious difficulties and restrictions encountered by the Mexican economy in using efficiently the oil derived financial surpluses. All available data point to the fact that the Mexican economy was not ready to enter a process of accelerated expansion. Most serious bottlenecks in the industrial sector were reflected in the extraordinary expansion of capital goods, machinery and equipment imports, the large purchases of luxury goods, the comparatively slow productivity growth vis-a-vis the requirements of the growth process, and the acute shortage of professionals and middle and high level technicians.

The political and economic costs of the oil boom and the accelerated GDP growth with an annual average of over eight per cent from 1977 to 1982 were extremely high. Even though oil exports value continued to increase, the foreign exchange revenue was not sufficient to pay for additional imports, which doubled between 1977 and 1981 as a result of trade liberalization. With a large balance-of-payment deficit, a rapidly growing foreign debt and an oil market witnessing declining prices, Mexico was forced to devalue the peso in February 1982. Keeping in mind that several decades of the reasonable monetary and financial stability conditioned Mexico to consider any peso devaluation as a major political and economic disaster, the long overdue devaluation of early 1982 seems to have been the major factor which led to the general economic crisis and forced the government to adopt a series of *ad hoc* measures after the initial panic at home and within the international banking community had subsided. Despite their immediate failure the measures set down in the short term *Programa Inmediato de Reordenación Económica* (the Emergency Programme for Economic Restructuring) were consolidated in 1983 into the new National Development Plan.[22]

In summary, although the import substitution model promoted until the early 1970s produced important results, such as high GDP growth rates and dynamic expansion in manufacturing, construction and oil and electric power sectors, serious difficulties continued to plague the Mexican economy during the short lived petroleum-led economic boom of the late 1970s. The loss of dynamism in the primary sector, particularly in agriculture; increased income deterioration affecting mostly but not exclusively the rural population; the malfunctioning of the industrial activities, which brought about increased dependence on imported inputs and especially capital goods; unemployment, low labour efficiency and absence of competitiveness accompanied the boom. The persistence of these phenomena pointed out a need for major changes in the economic policies used, with some minor adjustments, over the whole post-war period. These changes have never come.

This brief analysis confirms that the presence of growth process patterns without structural change instead of alleviating major economic and social problems aggravated them and intensified the excessive financial, economic and technological dependence upon the outside world.

IV   The technological development process

In the debate which has arisen concerning the economic development process in general and in developing countries in particular, technological development is one of the issues which has received the most attention in the past two decades.

The concept of technological development is closely related to that of domestic technological capability. Technology is defined as the set of social practices which transform scientific concepts into knowledge to be applied to production. In other words, in the case of the developing countries it involves the construction of social practices related to the organization and management of the productive process linked to the educational and R and D sectors.

If technology is defined in this way, then the concept of domestic technological capability can be defined as the ability to organize the productive process, absorb the external technological advances and use them for the purpose of expanding constantly the technological capacity of a society. In the light of the speed and the depth of the scientific and technological advances world over the build-up of domestic R and D capacity depends upon a technological learning process on many levels at the same time. These levels include the selection of the appropriate technology, the search for available technical alternatives in function of the resources endowment, the mastery and effective utilization of the technology adapted to the specific production conditions, the development of new or improved technologies and know-how through minor innovations, and conducting appropriate basic research activities.[23]

In using this concept, a country's technological development level can be measured by the degree to which the demand arising at each of these levels can be satisfied. Therefore, technology must be regarded as the result of the economic and social system which creates and utilizes it, rather than the combination of accidental factors.

To the extent that technological development and the rate of technical progress are determined by the socio-economic conditions of the overall development process, both of them ultimately depend on the development of industrial, educational, scientific and technological infrastructure.

1 Industrial infrastructure

From 1960 to 1985, total gross fixed investment rose from 34,100 to 154,500 million pesos at 1970 prices (Appendix - Table 8.17). Detailed information on the investment distribution by sectors of the economy is extremely sketchy. However, according to available data (Appendix - Table 8.18), the share of industrial investment in the total grew significantly until the late 1960s from 33 per cent in 1960 to 46 per cent in 1967; that of agricultural investment decreased from 12 per cent to 10 per cent respectively; that of transportation was reduced in the same proportion; that of housing hardly changed - 23 per cent and 22 per cent - and there was a significant reduction in the category of 'others' which accounted for the bulk of unproductive investment (20 per cent and 12 per cent).

Another disaggregation of investment in Mexico, corresponding to the 1960-78 period (Appendix - Table 8.19), reveals that the public sector's share was steadily increasing particularly during the early stages of the oil boom. In respect to private investment a key role was played by investment by foreign enterprises and capital, which constituted only approximately 25 per cent of private investment in the late 1960s.[24] In this respect it may be worth mentioning that although foreign direct investment did not play a decisive role in the investment financing it increased considerably, particularly until the beginning of the 1980s. According to the Banco de México data, foreign direct investment flows which amounted in 1960 to only US$68 million increased in 1980 to $1,254 million. After having reached their historical record in 1982 ($1,657 million) they declined abruptly to only $59 million in 1985 (Appendix - Table 8.20). Foreign enterprises were located in the most dynamic activities (industry and commerce) and expanded more rapidly than their domestic counterparts by the late 1970s, their investment share rose to between 36 per cent and 40 per cent of total private investment.

Investment breakdown by sectors and by investment sources, where once again only scanty information is available, shows interesting trends (Appendix - Table 8.21). According to 1975 figures, the only year for

26

which information seems to be reliable, the bulk of public investment went into the secondary sector (85.2 per cent), more than half of private investment into the tertiary sector (53.2 per cent) but only one-third of private investment into the secondary sector. Even though these estimates must be handled with reservations they indicate that domestic private capital lost ground in the most strategic sectors; traditional and/or unproductive branches were relegated to a secondary position, and the state and to a lesser extent foreign capital took the lead in the investment process.

According to data available for the 1957-81 period (Appendix - Table 8.22), investment financing came basically from domestic savings although in the 1970s the use of external savings started increasing as suggested by the fact that despite the relatively dynamic behaviour of domestic savings they have grown at a lower rate than total investment.

The evolution of investment in Mexico left its mark on the mix of products in the manufacturing industry and the capital goods sector in particular. The latter will be looked into in greater detail since it is the sector which by the intensive use of technology is expected to make the greatest contribution to creating domestic capability for technological advance.

An analysis of available data for domestic capital goods production (Appendix - Table 8.23) reveals that from 1960 to 1981, capital goods value rose steadily from 7,683.6 million pesos to slightly over 55,000 million pesos at 1970 prices. In 1982, their value dropped to 54,135.4 million pesos. The decline was even greater in 1983 when 43,607.0 million pesos of capital goods were produced, over 2,000 million pesos less than in 1978, and approximately 18,000 million pesos less than the record high in 1981. In 1985 the production of capital goods was estimated at 51,792 million pesos, suggesting increased use of available capacity under the imports cuts for the balance-of-payments reasons.

Several interesting conclusions can be drawn from the evolution of the capital goods sector during the period in question. First, its dynamic growth between the mid-1960s and the early 1980s was due to a considerable extent to the fact that almost 40 per cent of the gross fixed investment went into manufacturing of machinery and equipment[25] in response to the sustained increase in demand for these goods. Second, the dynamism of the industry during the above mentioned period was curbed substantially between 1979 and 1980 at the highest point of the oil boom period. Its annual growth rate in these years dropped to 1.3 per cent (Appendix - Table 8.24). Third, the imports of this industry accounted for 30 and 50 per cent of the total imports of goods over the 1970-1980 period (Appendix - Table 8.15). This behaviour of the industry reflected not only the constant growth of the aggregated demand for these goods and the insufficient domestic productive capacity, but also the high import component of the domestic production of capital goods.[26] Fourth, a close look at the composition of the capital goods (Appendix - Table 8.25) indicates that in 1970, 65 per cent

27

was accounted for by two branches: basic metal and metal products and automobiles. In 1985 their participation was practically the same (62.4 per cent of the total). Both branches are characterized by relatively simple production processes. At the same time the participation of the non-electrical machinery and equipment branch, usually considered as the heart of the capital goods sector, amounted to 11 per cent only in 1970. After a small but sustained expansion (12.5 per cent and 12.8 per cent in 1975 and 1980 respectively) it declined to 11.4 per cent in 1985, practically the levels of 1970. This branch, including production of machine tools considered of great importance, was technologically more complex. Fifth, looking at some estimates covering the 1970-83 period and related to the ratio between imports and demand for final capital goods (Appendix - Table 8.26), it is possible to sustain that the domestic capital goods production tends to be technologically simpler than the majority of imported capital goods incorporating more sophisticated technologies.

This situation is explained by the persistence until the early 1980s, of elevated profit margins in industries established in the early stages of the import substitution. High profits obtained in these industries have not created, however, an incentive for investing in technologically more complicated industries nor for facing risks involved in developing domestic technology and technological capability to apply them in the local production of capital goods. According to a recent detailed study, domestic enterprises which attempted to improve technology or invest in their own technological capability generally were not able to increase their profit margins. On the contrary, enterprises which relied more heavily on imported technology and lacked R and D programmes continue to show the highest profits.[27]

These findings would suggest that unless the market conditions or the profit opportunities of the innovating enterprises change, the chances of reducing Mexico's high technological dependence are very slim, because most domestic and foreign enterprises lack incentives to innovate. Moreover, the large presence of transnational enterprises in Mexico should be noted. In fact, private 'joint ventures' producing capital goods with participation of foreign capital and/or the transnationals' subsidiaries have used mostly foreign technologies. Only a small part of the technological problems have been resolved locally. One should remember that close relations between these enterprises or subsidiaries with their headquarters have practically blocked all technological activities in the enterprises located in Mexico.[28] At the present stage of the country's industrial development the Mexican subsidiaries are more interested in promoting manufacturing exports than import substitution in a market of limited size. For producing for exports, however, they count upon the large stock of technology and know-how within their own multinational systems.

In brief, for a number of reasons the degree of development of Mexico's capital goods industry clearly falls short of the industrial development image created by industrial production indicators, and shows a high degree of external dependence. Therefore, the question arises which factors have hampered the development of this industry, despite the economic growth and important advances in the industrialization process registered in Mexico in the post-war period.

The lag in Mexico's capital goods industry would seem to be permanently linked to the characteristics of the country's industrialization model. One of its key features was a priority offered to quantitative investment increase which promoted in turn capital goods imports. While the production of consumer non-durables followed by durables and intermediate goods was stimulated, the need for local manufacture of machinery and equipment was not perceived since it might have increased investment costs during the establishment of new manufacturing enterprises. It should be kept in mind also that the production level for the capital goods sector was considerably lower than that for the rest of the industry.[29]

The industrialization model adopted in Mexico is not solely responsible for the lag in the capital goods industry. Many other institutional factors have influenced the behaviour of different technology users (whether public enterprises, subsidiaries of transnational enterprises and domestic private firms) on the demand side, and have hindered to a varying degree local capital goods production.[30]

In conjunction, all these factors account for the slow and haphazard development of the capital goods sector. If one recalls - as stated at the outset of this chapter - that the capital goods sector makes the major contribution to creating domestic technological capability, then while it becomes obvious that Mexico's weak technological development can be related to the lag of this sector, at the same time the unsatisfactory performance of the educational system, and particularly technical schools, became a major obstacle to the appearance of the capital goods sector.

2 Education and human resources

Low labour productivity is one of the basic problems which the Mexican economy has had to face for a long time. Over the last three decades, labour productivity levels in the processing industry, measured as a quotient of its GDP and total employment of that sector, were very low (Appendix - Table 8.27). Between 1950 and 1955 the average labour productivity increased by 1.1 per cent annually. From the beginning of the 1960s the annual average productivity increased slightly from 3.6 per cent between 1961-65 to 4.3 per cent in 1966-70 when the productivity rate of growth became the highest for the whole 1950-85 period. This development was related to the interplay of two factors: the significant growth of investment at the end of the 1960s and the impact on the structure of manufacturing production of intermediate industries (particularly chemical, oil and plastics) and other new industries (machinery and equipment and automobiles). The dynamism registered at the beginning of the 1980s was later curbed. The annual productivity growth declined from 3.9 per cent between 1971-75 to 3.2 per cent between 1976 and 1980 and declined again to 1.2 per cent between 1981-85.

The low labour productivity performance in Mexico's manufacturing industry is corroborated by comparison with other regions with similar conditions. In Latin America as a region for example, labour productivity grew from 1970 to 1980 by 4.1 per cent a year and in Mexico by 3.6 per cent only (Appendix - Table 8.28). Obviously, no simple factor explains the low productivity problem of the Mexican economy. It reflects such factors at inter-sectorial and intra-sectorial heterogeneity expressing in turn the structural heterogeneity of the whole economy.[31]

Judging, however, by the Mexican economy's high investment growth rates, it is evident that capital density (fixed capital per person employed) has increased very rapidly in the past two decades. Therefore, noting that technical progress is incorporated, to a large extent, in new machinery and equipment, this factor can hardly be responsible for low productivity. Its origin can be found most probably in the inefficiency at all levels of management of productive processes and technologies available, rather than in a scarcity of natural resources or other inputs. Thus, it becomes necessary to look into the problem of manpower, training directly related to the quality of formal education, but transcending the latter to cover cultural patterns inherited from pre-industrial Mexico.

Since 1960, the Mexican government has made considerable efforts to expand the nation's educational system,[32] without being able to solve many major problems. According to official figures (Appendix - Table 8.29), total expenditures for public education increased significantly from 1,959 million pesos in 1960 and 7,817 in 1970 to slightly over 800,000 million in 1984 (in current pesos). Nevertheless, in 1980 the spending on education which accounted for approximately 2.5 to 3.0 per cent of GDP, was still short of internationally accepted targets. Moreover, after 1980 its share in the federal budget fell sharply, from 42.1 per cent in 1979 to 18.6 per cent in 1980 and only 17.2 per cent in 1984.

Between 1970-71 and 1985-86 the total number of students participating in the national educational system more than doubled, from 12 million to close to 26 million (Appendix - Table 8.30). Although primary school enrolment is nearing 100 per cent of the school-age population in urban areas, figures are considerably lower for rural areas, in which still over 40 per cent of Mexico's population lives. In both urban and rural schools the drop-out rate is high, especially in the latter. In most small towns and villages (and 30 per cent of Mexico's 75 million people live in communities of less than 10,000 inhabitants), no education is available after the fourth grade. Although the network of secondary and technical schools has expanded very rapidly, enrolment still represents only a small percentage of the potential population of between 12 and 18 years of age. This is also true of higher education. In 1970, the average number of years of schooling for people entering the labour force was 3.5 years. Whereas 27 per cent of them had no formal schooling, 30 per cent had completed only 1 to 3 years and another 30 per cent, from 4 to 6 years of elementary school. Only 10 per cent had gone beyond the primary education.[33]

Without forgetting that all educational levels are equally important from the viewpoint of manpower training within a modernizing and industrializing society, three levels only: a) technical education; b) training and skills upgrading; and c) higher education, will be briefly analyzed now.

a Technical education

Mexico's system of technical education can be traced to XIX century art and trade school. In the early 1920s, several technical and agricultural schools were founded to provide basic training in engineering and house construction. In 1932, the first secondary level technical schools appeared. The year 1937 marked the setting up of the National Polytechnic Institute (IPN) which included pre-vocational basic secondary schools, vocational or second-cycle secondary/upper middle level technical schools, as well as professional schools at the university level. In addition, the establishment of the IPN aimed at counteracting the traditional preference for humanities, law and medicine, taught at the National Autonomous University of Mexico (UNAM), and at satisfying the needs of a society starting the industrialization process.

In 1958, the Ministry of Public Education established the post of an under-secretary for technical and higher education. Between 1967 and 1969, a network of agricultural and technical schools was established. At the start of the following administration (1970-76) technical education was given considerable support as the Ministry of Education which expanded these type of schools at all levels. In 1975, a National Technical Education Council parallel to the National Education Council, was created to coordinate and promote technical education at secondary and higher education levels. In 1976, when the post of an under-secretary for higher education and scientific research was established, technical education received further emphasis by increased diversification in terms of curicula and regional decentralization.

In 1978, targets were established for the expansion of the education sector, including a 9-20 per cent increment in enrolments in terminal secondary; programmes for second-cycle secondary/higher middle level schools; a 70 percent efficiency increase at the terminal level of the technical education and the increase in social recognition for technical schools in general. In addition; professional education colleges were set up within a decentralized federal government agency. The innovative feature of these colleges was the attempt to link them to the productive activities through formal agreements between schools and enterprises.

31

Complete detailed information for enrolment patterns in technical education is available for the 1970-71 and 1978-79 school years only (Table 4.1) with partial data covering the 1982-83 cycle.

Between 1970-71 and 1978-79 the technical secondary level and the terminal middle level schools registered the highest increase in enrolment: technical secondary schools enrolment grew by over 400 per cent and terminal middle level schools by almost 1,400 per cent. At the secondary level enrolment increased particularly in the agricultural schools where the number of students increased from about 17,000 in 1970-71 to slightly more than 190,000 in 1978-79 and in industrial technical schools where the number of students increased from 68,000 to almost 247,000 respectively. Higher middle level technical schools also expanded enrolment during the same period by 240 per cent although its rate was lower than that of the growth of the total technical education system (280 per cent).

The higher education level of the formal technical school system experienced the lowest enrolment growth rates except in the on-the-job training centres, even though the number of students more than doubled during the same period (from 45,000 in 1970-71 to 110,000 in 1978-79).

The higher technical education consists of the National Polytechnical Institute (IPN) which, in addition to offering a bachelor's degree in 14 disciplines, counts with 10 post-graduate centres with 37 Master's and 10 Doctorates programmes, 48 regional technological institutes and 17 marine biology institutes, among others. Between 1970-71 and 1978-79, the IPN enrolment doubled as the result of an annual growth rate of 7.5 per cent. The 1978-79 enrolment of 77,000 students at IPN accounted for 70.5 per cent of all students in the technological area. However, the IPN's enrolment dropped to 53,000 students only in 1980-81.

According to recent studies,[34] the unfavourable results of technical education's expansion between 1960 and 1985 in Mexico could be attributed to various factors: no substantial difference seems to exist between the training given by technical and non-technical schools; income of technical school graduates is generally lower than that of general secondary school graduates; employers prefer to hire secondary school graduates rather than those finishing technical schools; the jobs obtained are inferior to the job-seekers' apparent qualifications or expectations (especially for women), and technical secondary school graduates prefer to pursue university studies. The combination of these factors have discouraged young people from the lower social strata from entering technical schools, especially since this type of education is not regarded as a means of upward mobility, the natural aspiration for most of the people seeking a technical education.

b Training and skills upgrading

In 1970, the number of technicians and workers engaged in the on-the-job training and skills upgrading courses was estimated at about 140,000.

32

TABLE 4.1

GROWTH OF TECHNICAL EDUCATION: 1970-78

Schooling level	1970-71		1978-79		% of total	Percentage increase 1970-78	Annual average increase rate of interest 1970-78
	Number of schools	Enrolment	Number of schools	Enrolment			
Training centres	27	21,811	33	27,067	3.3	24.1	2.7
Secondary level	189	84,852	1,032	446,966	54.7	426.8	23.1
Agricultural	87	16,816	734	192,998	23.6	1,047.7	35.7
Industrial	102	68,036	266	246,665	30.2	262.6	17.5
Fishing	-	-	32	7,303	0.9	-	-
Higher middle level	25	62,401	250	213,584	26.2	242.3	16.6
Terminal higher middle level	10	1,312	41	19,376	2.4	1,376.8	40.0
Higher education	25	45,051	80	109,295	13.4	142.6	11.7
Total	276	215,427	1,436	816,288	100.0	278.9	18.1

Source: Secretaría de Educación Pública, México.

Although this figure rose to 458,000 in 1985, this sector's relative share in the entire educational system increased only slightly from 1.4 per cent in 1980 to 1.8 per cent in 1985.

Notwithstanding acceptable growth in programmes and courses of this kind, as well as an increase in institutions and enterprises involved in the training effort over the past 15 years, the overall picture is not encouraging for a number of reasons.[35]

a) Enterprises did not allocate enough resources for training programmes (70 per cent did not even include them in the budget and 22 per cent allocated less then the equivalent of $5,000 in 1982).
b) Joint management-labour training committees functioned more in theory than in practice.
c) Courses for training and skills upgrading were seriously handicapped because the labour force had little or no formal schooling.
d) Unskilled workers received the least training.
e) Personnel turnover rates were high.
f) The business sector regarded training as the government's responsibility. Therefore, only the state-owned firms and a few transnationals such as Ford, Nestlé and Volkswagen, had training programmes.
g) Employees felt that the programmes benefited the company rather than the workers and union leaders often violated training agreements in favour of management.

Another study of the on-the-job training revealed in 1979[36] that:

a) None of the training facilities had obtained official approval for their curricula.
b) Some 65 per cent of the teachers had neither academic or pedagogical training nor any formal studies.
c) 63 per cent of the trainees took courses strictly to obtain better paying jobs.
d) Only 25 per cent of the trainees were satisfied with these courses although 90 per cent of them considered the available facilities as good.

In the light of these few enquiries into the on-the-job training and skills upgrading activities, it seems clear that their actual contribution to the technical improvement of the industrial labour force in the country continues, to say the least, to be marginal.

c Higher education

In 1985, 1,200,000 students were enroled in institutions of higher learning, including graduate schools, as compared with 271,275 students in 1970. Thus, the student population had practically increased fivefold in just fifteen years. The Mexican 'elitist' universities of the 1960s with 30,000 students, have become the 'universities of the masses', at least in the country's largest cities.

The following trends in university enrolment could be observed over the same period:

a) Strong and steady increases in the attendance numbers, especially in government owned higher education institutions and the teacher's colleges.
b) A drop in enrolment at the National Polytechnical Institute, IPN, which accounted for 70 per cent of all technological training at the university level until 1975. Moreover, enrolment in engineering, technology and natural and exact sciences decreased as compared with other study areas.
c) The National University of Mexico's share of enrolment within the higher education system fell from 58.4 per cent in 1960 to 27 per cent in 1970 and 13.6 per cent in 1985.
d) Private universities' (including those not approved officially) share of enrolment remained stable (11.5 per cent in 1970 and 13 per cent in 1985), even though the number of graduates in proportion to undergraduates was in them much higher than at the National University.

Although in the last ten years, the number of students in higher education grew in absolute numbers in all areas of study, nothing has been able to successfully counteract the continued strong preference for medicine, social sciences and administrative and business schools. 17 per cent of the total student body was studying medicine in 1970 and 14 per cent in 1985. In 1970, 40 per cent of students were enroled in social science faculties and administrative and business schools as compared with 43 per cent in 1985. The enrolment in engineering and technology in the broadest sense declined slightly from 32 per cent of student population in 1970 to 27 per cent in 1985.

The patterns of graduate studies did not change much until at least 1980. In that year, 25.8 per cent of the 82,344 graduates had studied medicine, 35.8 per cent were in social science and administrative and business schools and 25.3 per cent in the natural sciences. The relative number of undergraduates finishing the studies declined, however, drastically.

According to the Ministry of Education, the number of people receiving bachelor's degrees dropped between 1967 and 1978 from 58.2 per cent to 39.7 per cent of those who entered higher education schools five years earlier.

Graduate study level for Master's and Doctorate degrees, a relatively new area in Mexico, deserve some comments. In the 1975-76 academic year, total enrolment in Master's programmes was 7,550 whereas only 232 people were engaged in studies leading to a Doctorate. The largest number of graduate students again choose social sciences and administration (53 per cent of Master's and 50 per cent of Doctorates) while only 2.8 per cent of the Master's degrees and 14 Doctorate candidates were studying physics. The situation was even more dramatic in chemistry and mathematics. While each discipline accounted for less than 2 per cent of all Master's degrees candidates, 6 Doctorate degree candidates studies chemistry and 11 mathematics.

In brief, although because of explosive growth of the informal and formal educational systems at all levels, social, economic and cultural needs of the Mexican society have been met in quantitative terms to a large extent, certain levels and areas of study are practically non-existent in the absence of the resolution of most of the serious qualitative problems. The latter are a consequence of not only the phenomenal growth of the educational system, but also of improvised measures accompanying this quantitative expansion, and the lack of planning and coordination reflecting a kind of autonomy within which the educational system operates according to principles inconsistent with the needs of a modernizing society.

In 1985, Mexico's educational system was still structured like a kind of pyramid which at a closer look was rather similar to a sky-scraper. It is true that the structure had a very broad base composed of nursery and primary education (78 per cent in 1980 and just under 70 per cent in 1985), but even at that level a high drop-out rate, particularly in rural areas, prevailed; the intermediate level accounted for only 22.6 per cent of students at all levels in 1985 against 17.9 per cent in 1970; but more than one hundred universities, technological institutes and other centres of higher learning were attended by only 4.9 per cent of the educational pyramid members in 1985 (in contrast with 3.5 per cent in 1970), also with a high drop-out rate.

The problems facing the educational system in Mexico are easy to identify:

a) Despite the sizable increase in overall enrolment, the absolute number of those outside the education system is very high. In 1980, 22 million Mexicans had not finished even elementary school and over six million were illiterate.

b) The problems of access to elementary school are closely linked to the low incomes of the rural population. Although more education services have become available, most rural inhabitants only attend school for one to three years, generally in one-room school houses with barely educated and badly-paid teachers and extremely limited resources. The drop-out problem, absenteeism (often higher among teachers than students), belated entrance and inadequate learning processes still persist.

c) Although elementary education in urban areas is available to all children and average rates of attendance are high, serious shortcomings of quality of education and scholastic achievement have not been taken care of. The teaching quality of private schools is better than that of public ones, and scholastic achievement varies according to social class.

d) The probability of failure is higher at the beginning of each cycle or educational level than throughout the remaining grades of the same level. Likewise, the proportion of students who complete one level and go on to the next is also very high.

e) When education became 'mass education', the drop-out rates increased and the quality graduates declined.

f) Internal effects of migrations on education have not been evaluated as yet. In a country like Mexico, where significant internal migrations from the interior to the urban areas take place, it might be counterproductive to try to design and implement a rural education programme adopted to the requirements of the environment, since any children and young adults will eventually move to urban areas.

g) With regard to international migration, whose most dramatic expression is the brain drain, although Mexico counted until the early 1980s with more technicians and professionals educated abroad that the number of unskilled labour leaving the country for economic reasons, the situation has reversed itself in most recent years as a result of the deep economic crisis.

h) Education actually takes place inside the schools and higher level institutions. However, there is a tremendous gap between what people think should be done, what they say is being done and what really is being done within the educational system. This reality represents one of the weakest links in the entire educational chain, which effects educational quality at all levels in Mexico. Teaching methods in higher education are subject to the play of political interests, and graduates often take their places in life inadequately prepared professionally. In addition, when universities were opened to the masses, the answer to the problems created by dramatically higher enrolment was inadequate and continues to be limited, with marginal exceptions, to improvising the teaching staff.

3 Scientific and technological scene

Two issues have been singled out in discussions in the country about its scientific and technological backwardness: the technology transfer process and the domestic capability to adapt the foreign scientific and technological knowledge, whether embodied in imports of goods or acquired by other means.

The evaluation of the role played by foreign technology in Mexico's industrialization is very difficult because of the scant availability of corresponding data. It is particularly true for the period prior to the early 1970s, in which, on one hand, the government regarded the contribution of technological progress to the development process as relatively unimportant, and, on the other, public and private, domestic and foreign enterprises generally refused to collect and make public information related to technological aspects of their operations. The situation improved somewhat in the 1970s, thanks to the different laws implemented in the first half of that decade. An official policy in technology transfer was defined in November 1972, when a law providing for the approval of technology transfer contracts and another on the patents and trademarks use and exploitation were drafted at the then Ministry of Trade and Industry with the full support of the Presidency. Previously, the technology transfer has been taken care of by various measures included in industrial development legislation.[37] Until late 1972, the Mexican government confined its participation to monitoring the costs of acquiring technology abroad in foreign currency. It did not seem to be concerned with what these technologies really were and how they would function within Mexico's particular development characteristics nor did it offer to help the private sector to adapt imported technology to local conditions.

Even though the debate on the technology issue had educated both public opinion and the direct actors involved in the technology transfer process, the general trend towards dependence on imported technology continued. This is evident when the evolution of expenditure on technology is taken into account.

a Technology transfer

Between 1970 and 1978 total expenditures on technology, understood as the payment of royalties on technology transfer as well as independent consultants' fees for short term technical services, rose from $80.3 million to $208.9 million (Appendix - Table 8.31). Because not all technology transfer contracts were registered and the characteristics of the intra-company accounting practices of foreign subsidiaries were not considered, this figure can be considered as an approximation only. The technology transfer costs must be looked upon within a broader context of foreign exchange transfers by direct foreign investment in Mexico during the same period.

Their total foreign exchange transfers on current account increased between 1970 and 1978 from $357.5 million to $823.5 million and interest payments increased from $91.7 to $398.7 million. A large part of these payments also involved payments for technology.

There is no doubt that both foreign and domestic enterprises spend sizable amounts of money on imported technology. However, important differences existed between the two industrial groups due to varying degrees of technological intensity related to product types and the different magnitudes of the efforts to develop local technological capabilities (Appendix - Table 8.32).

In 1975, foreign enterprises - subsidiaries of transnational companies in the main - accounted for 60 per cent of all spending on technology. Most of these enterprises operated in technology-intensive sectors, such as basic chemical products, pharmaceuticals and synthetic fibres, the automotive industry and industrial chemicals (Appendix - Table 8.33). Domestic enterprises spent less on technology. Three quarters of their technology expenditure came from a limited number of the technology-intensive enterprises (Appendix - Table 8.34). The most important were domestic companies producing iron and steel (43.2 per cent), basic chemicals, pharmaceuticals and synthetic fibres (12.2 per cent); industrial chemicals and fibres (8.1 per cent), and electrical appliances (5.1 per cent).

In Mexico as in other developing countries, the purchase of technology abroad can be classified under the same categories: contractual agreements, payments for the use of patents, licenses and technical assistance, as well as those originating in direct foreign investment.[38] In Mexico each of these major modes was used according to its importance to a particular sector and the nature of ownership of the enterprises involved (domestic or foreign).[39]

According to data available at the National Technology Transfer Registry, 6,669 contracts had been registered by late 1979, of which 5,443 or 80 per cent were destined for manufacturing enterprises. Priority manufacturing sectors[40] accounted for 3,526 contracts or two thirds of all manufacturing contracts registered prior to 1979 (Appendix - Table 8.35), indicating that these sectors were responsible for the bulk of technological demand in the manufacturing industry. Foreign enterprises accounted for a sizable share (about 47 per cent) while the rest corresponded to domestic companies. Since these are global figures, they do not reflect variations in the degree of each sector's external technological dependence on both foreign and domestic companies. The dependence on domestic enterprises was high in pharmaceuticals, auto parts and electrical appliances; low in industrial chemicals and even lower in the iron and steel industry. The relatively reduced dependence of the last two sectors can be explained by the fact that even though both are technology-intensive their demand for technology was mainly satisfied by domestic suppliers. Thus the available evidence seems to support the argument that the accumulation and use of domestic technology can be facilitated by state participation in the industrialization process, as in the two examples given, if a certain amount of advanced technological capability already exists in the country.

A more detailed analysis of technological aspects of the technology transfer contracts and their subsequent use may help to establish their relationship with the build-up of domestic technological capability. In general, these contracts cover seven elements: trademarks, patents, unpatented technical assistance, know-how, basic and detailed engineering services, and management services.

The Mexican literature on the subject[41] which used the same classification as the National Technology Transfer Registry, (Appendix - Table 8.36) offers the following analytical conclusions:

a) The elements most frequently transferred were non-patented know-how and technical aid.

b) While trademarks appeared in about half of the contracts, patent licenses appeared in only 20 per cent.

c) Engineering services were least frequently mentioned and were appearing in only 10 per cent of the contracts.

d) The relative frequency of technological elements was almost the same in contracts established by foreign and domestic enterprises.

While in general terms, there was no significant differences in contract terms between foreign and domestic enterprises, it may be worth mentioning that the frequency of each technological element differed according to the sector considered. For example, for foreign enterprises, technical know-how was more frequent in capital and consumer goods industries, and the use of trademarks appeared more often in non-durables and capital goods. The situation was similar for domestic companies, except in non-durables, where the use of trademarks was more important.

For the purpose of this essay one of the most interesting features of the contracts analysis is the role played by Mexican R and D suppliers. The data available identifies two types of local suppliers, according to their degree of specialization and diversification. The first group consists of several large engineering and consulting firms which operate in different industrial sectors and technology markets at the same time. The domestic iron and steel industry signs half of their contracts with this group of suppliers. The oil and petroleum derivatives industry also falls within the same category, since the Mexican Petroleum Institute (IMP) has become the major source of know-how and technical assistance for the state-owned Petróleos Mexicanos. Although the IMP and other domestic suppliers meet only half of the hydro-carbons sector's technological demand, this fact represents a step in the right direction.[42]

When one looks at these problems from a different methodological viewpoint, like for example the evaluation of technology exports by different domestic enterprises between 1970 and the beginning of 1980, another study arrives at similar results.[43] Thus the technology exporting sector seems to reflect the areas in which the country has acquired technological capacity locally as the result of accumulated productive experience, technological efforts, supported in part by the state, and the skilling of domestic human resources. Such is the case of Mexican technology exports in the area of construction related to the development of engineering capacity in water works and pipeline construction. According to the same study almost all technology exports in the manufacturing sector originate in the mature industrial branches. It is even more interesting that some of the technology exports based upon local innovations are closely linked to the conditions surrounding the processing of domestically available natural resources. Such is the case of IMP (oil), HYLSA (natural gas), Cussi's (bagasse). In other cases technology experts were closely related to or derived from direct state intervention supporting the establishment of a domestic technological capacity.

Thus, it seems that despite industry's generalized and continuous technological dependence upon external sources, there are segments in which local sources of technology have begun to play a significant role. Although the technological learning process which is taking place is still insufficient, at least part of the Mexican industry has been able to advance in this respect.

b Domestic R and D activities

Domestic spending on science and technology increased very considerably at constant prices in the past 15 years from 772 million pesos in 1970 to 4,729 million pesos in 1985 (Appendix - Table 8.37). Its share of total federal expenditure budget rose from 0.15 per cent in 1970 to 0.51 per cent in 1985. Private expenditure on these activities continued to be very small.

Funds assigned to the National Technology Council (CONACYT), an agency created in 1970, grew slowly but steadily from 41 million pesos in 1971 to 505 million in 1985. In 1985 these resources represented a 0.06 per cent share in GDP, a 10.68 per cent share in total domestic spending and an 11.21 per cent share in total government expenditure for science and technology (Appendix - Table 8.38)

Until 1985 almost 95 per cent of all spending in the scientific and technological areas was made by the state. However, it would be more realistic to estimate it at about 90 per cent since official agencies do not usually record R and D outlays by private foundations and enterprises. Even so, science and technology depends heavily on federal government budget appropriations.

Over the last decade, substantive changes have occurred in the federal government's expenditure patterns for science and technology (Appendix - Table 8.39).

The share of basic research dropped from 5.4 per cent of the total in 1975 to 3.8 per cent in 1980 and to 8.5 per cent in 1985. Funding for applied research declined even more sharply from 30 per cent in 1975 to 10 per cent in 1980 and only 15 per cent in 1985. A similar pattern was observed in experimental development, which decreased from 13 per cent to 11.8 per cent and 11.5 per cent for 1975, 1980 and 1985 respectively.

Research on education share showed a cyclical pattern. Between 1975 and 1980, it jumped from 26.6 per cent to 56.2 per cent, only to fall to 22.2 per cent in 1985. It should be emphasized that the relative share of support activities (although it is unclear just what this classification refers to) for scientific and technological research, or 'associated activities', increased considerably from 16 per cent in 1975 to 13.3 per cent in 1980 and 45 per cent in 1985.

According to figures at current prices (Appendix - Table 8.40), the functional distribution of the government's R and D funding also varied significantly, reflecting the sudden priority changes of the subsequent plans and programmes.

In 1975, agricultural, industrial and educational research was assigned just under 70 per cent of fiscal resources, research related to health and social security matters received approximately 11 per cent, research on improvement of administration and management 13.6 per cent, and the remaining 5.7 per cent was dedicated to research on telecommunications and transport. By 1985, the industrial research share jumped to over 50 per cent; that of research on education fell to 2.5 per cent and agricultural research participated with 10.8 per cent, and that on telecommunications and transport practically disappeared (1.6 per cent).

Behind the relative growth of government spending on science and technology which did not exceed 0.58 per cent of GDP in its record years, one can detect a great emphasis put on expenditure for the institutional infrastructure devoted to scientific and technological research. No data are available, however, which would permit the evaluation of the extent to which the build-up of the infrastructure translated itself in the quantitative and qualitative research improvement.

Data for the 1982-83 academic year (Appendix - Table 8.41), which cover all institutions of higher learning engaged in research in exact and natural sciences, other government research institutes, private universities and approximately 70 per cent of private institutes and research centres, suggest that:

a) Notwithstanding the attempt to decentralize scientific and technological activities, 30 per cent of all institutions, centres and universities dedicated to research were concentrated in the Federal District and greater Mexico City.
b) Out of the 12,600 specialized personnel dedicated presumably to research less than 1,200 were doing full-time research.
c) The National University accounted for 14 per cent and the National Polytechnical Institute for 4.5 per cent of the total of the full-time researchers.

Sketchy information on scientific and technological output and productivity in Mexico may be worth presenting although they are very difficult to measure in a society which is still unaccustomed to R and D quality control.[44] In evaluating national scientific and technological output three indicators are used: only seven scientific magazines were published in Mexico in 1984; four monthly publications printed 20,000 copies each; and the total circulation of the remaining three did not exceed another 20,000 copies (Appendix - Table 8.42).

In comparison with other major countries even in Latin America, the number of scientific authors is very low. Between 1976 and 1983, their number in Mexico rose steadily from 606 to 1,060, 14.6 per cent of all publishing in Latin America and only 0.19 per cent worldwide. With regard to the ratio between projects, researchers and R and D spending vs. scientific authors, Mexico occupies an intermediate position in comparison with other Latin American countries. In Chile, for example, 2.0 projects, 4.9 researchers and $90,000 are required to produce one scientific author. At the other end of the spectrum, in Peru it takes almost 50 projects, 53 researchers and $710,000 to generate a scientific author. In Mexico, 14.6 projects, 11.2 researchers and $400,000 are needed to produce one author.[45]

Finally, from the total of 5,419 patent registration requests presented until the end of 1980, 704 requests originated with Mexican residents and

4,775 with non-residents (13 per cent and 87 per cent respectively). Of 2,523 patents granted, 174 were granted to residents and 2,349 to non-residents (69 per cent and 93.1 per cent respectively), (Appendix - Table 8.43).

An overall evaluation of the present R and D situation in Mexico indicates that despite some progress in the 1970s and the early 1980s, efforts thus far may have contributed relatively little to the scientific and technological advancement of the country. Mexico's scientific and technological community is small and heterogeneous and faces serious problems of linkages both with the education system and potential users. A high percentage of Mexico's research centres, including those located at universities, seem to neglect the fact that in order to create knowledge useful to the productive sector, appropriate formal links must be established with this sector and, in many instances, complete technological packages must be elaborated for potential clients.

The sectorial heterogeneity of the scientific effort is an even more critical issue than the geographical concentration of R and D centres. Certain areas of science, such as biology, have been well developed whereas others, especially in technology are extremely backward. According to experts in engineering, process design has an acceptable capability level whereas equipment design continues undeveloped and R and D in basic engineering has still to start.

V   Technological development policies

The need for an integrated science and technology policy, consistent with the country's economic, social and cultural requirements, started being perceived in Mexico only in the late 1960s. In spite of some progress made in this respect by the state and scientific community during the 1970s, one can hardly talk about the emergence of a long term policy in that field even though some components of such a policy do exist.

Among the various planning exercises, the most serious was the first one, *Plan Nacional Indicativo de Ciencia y Tecnología*.[46] This plan elaborated by the National Science and Technology Council and made public in 1976 was based on a thorough evaluation of the existing scientific and technological system. Some 300 leading scientists and technologists participated in its elaboration.

The analytical part of the plan confirmed that although scientific and technological activities had experienced constant expansion, their excessive dependence on science and technology advancement patterns in the industrialized countries resulted largely in the system becoming its copy. The system lacked financial support and manpower adequately trained in qualitative and quantitative terms. Financial resources, concentrated both geographically and institutionally, were inadequately distributed. Important research areas had been neglected and permanent links among R and D, education and production had not existed. The divorce between the technically complex needs of the productive system and activities of the scientific and technological community was encouraged by the structure and the preferences of the latter. Moreover, diffusion of the scientific and technological advances was very weak, limiting their impact on the educational system and hampering the transmission of knowledge to the productive sector. This situation was most serious in non-commercial agriculture and consumer goods manufacturing.

El Plan Nacional Indicativo de Ciencia y Tecnología (1976) was based on two premises: First, recognizing the increasing importance of science and technology in economic and social development, if considered imperative to organize systematically and institutionalize R and D activities. Second, in view of underdevelopment the relative shortage of financial resources and the magnitude of the needs of vast sectors of the population it embraced the idea of long term science and technology planning and of establishing R and D priorities.

This plan conceived science and technology planning as a permanent, flexible and participative exercise that would take care also of creating a demand for the domestically produced knowledge, given that this demand was being met mostly by external sources. The plan's basic goals were: scientific development, cultural autonomy and technological self-determination.

The national scientific and technological development policy required to gradually attain these objectives implied the following lines of action:

a) Incorporating science and technology policy into Mexico's overall development policy.

b) Establishing a science and technology development strategy related closely to the country's needs and objectives, without looking for the autarky in this field.

c) Overcoming scientific and technological backwardness and the lack of integration of the domestic scientific and technological system through a joint effort of the state, research institutions, the educational system and the productive sector.

d) Fostering science and technology in a context that would recognize their social value and especially, their importance in attaining long term national development objectives.

e) Striving for excellence in certain unexplored and underdeveloped areas of science, some of which were crucial in solving domestic problems.

f) Recognizing that the technological effort requires parallel and simultaneous action on different technological fronts.

In addition to establishing overall goals and policy guidelines, the plan addressed itself in detail to all aspects of the science and technology infrastructure problems, from manpower training, producing and maintaining R and D equipment and scientific instruments, to the advisable patterns of international cooperation. Goals and guidelines for action in this respect were set for the incoming six-year presidential term (1977-82).

The plan defined also policy objectives and guidelines in the exact and natural sciences, and the social sciences. A similar exercise was done for technological development for each priority productive sector. Furthermore, the plan quantified the expenditure needed to meet the outlined targets indicating that by 1982 it should rise to slightly over one per cent of GDP. The state's participation in funding R and D would be reduced and the private sector's share would increase.

The plan proposed institutional changes in the management of science and technology activities. The National Science and Technology Planning Commission was to be established with high level participants from the government, major public enterprises, higher education institutions, and users of science and technology in the productive sector. The commission's main task would consist of coordinating the science and technology permanent global planning efforts. Close links were to be established between the planning process and the social and economic development strategy.

The permanent planning process was to be divided into four phases:

a) Formulating long term (20-25 years) scientific and technological development strategy.
b) Defining a medium term (10 years) national R and D policy.
c) Preparing the subsequent national scientific and technological plans for five or six years.
d) Designing research programmes and projects at the institutional and sectorial levels for the duration of each plan.

The plan stressed the urgency of establishing mechanisms that would assure the effective implementation of the sectorial R and D programmes, coordinate them with the users whether in the educational or productive sectors, and link programming at the institutional and sectorial levels with the annual federal science and technology budgets. Finally, it was also proposed that the state design fiscal, financial and other incentives for private enterprises that would help them to develop their own R and D capability, increase the use of domestic R and D and contribute significantly to the national effort in the field of self-reliant science and technology development.

Since scientific and technological advance alone cannot resolve the major underdevelopment problems, even the best planning in this field followed by its implementation at the institutional and sectorial levels is a necessary but not sufficient condition to contribute meaningfully to the country's development. According to the 1976 plan scientific and technological policy was to be incorporated into the overall development strategy. In operative terms, it meant that while a set of direct policy instruments for science and technology had to be established, policy instruments in many other fields directly affecting science and technology advancement had to be redesigned as well. However, even if all this were done, the results of the planning exercises might not necessarily be spectacular due to the sharp changes which characterize the six-year political cycle in Mexico

In fact, the above described first attempt to start between 1973 and 1976 implementing a coherent, long term science and technology policy did meet with total failure. Such an outcome resulted from the complex interplay of power groups bent upon the defence of their own short term political and economic interests within a society almost totally incapable of appreciating the vital role played by science and technology in achieving some degree of the self-reliant development.

The following administration (1977-82) saw the appearance of the new National Science and Technology Programme for 1978-82. It was not only completely unrelated to the earlier CONACYT planning work but took the form of a disorganized directory of several thousands of isolated research projects submitted by the scientific and technological community members and devoid of any serious evaluation.[47]

The new programme, which ignored the recommendations of a 1976 plan submitted shortly before the change of government, provoked considerable criticism in the scientific community, as a convincing proof of the recurrent absence of continuity in scientific and technological policy. Similar critical opinions, expressed by many Mexican higher education institutions and technological and engineering associations, add to the impressive volume of judgments censoring the CONACYT's performance in the late 1970s. Even more serious, however, than the haphazard approach to the problems involved in elaborating scientific and technological research programmes, was the new programme's disregard for science and technology guidelines. It was reflected in documents presented by Mexico at the UN Conference on Science and Technology for Development, held in Vienna in August 1979.

The overall scientific and technological situation was resumed on the eve of the end of the 1977-82 administration by one of the leading Mexican social scientists in the following terms:[48]

a) While research proposals were incomplete, scientific and technological policy was considered as the domain of public sector spending policy. The complex interrelationship between science and technology and the development of society, economy and culture was not taken into account. No scientific and technological planning for development was pursued and science and technology were not included in the overall national planning even though the new Global Development Plan had been in force since 1979.

b) No evaluation had been made of the domestic scientific and technological effort, nor the impact of macroeconomic policy, especially of public sector investment and industrialization policies on technological decisions at a sectorial level and within production units had been considered. Inadequate linkages existed between partial science and technology programmes and the administrative and financial mechanisms (tariffs, licenses, interest rates, and credit, among others) responsible for most of the technological decisions. Technology transfer and industrial property policies were weak and ineffective.

c) Incentives for technological research were unsatisfactory with the possible exception of a few institutions with privileged budgets. Although the new set of fiscal incentives had been approved at the end of 1980, mechanisms for replacing even a small proportion of imported technology with domestic research and technological development efforts had not been established by 1982.

d) Despite the absence of coordination among CONACYT's actions some of them had a positive effect. Even though financial resources for science and technology had increased substantially, CONACYT did not satisfactorily perform its function as an overall coordinating agency for scientific and technological advancement.

e) The participation of the scientific community in science and technology was marginal.

f) The productive sectors, both public and private, continued to show indifference with regard to science and technology policy and domestic R and D expansion, partly because of ignorance. Some other factors related to the market conditions, contractual arrangements covering technology purchases, links with foreign enterprises, prejudices concerning domestic research capability and fears of risks accompanying innovation, played their negative role as well. Whatever the reasons were, the productive sector was not mobilized either to collaborate in the design of scientific and technological policy. Little technological innovation took place within enterprises and only exceptionally few of them supported domestic R and D within universities specialized in research centres.

The content of the most recent exercises in science and technology planning, the National Science and Technology Development Programme for 1984-88, confirms the persistence of serious problems in Mexico, arising from the lack of a long term approach to science and technology policy and making impossible self-reliant technological advancement.

The programme presently in force states at its outset that '...although it is based on a long term outlook it will remain in effect at least explicitly and on a compulsory basis, during the present administration only'.[49] Even though the strategic importance of scientific and technological activities is accepted by its authors, the programme runs the serious risk of becoming another piece of political rhetoric due to its limited scope, the absence of any permanent planning mechanism and the highly deteriorated economic and financial situation of the country. It is worth keeping in mind that the National Development Plan, formulated at the beginning of the present administration and containing policy strategies, objectives, targets and instruments, was discarded shortly after its public appearance in 1983. The reason was that the global plan became obsolete in the face of the 1982 economic crisis, complicated further by the magnitude of the country's external indebtedness and the behaviour of the international oil market.

All these circumstances seem to reinforce domestic and foreign doubts about the feasibility of a reasonably coherent and long term science and technology policy in Mexico.[50] If no progress in that respect was made when the Mexican Economy continued to grow rapidly, what progress can be expected at the time of the most serious crisis since the 1930s?

VI   Concluding assessment

Leaving aside the depth of the present crisis, one of the greatest obstacles facing science and technology policy design in Mexico arises from the difficulty to assess the impact of industrialization policies on science and technology development.

Until the beginning of the 1980s, industrial, monetary, fiscal and particularly foreign trade policies have not taken into account the need to accelerate scientific development and promote technological self-reliance in Mexico. Moreover, many of these policies have had a negative impact on scientific and technological advancement. The divorce between leading economic policy instruments and those designed to be applied to scientific and technological activities can be explained in part by the fact that scientific and technological policy was formulated only after the main lines of economic policy were agreed upon. Such sequence of policies reflected the position that the science and technology issues were external to the whole social and economic system, under the implicit albeit erroneous assumption that the results of R and D are incorporated into the economy via the accumulation process.

Since science and technology planning has not been regarded as essential for development, the initiatives aimed at the achievement of the technological self-reliance have never gone far beyond rhetorics. Except the 1976 CONACYT exercise the subsequent plans and the programmes for science and technology, elaborated in the past ten years within such a framework, have proven both insufficient and incomplete because scientific and technological policy has been viewed as just the building of research institutions to be taken care of by the public sector expenditure. In other words, contrary to what was happening elsewhere, including some newly industrialized countries, no systemic approach has been adopted in Mexico to scientific and technological activities.

Another feature of science and technology planning has been the lack of an objective assessment of efforts undertaken and their results. It is not just accidental that even the current national science and technology development programme is based on the inventory of available inputs of all sorts made in 1974.[51] Any planning exercise based on such outdated information must be biased and impossible to implement.

Still another shortcoming in the field of science and technology policy design in Mexico is the disregard of the dynamic relationship characterizing the science-technology-production-education sequence.[52] Practically all plans and programmes implemented to date, again with the exception of the still-born 1976 exercise, paid little attention to these relations perhaps because their authorship was left mostly to the bureaucrats completely unaware of the problems involved in science and technology management. In the programme presently in force, the treatment of the relationship between education at all levels, R and D and production of goods and services is superficial at best.[53] Consequently, it is not understood that the mere expansion of human and financial resources for scientific and technological activities does not ensure necessarily science and technology advancement. The progress in this respect depends more on linking educational, productive and scientific/technological systems than on the politically acceptable distribution of money to the existing isolated institutional structures or distributing scholarships abroad at random. As no country in the developing world can cover in our times the whole range of scientific and technological pursuits, the possibility of success along these lines can be discarded in a country of 80 million people and several thousand serious scientists and technologists.

Whatever its state of science and technology one has to remember that Mexico has undergone, since World War II, a broad transformation on many fronts. The country has attained an intermediate industrial development level and its population became predominantly urban. Although the state has been modernized also to a certain extent it remains locked within a one party system which has been designed for the mostly rural Mexico of the late 1920s.

Despite the progress in meeting society's basic needs, many significant deficiencies persist. Although the educational system has been largely expanded, it still takes the form of a disfunctional pyramidal structure and exhibits serious shortcomings from the viewpoint of access to education and its quality.

The capital-intensive industrialization based mainly on technology imports led to the emergence of three Mexicos: The modern private sector dominated by the largest transnational firms; the highly inefficient public industrial sector; and the host of small private domestically owned firms producing consumer non-durables and durable goods, facing a very uncertain future.

The growth model based upon import substitution and ensuing industrialization process has enabled Mexico to move ahead in the development process up to the point. The misadventures of the country during the short-lived oil boom (1977-81) indicate that the traditional growth model does not work any more. In the mid-1980s the Mexican society and economy are more dependent than ever before on the vagaries of the international economy and the policies of industrial countries. Perhaps the most important feature of this dependence is the absence of any correlation between macroeconomic growth performance and the progress in technological self-reliance. In other words, the modernization of productive structures was based mainly on imported technology and know-how, domestic creativity suffered greatly.

As this essay suggests Mexico's scientific and technological backwardness vis-a-vis more industrialized nations can be explained by the persistence of policies aimed at accelerating growth without structural change and by the subsequent lack of reasonably coherent long term science and technology strategies.

A serious economic crisis in 1982 makes the future of science and technology even more difficult. On the one hand, the crisis brought serious economic and financial restrictions which affect negatively national scientific and technological efforts. On the other, the rapid advance and spread of new technologies for producing goods and services in industrialized countries anticipate new trends in the international division of labour which will have a profound impact on Mexico and all other developing nations.

Mexico's present defence against the negative impact of the crisis on its infant scientific and technological development has three basic components: the effort to regain levels of federal budget allocations for science and technology; the more rational resources allocation in this field; and the design of a set of incentives to encourage investment in technological innovation by private enterprise. Two important restrictions complicate the situation. The first originates in the public finances disequilibrium and the macroeconomic approach underlying the state's scientific and technological efforts. Moreover, if public finances continue to contract and national income falls sharply, any increase in outlays for research and development in real terms will be impossible. Even if it were possible in theory, it will be displaced by the politically and socially urgent expenditure in other fields, particularly because they are absent in the country interest groups which would consider the expenditure on science and technology indispensable in the short run. Second, expecting that the private sector and particularly transnational enterprises will build in Mexico something close to a self-reliant scientific and technological capability amounts to believing in miracles. These two considerations seem to suggest that the future of technological transformation in Mexico is very bleak indeed.

VII Annex – Domestic technological capability: The contribution of the Instituto Mexicano del Petróleo (IMP) (Mexican Petroleum Institute)[54]

Judging by the participation in domestic gross product, the generation of revenues and employment and the multiple direct and indirect impact of its activities, the oil industry in Mexico represents the most important sector of the Mexican economy.

A fully vertically integrated state-owned enterprise, Petróleos Mexicanos (PEMEX), covers from the exploration and exploitation of hydrocarbons to production of basic petrochemicals, including domestic and foreign commercialization of all its products. Consequently, Petróleos Mexicanos is the key source of demand in the country for capital goods, machinery, equipment, know-how and technical assistance, all largely of foreign origin.

Instituto Mexicano del Petróleo (IMP) was established in the mid-1960s to stimulate and develop scientific and technological activities related to the exploitation of the country's hydrocarbon energy resources. Its main objective is to diminish the degree of Mexico's heavy dependence on foreign R and D in this field. While the IMP expansion is not representative of the Mexican science and technology advancement, this annex aims at providing some basic information about the range of the IMP activities, its achievements and its shortcomings in recent times.

The IMP achievements particularly in the 1970s and the early 1980s reflect to a considerable extent the highest priority given during the same period in Mexico to its oil industry.

The domestic R and D in this field received strong financial support at the expense of the R and D stagnation in other sectors of the economy. Moreover, the demand for energy-specific technologies increased considerably in response to the oil boom of 1976-82.

The IMP was able to meet the challenge thanks to the availability of highly qualified technical personnel. No less important were long-standing links with a number of specialized foreign enterprises traditionally providing Mexico with oil industry equipment and technical services. Some joint ventures helped considerably to strengthen domestic technological capability in the oil sector.

In 1938, as a result of the petroleum industry nationalization, Petróleos Mexicanos (PEMEX) appeared on the national scene as an integrated state-owned oil company heavily dependent upon equipment and other technology-intensive inputs, mostly of foreign origin. The obstacles due to the embargo policy applied by the countries of the former US, British and Dutch owners of the oil industry in Mexico brought about considerable constraints on the PEMEX productive capacity. The external technological dependence of the Mexican oil industry became so acute that those responsible for PEMEX started immediately a policy aimed at establishing a minimal domestic technological capability. It brought considerable results in the long run.

Forty-five years later, in 1983, the oil company had produced 2,750,000 barrels of crude oil and condensates and 4.25 billion cubic feet of natural gas per day, it counted with proven crude reserves of close to 72 billion barrels and operated 9 refineries and 92 petrochemical plants. This very large expansion of productive capacity and of production range reflected in part the accumulated experience of the technical personnel of PEMEX and the Instituto Mexicano del Petróleo (IMP) established in 1965.

Although the IMP contribution to the establishment of the domestic technological capability in the Mexican oil industry still falls short of its needs on many fronts, as is demonstrated by the analysis of the IMP activities carried on in the 1970s and the early 1980s in exploration, hydrocarbons production, refining and basic petrochemistry.

1 The IMP and local capabilities in exploration technologies

By 1970, five years after its establishment, the IMP was already involved, albeit on a very modest scale, in developing technologies. That year its *Subdirección de Tecnologiá de Exploración* (Exploration Technology Division) had a budget of 10 million pesos and some 180 technical and administrative employees. By 1982, the budget of that division had expanded at current prices seventy times although, according to official sources, its personnel did not increase significantly (by less than 50 per cent only).

In 1970, the technical, academic-level staff of the same IMP division concentrated mainly on widely-known abroad geological and geophysical technologies. Geology related activities of a varying nature were carried out at different technical levels. Geochemical analyses were made of ground and well samples; maps, photographs and drawings were also prepared. In 1973 still only 13 technical geological services were provided for distinct PEMEX entities, the main one being its Exploration Division.

Other IMP research activities and geophysical studies were even more limited in the early 1970s: only two computer programmes and three geophysical modeling research projects were developed. As in earlier years, no programme for designing exploration equipment or technologies existed. The same pattern of activities continues to 1980, the date at which only 12 projects for computer programmes, 11 research projects on geophysical models and 3 projects for developing new technologies were registered.

Nevertheless, during the 1973-82 period an annual average of 5 seismological processing services were carried out and during those 12 years 7 gravimetric services and 6 magnetometric services were provided to PEMEX. There were no services rendered in the fields of electrical methods or optical processes.

The majority of the services provided to PEMEX consisted of processing shooting points, updating programmes for gravimetric and magnetic interpretation, and the elaboration of geological-magnetic models. Seismological processing services were made available and continue to be provided to Central America (Jamaica, Costa Rica, Cuba and Nicaragua) and outside that region, to China and India. Quality control has been improved in respect to monitoring data and confirming the parameters of seismic sections of five petroleum-bearing zones: northern Mexico, Poza Rica, northeastern Mexico, southern Mexico and the Gulf of Mexico. From 1973 to 1982, PEMEX's exploratory activities were conducted principally in offshore zones; during the first year of this period, over 250,000 shooting points were processed. Throughout the period, that figure rose to two million.

The petroleum industry requires heavy investments in exploration in order to gather all the necessary data to take the right decision from the enormous ranges of possibilities open. In this area, the situation regarding local capabilities can be summed up as follows.

As of 1973, the IMP has already been capable of processing all the seismological data obtained in the field by PEMEX brigades, including those devoted to offshore exploration on the Mexican continental platform.

The Geophysical Data Processing Centre began to function in September of 1972 and, during the following six months, processed approximately 70,000 shooting points, equivalent to 15,000 kilometres of seismological exploration lines.

By 1978, that centre had already processed 80,000 kilometres of seismological lines. After operating for ten years, the centre - with its modern equipment - met in 1982 most of PEMEX's needs for seismological data processing, which allowed for better control and organization of information on the subsoil conditions and significant time and money savings. Before the setting up of the Data Processing Centre at the IMP all the geophysical information obtained by PEMEX through its onshore and offshore exploratory teams was processed in the United States.

However, from 1979 to 1982, Mexico was still dependent on foreign sources for software to process and analyze data on its subsoil. Since computer programme kits were imported from the USA, their users continued to lack detailed knowledge on how all those systems operate. While the Mexican oil industry learned how to utilize costly and sophisticated equipment and processes, it still continued to rely on very expensive innovations in software developed abroad.[55]

Since 1973, the ERTS-A satellite has been used to develop tectonic maps of northern Mexico. The first regional tectonic study covered the northern part of the State of Coahuila and the Sierra Madre Oriental, similar studies were continued in Baja California and Somora and others begun in Mexico's central region and the areas comprising Oaxaca and Chiapas in the south. Two years later, the National Energy Commission requested that the IMP initiate - in collaboration with the Western Geophysical Company - a study aimed at quantifying the country's hydrocarbon reserves. Using data from satellites and from radiometric geochronometry, work was pursued on diagenetic-stratigraphic, paleontological, palynological, geochemical and tectonic-petrographic studies on all the zones under the PEMEX explorations.

2 The IMP and local capabilities in exploitation technologies

In 1973, the activities of the IMP's Subdirección de Tecnología de Explotación (Exploitation Technology Division) were divided into four areas: oil deposits, drilling, evaluation of formations and corrosion. Among these activities the most important were the development of norms and quality control for drilling fluids. Experimental work was concentrated in the development of equipment to study phase behaviour of hydrocarbon mixtures, conduct tests for displacement in steady-rate flow; recover oil by steam infection and design means of thermal stimulation for oil and gas wells.

Insofar as the design and fabrication of equipment was concerned, for the first time the following were made available: constant pressure test-porosimeters, gas permeameters, mercury distillers, flash separators and other items at a similar technology level. An electrical impulse coder and recorder was built for PEMEX and the repair and maintenance servicing was provided for the PEMEX equipment and to private contractors.

In addition, packers, foaming agents, paraffin and scale crust inhibitors, new and basic demulsifiers, surfactants, muds and lubricants were developed. By 1974 the Exploitation Technology Division had already licensed to PEMEX three of the IMP patents, including the patent for foaming agent (IMP-EP-302).

One of the most intense activities of this division was the development and application of mathematical models to studies of oil fields. Efforts were directed most of all to numerical simulation of the behaviour of oil and dissolved gas deposits, saturated and undersaturated reservoirs and those subject to water programmes were used to design primary foundations and to analyze logs of mechanically-pumped wells. Similarly, work continued in the areas of theoretical and experimental research in order to come up with more suitable methods for oil displacement.

In 1975, work began toward developing models for studying the motion of waves on offshore platforms, so as to obtain information applicable to the design of such platforms. These efforts made possible the design of alternating current potentiometers, more precise digital and inductive wave sensors, temperature controllers and a prototype of a two-channel laboratory recorder.

From 1973, the number of ongoing projects run by the division began to rise sharply. In just three years they tripled, from 35 in 1973 to 106 in 1976. The opposite was the case with regard to the number of projects completed during that same time span. Whereas in 1973, 38 projects reached their conclusion, in 1976 only 23 did so. Detailed information on more recent years is not available, although in 1982 the IMP Exploitation Division ran 174 ongoing projects.

While from 1976 on, the already scant activity of basic and applied research dropped, most efforts were directed toward the evaluation of oil producing fields.

An almost constant feature of the activities reported by this division during the 1973-82 period has been the large quantity of projects on designing and fabricating equipment and mechanisms for both the IMP itself and several PEMEX departments. If significant advances were made in equipment design and construction, these necessarily were to be reflected in the IMP commercialization indexes. Unfortunately, there is not enough data to determine that commercialization capability.

Research in the area of exploitation consisted of geological studies and studies on the primary and secondary behaviour of reservoirs, the analysis of rocks and fluids, and the development of mathematical models applicable to problems in petroleum engineering. Electronic calculation programmes were worked out for models that analyze the flow of hydrocarbons in different types of seepage; research and development of new methods for ascertaining the most important petrophysical properties of porous media was encouraged, as well as the study and optimization of hydraulic fracturing. In addition, developmental and experimental work was done on chemical products needed in the different phases of production and quality control for the preparation of drilling muds and foundations.

Despite the above, basic research did not have high priority at the IMP Exploitation Division. Limited basic and applied research endeavours were defined largely by the interest and support of top officials. The few projects instigated on the initiative of the IMP staff, were extremely susceptible to intra-institutional conflicts and to PEMEX policy priorities.

In 1978, PEMEX began to request the IMP Exploitation Division that it dedicates itself to solving problems related to the exploitation of volatile oil deposits located in the cretaceous zones of Chiapas and Tabasco. The division responded by elaborating mathematical models to simulate the behaviour of those oil deposits. This change in R and D priorities involved the use of considerable human and financial resources and affected negatively the progress of a few projects for constructing equipment carried out at that time.

In 1979, in view of the importance which PEMEX assigned to the offshore production of hydrocarbons from the Campeche Bay, the IMP established a joint coordinating body with PEMEX for this purpose. In 1981, when it was confirmed that most of the crude oil produced in the new fields in Mexico was located in fractured deposits and that nowhere in the world was there to be found a totally satisfactory model for analyzing the development of such deposits, the IMP devoted considerable efforts to theoretical studies on the phenomenon of the flow of fluids through these porous and permeable media and on the initial aspects of a mathematical simulation of such flows. These efforts resulted in mathematical models enabling PEMEX to obtain useful and interesting findings and data on some wells in different production zones.

By 1982, the growing demand for services by PEMEX had led the IMP to a more intensive use of the models and computer programmes. In addition, its services for PEMEX, involving the codification, digitization, transcription and processing of data coming from geographical records kept on wells, including bottom-whole pressure readings, expanded considerably.

The IMP Exploitation Technology Division has also conducted studies geared to automating drilling activities. As of 1973, several projects were launched to improve automatic oil-well drilling systems. The experience gathered between 1965 and the mid-1970s has allowed the IMP to calculate variables in the case of well drills, and install and calibrate electrical recorders and automatic boring rigs. However, the IMP's limited ability to design and foster the fabrication of these types of equipment has become very apparent. Work has been concentrated on the evaluation of automatic drilling equipment acquired abroad. The division has not sponsored any project for disseminating information on the design and fabrication of automatic drilling equipment, although it has carried out research projects for equipment used to analyze fluids, heaters, special-range voltage sources, sensors, and resistivity-meters.

Technical services rendered by the IMP in this field to private industry can be summed up as follows: analysis, assessments and repairs of viscometers and the sale of products such as barite and clay.

In brief, from 1979 to 1982 the division concentrated its efforts on meeting the demands posed by PEMEX, which virtually led it to neglect its relations with private oil capital goods industry, which even before were not very significant. All this being kept in mind, by 1982 the IMP Exploitation Technology Division had achieved significant operational mastery of the technologies associated with oil production.

The participation of the IMP Exploitation Project Engineering Division also had a bearing on exploitation capabilities in that it developed general programmes for producing hydrocarbons, feasibility studies, basic and detail engineering, procedures for obtaining equipment and materials, and supervised project elaboration and control. Other projects also received a great deal of attention: those concerned with facilities for handling, transporting and distributing crude oil and gas in both onshore and offshore fields.

3 The IMP and local capabilities in refining technologies and basic petrochemistry

In the field of process engineering, the IMP had already licensed by 1973 four plants for the catalytic hydrodesulfurization of gasoline and intermediate distillates, with an initial capacity of over 100 barrels a day.

In conjunction with Universal Oil Products, the IMP also developed a process known as DEMEX licensed to PEMEX to be used in a plant with a 40,000 barrel a day capacity, located at Ciudad Madero. The process allows for selective demetallization of residual products that are to be subjected to desulfurization of disintegration processes. Several petrochemical processes were also developed, such as those relating, among others, to the production of low cost reticulable polyethylene and polyethylene-asphalitic resins.

Closely linked to these processes is that of developing catalysts, some of which have been put onto the market, such as those for catalytic hydrodesulfurization. In 1973 preliminary studies were begun by means of a reduction in the volume of sulphur in automobile fuel. In the field of refining and petrochemistry, experimental pilot plants had been set up with highly specialized analytical equipment and instruments, to perform research functions.

Eight years after its establishment, the IMP had managed to substitute a considerable number of imports of chemical, agents and additives used in dehydrating crude oil, deparaffinization, the reduction of freezing temperatures, hydraulic fracturing, smoke suppression in diesel motors, the retardation of the hardening of concrete, corrosion inhibition in systems, etc. During the same period the IMP began to license its technologies for use in secondary petrochemical industries and in the chemical industry both in Mexico and abroad. The Demex and IMPEX processes constituted the IMP's response to PEMEX's requirements, in that the new technical processes permitted to obtain from Mayan heavy crude (24° API) yields of products similar to those produced from lighter types of oil. The DEMEX and IMPEX processes allow for the elimination of metals and asphaltenes from the residue formed during high-vacuum distillation. As the application of this new technology has turned out to be very expensive, its use has been very limited.

In 1982 the same IMP division had completed designs for refining plants, some petrochemical plants, and other facilities. The number of projects for design of these industrial facilities surpassed 150 and represented an overall investment of more than 740 billion pesos. And even though Mexico still relies on basic engineering know-how from abroad - and, consequently, on foreign materials and equipment for the facilities that have been designed locally - the progress made until that year meant a saving of some $450 million in the area of engineering and approximately $100 million in technology royalties.

Basic engineering of refining and petrochemical technology carried out in Mexico has led to the development of process simulators adapted to undertake physical and energy balance sheets on all the operations involved in separation, distillation and absorption processes, 'flash' calculations, optimization of heat exchangers and calculation of the thermophysical properties of the compounds handled most frequently in the petroleum industry.

The development of industrial project engineering of basic petrochemicals has been a rapidly expanding field. Despite that fact, the results have not been very promising, except as regards the attainment of certain levels of capability in training technical teams and highly specialized labour for the construction of petrochemical plants.

The IMP continues studies aimed at achieving greater efficiency in the utilization of energy sources in physicochemical processes, as well as greater knowledge of molecular and catalytic processes. Other efforts are directed toward research on materials and toward the study of atmospheric pollution for the purpose of diminishing the effect of heavy crude oils on the environment.

Up until the beginning of 1985, the IMP Industrial Promotion and Production Division had processed 223 patent requests in Mexico and 59 from abroad. Of these, 57 were for refining and petrochemical processes, 97 were for chemicals and additives, 47 for catalysts and methods for obtaining them, and another 22 for other types of processes.

Prominent among all the patents licensed were the technologies involved in the DEMEX and IMPEX processes.

Of the 223 patent registrations requested by the IMP within Mexico, 94 have been granted. Moreover the IMP has presented requests for 59 patents in 21 foreign countries, of which 24 have been granted.

According to data from the IMP, a diagnosis of the petroleum and basic petrochemical industries' technological capacities in 1981 shows that approximately 82 per cent of the demand for technology was met at the local level and the remaining 18 per cent came from abroad. In the realm of engineering, 91 per cent of the oil industry needs were met from domestic sources. With regard to the design of capital goods, technological advance stayed behind since only 45 per cent of the designs came from local sources.

In conclusion the IMP has achieved significant progress in the operational mastery of technologies associated with the exploitation of hydrocarbons, but its capabilities for research and the design and fabrication of prototypal equipment, as well as its ability to advise local producers of goods and services for the petroleum industry, is still limited.

While the 1980 Mexican Energy Programme acknowledged the fact that self-sufficiency in the field of energy could only be maintained through active local participation in technological advance, it did not propose the policy guidelines in this respect for the energy subsector as a whole, let alone for the oil subsector. All it did was to take for granted that the state had several entities specifically devoted to scientific and technological research - the IMP, the Instituto de Investigaciones Eléctricas (IIE) (Institute for Electrical Research), the Instituto Nacional de Investigaciones Nucleares (ININ) (National Institute for Nuclear Research) - and assumed that the National Council on Science and Technology (CONACYT) would support the universities and research institutes so that energy-related disciplines would receive greater emphasis.

As regards the general policies followed during the period of rapid expansion of the petroleum industry (1977-82), the IMP played an important - although secondary - role without any normative effect upon technological decision-making that would have allowed for a gradual substitution of foreign participation in the development of the petroleum industry's different branches. This secondary role played by the IMP was due, basically, to PEMEX's tendency to turn to foreign countries to meet its needs for technology, reasoning that as soon as possible oil had to become the pillar of the development of the Mexican economy.

VIII Appendix

TABLE 8.1

INSTALLED ELECTRIC ENERGY CAPACITY
(THOUSANDS KW)

	Total a)	Hydro	Termo
1937	629	372	257
1940	681	389	292
1945	720	428	292
1950	1,235	607	628
1955	1,930	922	1,008

Source: Nacional Financiera, S.A., Statistics on the Mexican Economy, 1977.
Note: a) Operating capacity.

TABLE 8.2

ELECTRIC ENERGY PRODUCTION
(MILLION KWH)

	Total a)	Hydro	Termo
1937	2,480	1,822	658
1940	2,529	1,698	831
1945	3,069	2,092	977
1950	4,423	1,949	2,474
1955	7,002	3,447	3,555

Source: Table 8.1.
Note: a) Net generated total.

TABLE 8.3

ELECTRIC ENERGY SUPPLY AND CONSUMPTION
(MILLION KWH)

	Generation (1)	Imports (2)	Total Supply (1) + (2) = (3)	Consumption (4)
1940	2,529	21	2,550	2,276
1945	3,068	59	3,127	2,751
1950	4,423	125	4,548	4,187
1955	7,002	302	7,304	6,789

Source: Table 8.1.

TABLE 8.4

RAILWAY SERVICES: 1937-55

	Passengers a)	Goods b)
1937	1,719	5,381
1940	1,844	5,810
1945	3,405	8,024
1950	3,025	8,391
1955	3,764	10,961

Source: Table 8.1
Note: a) Millions of passengers/km transported.
        b) Millions of tons/km transported.

TABLE 8.5

ROAD NETWORK: 1937-55

	Total	Paved
1937	7,510	3,004
1940	9,929	4,781
1945	17,404	8,163
1950	21,422	13,585
1955	27,431	18,528

Source: Table 8.1

TABLE 8.6

MOTOR VEHICLES IN CIRCULATION: 1937-55

	Total	Automobiles	Buses	Trucks
1937	120,390	78,155	8,489	33,746
1940	145,708	93,632	10,141	41,935
1945	185,538	113,317	12,407	59,814
1950	302,798	173,080	18,466	111,252
1955	550,646	308,097	22,320	220,229

Source: Table 8.1

TABLE 8.7

EVOLUTION OF THE MANUFACTURING INDUSTRY: 1950-70

	Percent changes				Growth attributable to: (percentages)		
Period	RG	E	F	EF	Increased employ-ment	Increased pro-ductivity	Repro-duction made
1950-55	33.4	26.4	5.5	1.5	85	15	extensive
1955-60	24.9	25.3	7.6	1.9	77	23	extensive
1960-65	54.9	30.0	19.1	5.7	61	39	extensive
1965-70	51.2	22.4	23.5	5.3	49	51	mixed a)

Source: Valenzuela, José (1984), 'Determinantes del crecimiento y modalidades de la reproducción', La industria mexicana: tendencias y problemas, Universidad Autónoma Metropolitana, México.

Note: RG Percentage output change.
E Percentage employment change.
F Percentage producitivity change.
a) Relative equality between the extensive and intensive growth components.

TABLE 8.8

PRICE INDEXES: 1960-85
(1970=100)

	Consumer prices a)	Wholesale prices b)	Producer prices c)	GDP deflator at 1970 prices
1960	-	79.0	-	70.8
1961	-	79.7	-	73.2
1962	-	81.2	-	75.4
1963	-	81.6	-	77.8
1964	-	85.1	-	82.2
1965	-	86.7	-	84.1
1966	-	87.8	-	87.4
1967	-	90.3	-	89.9
1968	92.0	92.0	-	92.1
1969	93.5	94.4	-	95.7
1970	**100.0**	**100.0**	-	**100.0**
1971	105.3	103.7	-	104.5
1972	110.5	106.7	-	110.3
1973	123.8	123.4	-	123.9
1974	153.3	151.2	-	153.7
1975	176.5	167.1	-	179.3
1976	204.3	204.3	-	218.2
1977	263.5	288.4	-	288.2
1978	309.6	333.9	-	340.4
1979	365.9	395.0	-	410.9
1980	462.2	490.7	**100.0**	508.0
1981	591.6	611.0	125.5	646.6
1982	939.9	953.7	197.7	1,042.1
1983	1,897.5	-	394.1	2,002.3
1984	3,139.6	-	644.8	3,238.7
1985	4,952.6	-	1,001.0	5,000.7

Source: Banco de México, 'Serie Histórica, Precios and Informe Anual 1985'.

Note: a) Calculated since 1968 in accordance with historical series of Banco de México.
   b) In Mexico City until 1982, discontinued afterwards.
   c) Calculated only since 1980 (base year 1980).

66

TABLE 8.9

GROSS DOMESTIC PRODUCT: 1960-65
(MILLION PESOS AT 1970 PRICES)

	Gross domestic product
1960	212,586
1965	299,676
1970	444,271
1975	609,976
1980	841,854
1985 a)	911,544

Source: Nacional Financiera, S.A. (NAFINSA), op. cit., ed. 1984, Mexico 1984.

Note: a) Preliminary.

TABLE 8.10

PER CAPITA GDP: 1960-65
(CURRENT PRICES AND 1970 PRICES)

	Current prices	1970 prices
1960	4,302	6,081
1965	6,087	7,311
1970	9,001	8,681
1975	18,902	10,140
1980	63,079	12,086
1985 a)	584,932	11,696

Source: NAFINSA, op. cit., ed. 1981, pp. 21-2, ed. 1984, pp. 67-8 and Banco de México.

Note: a) Preliminary.

TABLE 8.11

MANUFACTURING OUTPUT BY INDUSTRIAL BRANCHES: 1960-85 a)
(MILLIONS OF 1970 PESOS)

	1960	1965	1970	1975	1980	1985 b)
Manufacturing output	40,861	62,931	105,203	148,057	209,682	223,991
Foodstuffs, beverages and tobacco	15,000	19,685	29,373	37,789	49,444	56,956
Textiles, garments and leather	7,675	12,344	15,520	20,193	26,047	26,027
Wood and wood products	1,265	1,473	3,607	4,644	6,969	6,278
Paper, paper products, printing and book publications	2,049	3,813	5,685	7,168	10,818	11,877
Chemical products, oil derivatives, rubber and plastics	4,638	6,756	18,432	29,605	45,319	55,343
Mineral non-metallic products except oil and carbon derivatives	1,669	2,798	6,088	8,727	11,847	12,534
Basic metal industries	3,962	6,048	5,855	8,165	11,822	11,513
Metal products, machinery and equipment	3,722	8,638	18,832	29,456	44,456	40,279
Other manufactures	881	1,376	1,811	2,310	2,960	3,184

Source: SPP, 'Sistema de Cuentas Nacionales de México 1970-1978', vol. III section 1, 1979-1981 vol. II section 12, 1981-1983; the data for 1960 and 1965 were constructed by the author to be compatible with the NAFINSA, op. cit. 1984 Edition and the SPP data, op. cit. 1985 Edition.

Note: a) In accordance with the classification used by the Mexican National Accounts System 1970-83, elaborated at the Ministry of Budget and Programming (SPP).

b) Preliminary.

TABLE 8.12

LABOUR FORCE BY SECTORS: 1960-85
(THOUSANDS OF PERSONS AND PERCENTAGES) a)

	1960		1965		1970		1975		1980		1985	
	b)	%	b)	%	b)	%	b)	%	b)	%	b)	%
Labour force	11,274	100.0	12,265	100.0	13,343	100.0	16,334	100.0	19,951	100.0	23,810	100.0
Primary sector	6,097	54.1	5,616	45.8	5,004	37.5	5,676	34.7	6,384	32.0	6,786	28.5
Industrial sector	2,144	19.0	2,584	21.1	3,083	23.1	4,011	24.6	5,187	26.0	6,429	27.0
Extractive and energy industry c)	183	1.6	210	1.7	240	1.8	351	2.1	499	2.5	631	2.6
Manufacturing	1,553	13.8	1,880	15.3	2,251	16.9	2,889	17.7	3,691	18.5	4,548	19.1
Construction	408	3.6	494	4.0	592	4.4	771	4.7	997	5.0	1,250	5.2
Services	3,033	26.9	4,065	33.1	5,256	39.4	6,674	40.9	8,380	42.0	10,595	44.5

Source: NAFINSA, op. cit. 1984 Edition.

Note: Percentages may not add to 100.0 due to rounding up of partial figures.
a) On June 30 of each year and estimates for 1985.
b) Thousands of persons.
c) Includes mining, petroleum and coal and electricity.

69

TABLE 8.13

CHANGES IN THE GDP STRUCTURE AND FOREIGN TRADE: 1960-85
(PERCENTAGES)

	1960	1965	1970	1975	1980	1985
Total gross domestic product a)	100.0	100.0	100.0	100.0	100.0	100.0
Primary sector	15.9	14.4	12.2	10.3	9.0	9.4
Industry	29.2	31.1	32.4	33.4	35.1	34.9
Mining	4.9	4.7	2.5	2.4	3.2	3.8
Manufacturing	19.2	21.0	23.4	24.3	24.9	24.6
Construction	4.1	4.0	5.3	5.4	5.5	4.7
Electricity	1.0	1.4	1.2	1.3	1.5	1.8
Services sector	55.9	55.4	56.3	57.5	57.2	57.1
Total goods exports b)	100.0	100.0	100.0	100.0	100.0	100.0
Agricultural	56.4	57.1	41.5	28.5	10.1	6.0
Industrial	43.6	42.8	36.8	67.3	89.9	94.0
Mining	20.8	18.0	12.5	24.9	67.8	69.9
Manufacturing	22.8	24.8	24.3	42.4	22.1	24.1
Non-classified exports	0.0	0.0	21.7	4.2	0.0	0.0
Total goods imports b)	100.0	100.0	100.0	100.0	100.0	100.0
Consumer goods	18.7	19.1	21.5	9.1	12.1	8.0
Intermediate goods	34.0	35.3	32.4	44.1	59.6	68.1
Capital goods	47.2	45.5	46.1	36.3	27.2	23.9
Non-classified articles	0.0	0.0	0.0	10.4	1.2	0.0

Source: NAFINSA, op. cit., Editions 1981, 1984 and SPP, op. cit. 1985.

Note: Total may not add to 100.0 due to the rounding up of partial figures.
0.0 = Insignificant per cent, smaller than 0.1%.
a) Based on the value of 1970 pesos.
b) Based on the value in US$ million.

TABLE 8.14

MERCHANDISE EXPORTS BY SECTORS OF ORIGIN: 1960-85
(US$ MILLIONS)

	1960	1965	1970	1975	1980	1983	1984	1985
Total exports (f.o.b.)	738.7	1,101.3	1,373.0	2,861.0	15,307.5	21,398.8	24,196.0	21,866.4
Agriculture (agriculture, livestock, forestry and fishing)	416.6	629.1	570.2	814.8	1,545.9	1,284.8	1,460.8	1,322.7
Industrial	321.8	471.4	502.0	1,924.7	13,756.6	20,109.4	22,735.2	20,543.7
Extractive	153.2	197.8	171.9	712.7	10,373.7	15,590.1	17,140.4	15,277.1
Manufacturing	168.6	273.6	333.1	1,212.0	3,382.9	4,529.3	5,594.8	5,266.6
Foodstuffs, beverages and tobacco	72.9	101.0	136.1	233.9	770.2	707.3		
Textiles, garments and leather products	28.9	26.2	30.9	141.1	201.0	159.6		
Wood industry	0.9	3.1	5.9	25.0	57.9	71.1		
Paper, printing and publishing industry	3.1	5.7	17.4	23.0	86.2	60.0		
Petroleum derivatives	12.2	17.3	30.7	25.1	426.9	737.8		
Petrochemicals	-	1.2	1.5	14.4	116.7	120.6		
Chemicals	18.2	43.5	60.3	182.6	394.6	486.1		
Plastic and rubber products	-	-	-	7.2	21.3	36.9		
Other non-metallic mineral products	4.5	9.6	11.5	28.3	129.0	204.5		
Steel and iron industry	3.4	23.3	34.8	38.1	71.5	293.2		
Metallurgic industry	0.4	2.5	0.4	2.8	121.2	551.2		
Metal products, machinery and equipment	1.5	1.6	3.6	269.8	938.3	1,071.4		
Other manufacturing industries	22.5	38.6	0.0	220.7	48.1	29.7		
Non-classified exports	0.4	0.7	297.8	121.5	5.3	4.6		

Source: Banco de México, 'Serie Estadísticas Históricas Balanza de Pagos' (1960-65) and 'Informe Anual', various years.
Note: Totals may not sum up due to the rounding up of partial figures.   - means no exports;   0.0 means non-significant exports.

TABLE 8.15

MERCHANDISE IMPORTS BY MAJOR CATEGORIES: 1960-85
(US$ MILLION)

	1960	1965	1970	1975	1980	1985
Total imports	1,186.4	1,559.6	2,460.8	6,580.2	18,486.2	13,460.4
Consumer goods	222.0	298.5	528.0	599.9	2,231.0	1,075.0
Intermediate goods	404.0	550.7	797.9	2,903.1	11,014.9	9,162.3
Capital goods	560.4	710.4	1,134.8	2,390.7	5,024.6	3,223.1
Non-classified articles a)	0.0	0.0	0.0	686.4	215.7	0.0

Source: Banco de México, 'Serie Estadísticas Históricas Balanza de Pagos'
(1950-69) and 'Informe Anual', various years.

Note: Totals may not sum up due to rounding up of partial figures.
   a) Not considered in the historical balance of payments series nor in 1985
   Annual Report.

TABLE 8.16

TRADE BALANCE: 1960-85
(US$ MILLION)

	Exports	Imports	Balance
1960	738.7	1,186.5	-447.8
1965	1,101.3	1,559.6	-458.3
1970	1,372.9	2,460.8	-1,087.9
1975	2,861.0	6,580.2	-3,719.2
1980	15,307.5	18,486.2	-3,178.7
1985	21,866.4 a)	13,460.4 a)	8,406.4

Source: Banco de México, 'Serie Estadísticas Históricas Balanza de Pago'
(1950-69), 'Informe Anual', various years.

Note: The minus sign reflects deficit.
   a) Preliminary

72

TABLE 8.17

GROSS FIXED CAPITAL FORMATION: 1960-85
(MILLIONS OF 1970 PESOS)

	1960	1965	1970	1975	1980	1985
Total gross fixed capital formation	34,100.3	52,173.1	88,660.6	132,316.1	197,364.5	154,497.6
Construction	18,774.1	27,140.2	50,209.4	71,020.8	103,788.5	93,804.8
Domestic machinery and equipment a)	6,316.8	10,739.7	22,017.9	36,445.6	54,318.2	45,992.4
Imported machinery and equipment a)	8,054.8	12,886.9	15,854.7	23,941.3	38,319.9	14,700.4
Others b)	954.5	1,405.1	578.6	908.4	937.9	n.a. c)
Public d)	11,197.9	15,368.7	29,249.9	54,732.9	84,870.3	55,647.7
Private	22,902.4	36,804.5	59,410.9	77,583.2	112,494.2	99,029.9
Total	34,100.3	52,173.2	88,660.8	132,316.1	197,364.5	154,497.6

Source: Banco de México, Producto Interno Bruto y Gasto, Cuaderno 1970-78, Serie Información Estadística; and Secretaría de Programación y Presupuesto, INEGI, 'Sistema de Cuentas Nacionales de México', Tomo I, Resumen General, 1970-82 and Estimaciones Preliminares 1984-85.

Note: n.a. means not available.
  a) Includes transport equipment.
  b) From 1960 to 1969 its content unknown. From 1970 onwards until 1980 includes land improvement and development for agricultural purposes and imports of livestock for reproduction.
  c) Included in the categories of construction and machinery and equipment imports.
  d) Covers the public investment actually disbursed except in 1960 when it covers the authorized public investment in absence of more correct data.

73

TABLE 8.18

SECTORIAL DISTRIBUTION OF GROSS FIXED INVESTMENT: 1953-67
(PERCENTAGES)

	1953	1960	1967
Agriculture	17	12	10
Industry	40	33	46
Transport and infrastructure	15	12	10
Housing	17	23	22
Others	11	20	12
Total	100	100	100

Source: Fitzgerald, E.V.K. (1979), 'Patterns of Saving and Investment in Mexico: 1939-1976', Cambridge University Press, Cambridge.

TABLE 8.19

PUBLIC AND PRIVATE INVESTMENT
(PERCENTAGES)

	Public a)	Private b)	Total
1960-69	39.9	60.5	100
1970-78	45.1	54.9	100
1978	49.4	50.6	100

Source: Banco de México.

Note: a) Federal public investment
b) Calculated as residual.

TABLE 8.20

DIRECT FOREIGN INVESTMENT
(CURRENT MILLION DOLLARS)

Year	Amount
1960	67.9
1965	152.6
1970	184.6
1975	204.1
1980	1,254.0
1981	1,188.7
1982	1,657.3
1983	1,006.1
1984	777.6
1985	59.4

Source: Banco de México, 'Balanza de Pagos, Serie Histórica', 1986.

TABLE 8.21

SECTORIAL DESTINATION OF THE GROSS FIXED INVESTMENT
(PUBLIC a) AND PRIVATE: 1975)
(PERCENTAGE)

Sector	Public	Private
Primary b)	6.3	12.4
Secondary c)	85.2	34.4
Tertiary d)	8.4	53.2
Total	100.0	100.0

Source: Valenzuela, J.F.(1986), 'El capitalismo mexicano en los ochenta', ERA Editors, Mexico, p. 57.

Note: a) Total (includes federal gross fixed investment).
b) Agriculture and mining.
c) Manufacturing, electricity, petroleum, communication and transport.
d) Commerce, services (including housing) and others.

TABLE 8.22

INVESTMENT FINANCING
(CURRENT PESOS)

	Domestic savings	External savings
	(GDP percentage)	
1957-66	15.1	1.8
1967-71	17.0	2.2
1972-76	17.7	3.3
1978-81	22.9	4.5

Source: From 1957 to 1976, Fitzerald, E.V.K., op. cit.; for 1978-81, Valenzuela, J., op. cit.

TABLE 8.23

GROSS DOMESTIC PRODUCTION OF CAPITAL GOODS: 1960-85
(MILLIONS OF 1970 PESOS)

	1960	1965	1970	1975	1980	1985
Total	7,683.6	14,686.1	24,688.0	37,620.7	56,277.5	51,792
Basic metal industries and metal products	3,961.9	6,047.6	11,095.0	14,542.3	20,365.9	18,571
Steel and iron industries	n.a.	n.a.	4,753.0	6,667.2	9,722.8	9,578
Basic non-ferrous metal industries	n.a.	n.a.	1,102.0	1,497.6	2,099.0	1,935
Metal furniture	n.a.	n.a.	1,152.0	1,271.6	1,592.9	1,035
Metal structures	n.a.	n.a.	953.0	1,200.6	1,436.8	1,257
Other metal products, except machinery	n.a.	n.a.	3,135.0	3,905.3	5,514.4	4,766
Machinery and equipment	3,721.7	8,638.5	13,593.0	23,078.4	35,911.6	33,221
Non-electrical machinery and equipment	788.1	2,122.5	2,717.0	4,681.9	7,206.2	5,898
Electric machinery and appliances	1,265.5	3,214.0	1,152.0	1,579.4	2,747.0	2,690
Electric domestic appliances	n.a. a)	n.a. a)	899.0	1,843.4	3,268.6	2,365
Electronic equipment and appliances	n.a.	n.a.	2,115.0	3,316.3	5,732.9	4,949
Other electric equipment	n.a. a)	n.a. a)	1,084.0	1,464.3	2,348.0	2,507
Automobiles	881.4	1,910.8	2,623.0	5,458.7	7,877.2	7,141
Automobile bodies, motors, parts and accessories	n.a. b)	n.a. b)	2,318.0	3,776.8	5,600.7	6,566
Transport equipment and material	786.7	1,391.2	685.0	957.6	1,131.0	1,105

Source: Elaborated with Banco de Mexico data, contained in respective Annual Reports.

Note: Totals may not sum up due to the rounding up of partial figures.
n.a. means not available because in these years, central bank classification did not provide any detailed information.
a) Included in machinery and electric equipment category.
b) Included in transport equipment and material category.

TABLE 8.24

AVERAGE ANNUAL GROWTH RATES OF THE CAPITAL GOODS
PRODUCTION: 1960-85
(PERCENTAGES BASED ON MILLION PESOS AT 1970 PRICES)

	1960-69	1970-75	1976-78	1979-82	1983-85
Total	11.8	8.8	8.5	1.3	9.0
Basic metal industries and metal products	8.7	5.6	8.2	0.0	3.8
Steel and iron industries	n.a.	7.0	14.5	-0.6	4.5
Basic non-ferrous metal industries	n.a.	6.3	2.4	-1.7	7.9
Metal furniture	n.a.	2.0	4.3	-2.2	2.3
Metal structures	n.a.	4.7	-5.9	5.9	1.8
Other metal products, except machinery	n.a.	4.5	5.2	0.9	1.9
Machinery and equipment	14.4	11.2	8.6	2.1	12.2
Non-electrical machinery and equipment	13.7	11.5	7.1	-0.2	8.2
Electric machinery and appliances	14.3	6.5	12.4	4.9	11.9
Electric domestic appliances	n.a. a)	15.4	12.3	5.4	-7.0
Electronic equipment and appliances		9.4	7.3	-3.7	4.0
Other electric equipment	n.a. a)	6.2	9.2	7.6	11.6
Automobiles	16.7	15.8	9.9	0.9	30.8
Automobile bodies, motors, parts and accessories	n.a. b)	10.3	10.4	3.6	20.5
Transport equipment and material	12.2	6.9	-6.1	12.8	-3.2

Source: Table 8.23.

Note: n.a. means not available.
  0.0 Not significant percentage, smaller than 0.1%.
  (-) Indicates a decline.
  a) Included in electric machinery and appliances.
  b) Included in transport equipment and material category.

77

TABLE 8.25

STRUCTURE OF THE PRODUCTION OF CAPITAL GOODS: 1970-85
(PERCENTAGE)

	1970	1975	1980	1985
Total	100.0	100.0	100.0	100.0
Basic metal industries and metal products	45.0	38.7	36.2	35.9
Non-electrical machinery and equipment	11.0	12.5	12.8	11.4
Electrical machinery a)	21.3	21.9	25.0	24.2
Automotive industry b)	20.0	24.5	23.9	26.5
Other transport equipment	2.7	2.5	2.1	2.0

Source: Table 8.23.

Note: a) Includes electrical machinery and appliances, electric domestic appliances and electronic equipment and appliances.

b) Includes automobiles, motors, parts and accessories, and the production of other transport equipment (ships, railways and airplanes.)

TABLE 8.26

IMPORTS/DEMAND RATIO IN FINAL CAPITAL GOODS: 1970-83
(PERCENTAGES)

	1970	1975	1980	1983
Metal products	17.8	22.0	25.7	22.5
Non-electrical machinery	58.7	54.4	62.1	55.6
Electrical machinery	34.5	26.9	31.3	24.9
Transport equipment	45.9	33.9	30.6	21.3

Source: NAFINSA/ONUDI, 'México: Los bienes de capital en la situación económica presente', México, 1985, p. 84.

TABLE 8.27

DYNAMICS OF LABOUR PRODUCTIVITY IN MANUFACTURING INDUSTRY

	Annual average per cent increase
1951-55	1.1
1956-60	1.5
1961-65	3.6
1966-70	4.3
1971-75	3.9
1976-80	3.2
1981-85	1.2

Source: For the years 1951-70: (GDP data at constant prices) Banco de México.
For the years 1971-85: (employment data), Secretaría de Programación
y Presupuesto, op. cit., 1985.

TABLE 8.28

LABOUR PRODUCTIVITY

Industrial market economy countries	4.3 %
Centrally planned economies	7.7 %
Latin America (1970-80)	4.1 %
Mexico (1970-80)	3.6 %

Source: ONUDI, 'La industria mundial desde 1960, progresos y perspectivas', U.N.,
New York, 1979, p. 251; and CEPAL, 'Proyecciones del desarrollo
latinoamericano en los años ochenta', Santiago de Chile, 1981, p. 55.

TABLE 8.29

FEDERAL EXPENDITURE FOR EDUCATION: 1960-84 a)
[MILLIONS OF CURRENT PESOS AND PERCENTAGES)

	Total federal budget b) (1)	Education expenditure c) (2)	Education expenditure in total budget expenditure (1/2)
1960	8,011	1,959	24.5
1961	8,391	2,196	26.2
1962	9,397	2,513	26.7
1963	10,174	2,877	28.3
1964	12,719	3,728	29.3
1965	12,206	4,075	33.4
1966	14,173	4,697	33.1
1967	15,601	5,261	33.7
1968	18,055	5,819	32.3
1969	20,905	7,073	33.8
1970	22,613	7,817	34.6
1971	25,550	9,445	37.0
1972	34,987	11,760	33.6
1973	43,700	15,140	34.6
1974	55,231	20,795	37.6
1975	77,569	31,115	40.1
1976	102,598	42,496	41.4
1977	137,742	61,761	44.8
1978	178,701	77,562	43.4
1979	244,267	102,955	42.1
1980	753,564	139,971	18.6
1981	1,092,738	220,466	20.2
1982	1,818,460	368,608	20.3
1983	2,923,427	488,667	16.7
1984	4,818,493	826,712	17.2

Source: NAFINSA, op. cit., Edición 1981
From 1960 to 1969: José López Portillo, 'Primer Informe de Gobierno, 1977',
Anexo II, vol. 1; y Miguel de la Madrid, 'Tercer Informe de Gobierno, 1985',
Anexo Histórico-Estadístico, Sector Educación.

Note: a) Covers the actual federal expenditure only.
b) Excludes investment, non-sectorialized expenditure and external
debt service.
c) Expenditure in the public education sector.

TABLE 8.30

EXPANSION OF THE ENROLMENT AND THE TERMINATION OF STUDIES IN THE MEXICAN EDUCATIONAL SYSTEM

	Students	1960	1965	1970-71	1975-76	1980-81	1985-86 a)
Pre-school education	Enrolled E	229,535	325,405	400,138	537,090	1,071,619	2,407,500
	Terminated T						
Primary education	E	4,762,062	7,262,847	9,248,190	11,461,415	14,666,257	15,050,793
	T	n.a.	n.a.	792,577	1,090,496	1,955,622	1,946,280
Training of labour force	E	n.a.	n.a.	147,752	243,074	369,274	458,391
	T	n.a.	n.a.	n.a.	27,188	31,057	43,768
Secondary education b)	E	189,774	542,319	1,767,424	1,898,053	3,033,856	4,147,832
	T	n.a.	n.a.	374,663	431,500	745,507	1,109,427
Professional education (technical middle)	E	88,900	188,502	33,861	78,382	122,391	344,738
	T	n.a.	n.a.	8,048	11,750	17,864	56,651
Higher middle education c)	E	25,990	100,919	343,573	770,555	1,284,285	2,007,065
	T	n.a.	n.a.	82,100	128,651	280,284	372,800
Teachers' training colleges	E	36,242	69,032	55,943	111,502	207,997	125,800
	T	n.a.	n.a.	16,392	16,440	51,618	63,242
Higher education	E	30,538	130,848	271,275	543,202	935,789	1,193,281
	T	n.a.	n.a.	27,312	52,866	82,344	123,265
Total	Total	5,363,041	8,619,872	12,268,156	15,643,273	20,617,849	25,735,400
Enrolment in higher education (study area)	Total d)	n.a.	n.a.	252,236	501,250	816,281	1,082,281
Natural and exact sciences		n.a.	n.a.	10,412	36,639	47,177	32,767
Medicine		n.a.	n.a.	43,974	95,463	170,311	156,265
Agricultural and veterinary sciences		n.a.	n.a.	9,068	22,010	58,993	102,246
Engineering and technology		n.a.	n.a.	81,870	153,837	222,843	296,203
Social and administrative sciences		n.a.	n.a.	100,090	188,072	308,148	462,561
Education and arts		n.a.	n.a.	6,822	5,229	8,709	32,239

Source: NAFINSA, 'La Economía Mexicana en Cifras', ed. 1981; José López Portillo, '1er Informe de Gobierno', Anexo I, 1977; y Miguel de la Madrid, Tercer Informe de Gobierno', Anexo sector educativo, 1985.

Note:
a) Estimated figures.
b) Only in public schools.
c)
d) Includes other institutes and centres not registered in the higher education category.

TABLE 8.31

TECHNOLOGY TRANSFER PAYMENTS AND OTHER FOREIGN EXCHANGE TRANSFERS ABROAD BY DIRECT FOREIGN INVESTMENTS: 1950-78
(US$ MILLION)

	Total	Remitted profits a)	Interest	Royalties	Technical assistance and other payments b)
1960	131.0	72.2	19.7	18.7	20.4
1965	174.8	83.3	26.0	21.3	44.2
1970	357.5	145.4	91.7	40.1	80.3
1971	383.0	150.3	98.3	n.a.	134.4 c)
1972	451.5	193.7	121.9	n.a.	135.9 c)
1973	528.4	228.2	161.5	n.a.	138.7 c)
1974	633.7	231.0	248.0	77.8	76.9
1975	632.6	197.8	251.3	51.0	132.5
1976	813.3	327.6	296.1	n.a.	189.6 c)
1977	682.0	171.8	320.1	n.a.	190.1 c)
1978	823.1	215.5	398.7	n.a.	208.9 c)

Source: SPP 'Información sobre las relaciones económicas de México con el exterior', 1980.

Note: a) Excludes payments abroad on the account of debt and includes the disposal of accumulated profits.

b) Includes services, provision of information and training at all levels through transfer of scientific and technological knowledge or specific technical assistance activities.

c) Includes interest and royalties payments.

TABLE 8.32

GROSS PRODUCT AND TECHNOLOGICAL EXPENDITURE OF FOREIGN-OWNED AND DOMESTIC ENTERPRISES: 1975
(MILLIONS OF PESOS)

	Total	Foreign-owned enterprises	Domestic enterprises
Gross product	318,325.0	111,612.8	206,712.2
%	100.0	35.1	64.9
Technological expenditure	2,281.3	1,358.1	923.2
%	100.0	59.5	40.5

Source: Unger, Kurt (1985), 'Competencia monopólica y tecnología en la industria mexicana', El Colegio de México.

TABLE 8.33

TECHNOLOGICAL EXPENDITURE OF FOREIGN-OWNED ENTERPRISES
IN TECHNOLOGY INTENSIVE SECTORS: 1975   a)
(MILLIONS OF PESOS)

	Technological expenditure	Per cent
Production goods		
Capital goods		
Non-electrical machinery	120.2	8.8
Intermediate goods		
Basic chemicals, basic pharmaceuticals		
and synthetic fibres	355.6	26.2
Pharmaceuticals	168.8	12.4
Chemicals for industrial uses and fibres	186.8	13.8
Glass	53.5	3.9
Foodstuffs for animals	45.3	3.3
Consumer goods		
Non-durables		
Milk products	53.6	3.9
Soaps and detergents	98.5	7.3
Durables		
Automobile industry	286.3	21.1
Electric industry	169.3	12.5
Total technology intensive sectors	1,182.3	87.1

Source: Ibid. Table 8.32.

Note: a)   Technology intensive sectors are those which spent on technology in 1975
over 45 million pesos each, the equivalent of over 3% of total of
expenditure of the foreign-owned enterprises.

TABLE 8.34

TECHNOLOGICAL EXPENDITURE OF DOMESTIC FIRMS
IN TECHNOLOGY INTENSIVE SECTORS: 1975 a)
(MILLIONS OF PESOS)

	Technological expenditure	Per cent
Production goods		
Capital goods		
Non-electrical machinery	31.8	3.4
Intermediate goods		
Basic chemicals, basic pharmaceuticals		
and synthetic fibres	114.0	12.3
Pharmaceuticals	39.1	4.2
Chemicals for industrial uses and fibres	74.9	8.1
Iron and steel (laminated)	399.0	43.2
Consumer goods		
Non-durables		
Milk products	28.9	3.1
Plastic and glass industry	41.4	4.5
Durables		
Automobile industry	31.2	3.4
Electric industry	47.2	5.1
Total technology-intensive sectors	693.5	75.3

Source: Ibid, Table 8.32.

Note: a) Technology intensive sectors are those which spent in 1985 over
           28 million pesos on technology each, the equivalent of 3% of the total
           expenditure of the domestic firms.

TABLE 8.35

NUMBER OF REGISTERED TECHNOLOGY TRANSFER CONTRACTS: 1979

	Contracts Number	Contracts Per cent
Priority sectors	3,526	64.8
Non-priority sectors	1,917	35.2
Total in manufacturing activities	5,443	100.0

Source: Ibid. Table 8.32.

TABLE 8.36

FREQUENCY OF TECHNOLOGICAL ELEMENTS IN THE CONTRACTS OF EACH ENTERPRISE IN FOUR INDUSTRIAL GOODS GROUPS: 1979

	Number of contracts	P %	M %	K %	TA %	BE %	DE %	S %	Number elements
All manufactured goods	3,526	22	46	67	53	13	9	10	7,786
Production goods	2,259	21	42	68	53	17	12	10	5,035
Capital goods	649	25	51	70	59	12	8	13	1,547
Intermediate goods	1,610	19	39	67	51	18	13	9	3,488
Consumer goods									
Non-durables	636	19	61	58	45	4	3	13	1,294
Durables	631	32	44	69	60	9	7	10	457

Source: Secretaría de Patrimonio y Fomento Industrial.

Note: P = Licenses for use of patents.
       M = Licences for use of trademarks.
       K = Non-patented know-how.
       TA = Technical assistance.
       BE = Basic engineering.
       DE = Engineering of details.
       S = Management services.

TABLE 8.37

MAJOR INDICATORS OF DOMESTIC EXPENDITURE IN
SCIENTIFIC TECHNOLOGICAL ACTIVITIES: 1970-85
(MILLIONS OF 1970 PESOS)

	GDP	TFE	TDES & T	TFES & T	ENS & T
1970	444,271	109,238	772	656	-
1975	609,976	298,847	2,161	1,837	177
1980	841,855	350,412	4,548	3,954	361
1985	884,761 a)	437,867 b)	4,729 b)	4,504 b)	505 b)

Source: Dirección de Programacion, 'CONACYT en Cifras, 1984'. CONACYT,
México, and SPP Informes de Gobierno, Anexos Programáticos para
1985, México, 1985.

Note: GDP = Gross domestic product.
1970 Banco de México (Annual reports).
1975-85 Informes de Gobierno, Anexos Programáticos, SPP.

TFE = Total federal expenditure.
1970 Cuenta Pública, SHCP-SPP.
1975-85 Informes de Gobierno, Anexos Programáticos, SPP.

TDES & T = Total domestic expenditure for science and technology.
Dirección de Programación - CONACYT.

TFES & T = Total federal expenditure for science and technology.
1970-80 SPP-CONACYT Group.
1980-85 Informes de Gobierno, Anexos Programáticos, SPP.

ENS & T = Expenditure of National Science and Technology Council
Dirección de Programación - CONACYT.

a) Preliminary data.

b) Expenditure originally approved.

TABLE 8.38

NATIONAL SCIENCE AND TECHNOLOGY COUNCIL EXPENDITURES
(PERCENTAGE)

	GDP	TFE	TDE	TFES & T
1970	-	-	-	-
1975	0.03	0.08	8.18	9.63
1980	0.04	0.10	7.93	9.12
1985	0.06	0.12	10.68	11.21

Source: Ibid. Table 8.37.

Note: GDP = Gross domestic product.
1970 Banco de México (Annual reports).
1975-85 Informes de Gobierno, Anexos Programáticos, SPP.

TFE = Total federal expenditure.
1970 Cuenta Pública, SHCP-SPP.
1975-85 Informes de Gobierno, Anexos Programáticos, SPP.

TDES & T = Total domestic expenditure for science and technology.
Dirección de Programación - CONACYT.

TFES & T = Total federal expenditure for science and technology.
1970-80 SPP-CONACYT Group.
1980-85 Informes de Gobierno, Anexos Programáticos, SPP.

TABLE 8.39

FEDERAL EXPENDITURE IN SCIENCE AND TECHNOLOGY
(MILLIONS OF CURRENT PESOS)

	1975	1980	1985 a)
Basic research	179	756	6,774
Applied research	1,051	3,826	28,501
Experimental development	444	2,380	21,801
Education	884	11,284	42,251
Diffusion	195	336	5,006
Associated activities	560	1,506	85,516
Total	3,313	20,088	189,849

Source: Ibid. Table 8.37.

Note: a) As originally approved.

TABLE 8.40

FUNCTIONAL DISTRIBUTION OF THE PUBLIC SECTOR IN SCIENCE AND TECHNOLOGY (MILLIONS OF CURRENT PESOS)

	1975	1980	1985 a)
Agriculture and forestry	765	5,453	20,597
Industry	806	3,731	94,491
Education	737	5,746	4,712
Health and social security	364	4,424	33,010
Transport and communications	189	62	3,070
Fishing		536	1,650
Administration b)	452	-	-
Government research		136	2,370
Economic policy	-	-	26,621
Labour policy	-	-	573
Urban development and ecology	-	-	553
Trade and industrial development	-	-	2,009
Tourism	-	-	193
Total	3,313	20,088	189,849

Source: Ibid. Table 8.37.

Note: a) As originally approved.
   b) Starting in 1978 included under government research.

TABLE 8.41

SCIENTIFIC AND TECHNOLOGICAL CENTRES AND THEIR PERSONNEL: 1982-83 a)

Institution	Number	Personnel
National University of Mexico	18	1,772
National Polytechnical Institute	8	527
Autonomous Mexico City University	-	n.a.
University in the interior	52	1,858
Technological Institute in Mexico City and the interior	20	805
Federal public sector institutions	35	4,906
Private centres and institutions	31	2,748
Total	164	12,616

Source: Elaboración propia con datos de CONACYT, 'Catálogo de Centros e Institutos de Investigación Científica y Desarrollo Tecnológico en México', Mexico, 1984.

Note: a) Information covers exclusively the institutions dedicated to research in the exact and natural sciences. Institutions and personnel dedicated to research in social and liberal science are omitted due to the incomplete coverage.

TABLE 8.42

SCIENTIFIC PUBLICATIONS IN MEXICO: 1984
(PERIODICITY AND NUMBER OF COPIES)

Publication	Periodicity	Copies
Información Científica y Tecnológica	Monthly	35,000
Voces de Teléfonos de México	Monthly	24,000
Computer World/Mexico	Monthly	10,000
Compumundo	Monthly	10,000
Ciencia y Desarrollo	Bimonthly	7,500
010 Revista de Computación	Bimonthly	5,000
El Universo	Quarterly	n.a.

Source: Banamex, 'México Social 1984'.

Note: n.a. means not available.

TABLE 8.43

APPLICATIONS FOR REGISTRATION OF PATENTS
TO THE END OF 1980

	Total	Residents	Percentage	Non-residents	Percentage
Patents requested	5,419	704	13.0	4,775	87.0
Patents granted	2,349	174	6.9	2,349	93.1

Source: Sagasti, Francisco; Fernando Chaparro, Carlos E. Paredes Y Hernán Jaramillo 'Un decenio de transición. Ciencia y Tecnología en América Latina y el Caribe durante los setenta', GRADE, Lima, Peru, 1983.

Notes

1. Streeten, Paul (1985), 'Self-Reliant Industrialization', in Wilbur, Charles K. (ed.), *The Political Economy of Development and Underdevelopment*, London.
2. For evidence to that effect see Wionczeck, Miguel S. (1976), 'El crecimiento latinoamericano y las estrategias de comercio internacional en la posguerra', in Díaz Alejandro, Carlos, F., Teitel, Simón S. and Tokman, Víctor E. (eds) *Política económica en centro y periferia*, Fondo de Cultura Económica, Lecturas 16, México, pp. 234-74.
3. Even in the case of water it is more likely that water distribution policies followed in post-revolutionary Mexico were more responsible for the appearance of two agricultures (commercial and subsistence) than the water resource shortages. For details see Wionczek, Miguel S. (1982), 'The roots of the Mexican Agricultural Crisis: Water Resources Development Policies (1920-1970)', *Development and Change*, vol. 13, The Hague.
4. Such understanding could not have emerged as long as the country was run by the self-perpetuating political elites of traditional politicians never exposed in their formative years to the issues involving technological progress and modernization, supported by economists and other technocrats competent to a different degree in macroeconomic neoclassical analysis and policy design. Neither of

these two segments of the coalition ruling modern Mexico were able to incorporate in their planning strategies science and technology as a major factor of self-reliant development and social modernization. See Wionczek, Miguel S. (July-September 1980), 'On the Viability of a Policy for Science and Technology in Mexico', *Society and Science*, vol. 3, no. 3, pp. 1-24. New Delhi.

5. NAFINSA (Nacional Financiera, S.A.) (1977), *Statistics on the Mexican Economy*, Mexico, D.F.

6. To facilitate comparisons, all figures in this chapter are given in 1960 pesos.

7. Solís, Leopoldo, (1970), *La realidad económica mexicana: retrovisión y perspectivas*, Siglo Veintiuno Editores, Mexico, D.F., pp. 148-83.

8. Valenzuela, José F. (October 1983), 'Sustitución de importaciones y desarrollo industrial en México', *Comercio Exterior*, vol. 33, no. 10, pp 938-42, Mexico, D.F.

9. Wionczek, Miguel S. (April-June 1986), 'Industrialización, capital extranjero y transferencia de tecnología: la experiencia mexicana, 1930-1985', *Foro Internacional*, El Colegio de México, vol. XXVI, no. 49, pp. 550-66, Mexico, D.F.

10. In 1950 *Nacional Financiera* managed investment funds of about 1,200 million pesos - 18 per cent of the total public banking institutions.

11. In 1930 the country had 550 km of paved roads and 80,000 motor vehicles.

12. Ros, Jaime and Vázquez, Alejandro (1980), 'Industrialización y comercio exterior, 1950-1977', in *Economía mexicana: Análisis y perspectivas*, CIDE, no. 2, pp. 27-56. México, D.F.

13. CEPAL/ECLA (1952), *El desequilibrio externo en el desarrollo latinoamericano: El caso de México*, vol. 2, México, D.F. (mimeo). Its principal authors were Celso Furtado, Juan Noyola and Osvaldo Sunkel, all CEPAL/ECLA staff members.

14. For a detailed study of the economic planning attempts between the 1930s and the mid-1960s see Wionczek, Miguel S. (1963), 'Incomplete Formal Planning: Mexico', in Hagen, Everett E. (ed.) *Planning Economic Development*, pp. 150-82, Richard D. Irwin Inc., Homewood, Ill.

15. Some comparative data about the manufacturing industry's productivity, measured as the ratio of the GDP and total employment show that respective growth rates are as follows: Mexico (1950-70) - 2.7 per cent; industrial Western Europe (1951-68) - 4.5 per cent; Southern Europe (1951-68) - 5.9 per cent; Eastern Europe (1951-68) - 5.5 per cent; and Latin America (1950-68) - 3.7 per cent. UNIDO (1979), *World Industry since 1960 - Progress and Prospects*, p. 251, New York, and CEPAL (1981), *Proyecciones del desarrollo latinoamericano en los años ochenta*, Santiago de Chile.

16. The share of education expenditures in the federal budget rose from about 10 per cent in 1930 to 17 per cent in 1955, accounting for 2 per cent of GDP in that second year.
17. Reynolds, Clark W. (1973), *La economía mexicana: su estructura y crecimiento en el siglo XX*, p. 228, Fondo de Cultura Económica, México.
18. To facilitate comparisons, hereafter most of the figures are given in 1970 prices. When this data is not available, the rate used is indicated. See Appendix - Table 8.8 which gives price indices from 1960 to 1985.
19. For additional information see Green, Rosario (1976), *El endeudamiento externo de México, 1940-1973*, El Colegio de México, Mexico; and Zedillo Ponce de León, Ernesto (1985), 'The Mexican External Debt: The Last Decade', in Wionczek, Miguel S. (ed.) in collaboration with Luciano Tomassini, *Politics and Economics of External Debt Crisis. The Latin American Experience*, Westview Press, Boulder and London.
20. The administrative reform was to make the goverment's bureaucracy more efficient by eliminating duplication in public agencies as well as streamlining inefficient state enterprises. The Planning and Budget Ministry was created at the same time.
21. According to available figures, the ratio between the amount of deposits in the domestic banks and the GDP dropped from 31 per cent in 1969-73 to 26 per cent during the second half of the 1970s. This trend explains the credit shortage despite the inflow of petro-dollars.
22. Poder Ejecutivo Federal (May 1983), *Plan Nacional de Desarrollo 1983-1988*, Mexico.
23. Lorentzen, Anne (February 1986), *Capital Goods and Technological Development in Mexico*, CDR Research Report, no. 7, pp. 57-8, Copenhagen.
24. Fitzgerald, F.V.K. (1979), *Patterns of Saving and Investment in Mexico: Mexico, 1939-1976*, p. 16, Cambridge, MA.
25. NAFINSA-ONUDI, (1985), *México: los bienes de capital en la situación presente*, p. 77, Mexico.
26. Lorentzen, Anne, op. cit., pp. 39-41.
27. Unger, Kurt (1985), *Competencia monopólica y tecnológica en la industria mexicana*, El Colegio de México.
28. Lorentzen, Anne, op. cit., p. 60.
29. NAFINSA, CEPAL (1975), 'Condiciones de acceso de los bienes de capital al mercado de los países miembros', in *Mercado de Valores*, no. 37, Mexico.
30. Fajnzylber, Fernando (1983), *La industrialización trunca de América Latina*, Nueva Imagen, Capítulo III, Mexico.
31. Valenzuela, Feijóo (1986), *El capitalismo mexicano en los ochenta*, Ediciones Era.

32. Mexico's educational system is structured as follows: nursery school (3-5 years of age); primary school, six years of study; basic secondary school, includes 'preparatoria' college-preparatory, professional, technical and *terminal* schools, generally three years of study; teacher-training institutions of three levels: secondary, post-secondary and graduate; university or its equivalent in regional technological institutes or similar centres, four or five years of study; and graduate school, two to four years of study.

33. Urquidi, Víctor L., 'La expansión de la educación técnica en México desde 1970: Una apreciación preliminar', a paper presented at the Seminar on Reforming the Educational System and Training for Industrial and Technological Development. International Educational Planning Institute, Paris, 27 October 1980.

34. See Muñoz, Izquierdo, Rodríguez, Carlos y Pedro Gerardo (1980), 'La enseñanza técnica: canal de movilidad social para los trabajadores', *Revista Latinoamericana de Estudios Educativos*, Centro de Estudios Educativos, Mexico.

35. See a survey made in 23 cities by sampling the food processing, textiles, rubber products, meat manufacturing, publishing and construction industries and the trade and services sector, published in *Revista Mexicana de la Construcción*, no. 327, January 1982, Mexico.

36. Procuraduría Federal del Consumidor (Consumer Protection Institute) (1979), *Escuelas Particulares Especializadas*, Mexico, D.F.

37. For a concise account of the evolution of the technological policies of the Mexican government prior to the early 1970s see, Wionczek, Miguel S., Bueno, Gerardo and Navarrete, Jorge Eduardo (1974), *La transferencia internacional de tecnología. El caso de México*, FCE, Mexico.

38. See Cooper, Charles and Sercovitch, Francisco (1970), *The Mechanisms for Transfer of Technology from Advanced to Developing Countries*, SPRU, University of Sussex; and Emmanuel, Arghiri (1981), *Téchnologie Appropiée ou Téchnologie Sous-Developpée*, P.U.F., France.

39. For details see Unger, Kurt, op. cit., p. 95, who used figures covering all technology transfer contracts in manufacturing registered in the National Technology Transfer Registry, during the 1970s. See also Nadal, Alejandro (1977), *Instrumentos de política científica y tecnológica en México*, El Colegio de México, and Alvarez Soberanis, Jaime (August 1976), 'Justificación de una política que destruya el uso de marcas extranjeras en México', in *Comercio Exterior*, vol. 26, no. 8, pp. 940-51. Mexico.

40. Including capital and intermediate goods and consumer durables and non-durables.

41. Studies quoted in footnote 39.

42. See Chapter VII, Annex - Domestic Technological Capacity: The case of Instituto Mexicano del Petróleo, (IMP).

43. Dahlman, Carl J. and Cortés, Mariluz (May-June 1984), 'Mexico', in Lall, Sanjaya (ed.) 'Exports of Technology by Newly-industrializing Countries', *World Development*, vol. 12, no. 5/6, special issue, pp. 601-24, Pergamon Press. The authors propose that the exports of technology from developing countries be seen as the result of a gradual accumulation of human and physical capital that underlies the process of economic development. This suggests that a developing country's exports of technology may be a convenient starting point for a study of the development of local technological capability.

44. Hodara, Joseph (May-June 1984), 'La medición del avance científico en América Latina', in *Revista CONACYT*, pp. 80-8, Mexico.

45. See Sagasti, Francisco and Cook, Cecilia (December 1985), *Tiempos difíciles: Ciencia y tecnología en América Latina durante el decenio de 1980*, GRADE, Lima.

46. CONACYT (1976), *Política nacional de ciencia y tecnología: estrategias, lineamientos y metas*, México; and (1976), *Plan Nacional Indicativo de Ciencia y Tecnología*, México.

47. A sympathetic outside observer ventured the opinion that 'the way that projects within the programme were selected by the research entities themselves and classified into nine broad categories of priorities was apparently a method chosen in order to affect the power interests within the scientific community as little as possible', James, Dilmus D. (March 1980), 'Mexico's Recent Science and Technology Planning', *Journal of Inter-American Studies and World Affairs*, Miami, Fl.

48. Urquidi, Víctor L., *La necesidad de una política integral de ciencia y tecnología para el desarrollo*, a paper presented at the IEPES meeting on Science and Technology, San Luis Potosí, 23 March 1982.

49. Poder Ejecutivo Federal (May 1983), *Programa Nacional de Desarrollo 1983-1988*, pp. XI and XII.

50. See, among others, James, Dilmus D. op. cit., Del Río, Fernando and Malo, Salvador (1979), 'Mexico', in Greenberg, Dawid S. (ed.), *Science and Government Report - International Almanac 1978-1979*, Washington D.C. and Babatunde, Thomas D. and Wionczek, Miguel S. (eds) (1979), *Integration of Science and Technology with Development*, Pergamon Press, New York - Oxford - Toronto.

51. Poder Ejecutivo Federal, op. cit, p. 70.

52. See Wionczek, Miguel S. (1981), *Capital y tecnología en México*, Miguel Angel Porrua, Mexico, and Urquidi, Víctor L., *La necesidad de una política integral de ciencia y tecnología para el desarrollo*, a paper presented at the IEPES meeting on Science and Technology, San Luis Potosí, 23 March 1982.

53. According to Hodara, this weakness can be seen in at least three critical links of the connections which open and multiply 'thresholds', confront 'entrance barriers' and optimize 'critical masses'.

54. This annex is based on a study by Rogelio Ruíz 'La capacidad tecnológica nacional y la dependencia tecnológica del exterior: el caso

del sector de hidrocarburos' (Domestic technological capacity and technological dependence on foreign sources: the case of the hydrocarbon sector), elaborated by El Colegio de Mexico's Energy Programme within the framework of the project 'La industria petrolera, el Estado y el sindicato petrolero, 1970-1985', (The Petroleum Industry, the State and the Oil Trade Union, 1970-1985).

55. García-Colín Scherer, Leopoldo. (1979), 'La ciencia y la tecnología del petróleo: situación actual y perspectivas futuras en México', in *Las perspectivas del petróleo mexicano*, pp. 65-82, El Colegio de México, Centro de Estudios Internacionales.

References

Alvarez Soberanis, Jaime (August 1976) 'Justificación de una política que destruya el uso de marcas extranjeras en México', in *Comercio Exterior*, vol. 26, no. 8, Mexico.

Babatunde, Thomas D. and Wionczek, Miguel S. (eds) (1979), *Integration of Science and Technology with Development*, Pergamon Press, New York-Oxford-Toronto.

Barker, T. and Brailovsky, Vladimiro (August-December 1983), 'La política económica entre 1976 y 1982 y el Plan Nacional de Desarrollo Industrial', in *Investigación Económica*, no. 166, Facultad de Ciencias Económicas, Universidad Nacional Autónoma de México, pp. 273-17.

Bell, Martin (ed.) (February 1985), *The Great Experiment: Harnessing Science and Technology to Third World Development. A Review of Policy and Policy Analysis Science The 1950s*, SPRU, University of Sussex.

Bhagavan, M.R. (March 1980), *Technological Transformation of Developing Countries*, Economic Research Institute, Stockholm School of Economics, Sweden.

Blomström, Magnus (1983), *Foreign Investment, Technical Efficiency and Structural Change. Evidence from the Mexican Manufacturing Industry*, Ekonomiska Studier Utgivna av National Ekonomiska Institutionen vid Göteborgs Universitet, Sweden.

Blomström, Magnus, 'Technology Policy in Development Possibilities and Constraints', a paper presented at the meeting: Towards a Dialogue between Technologies Produced by Different Cultures, organized by OLKOS and Istituto di Sociologia, University of Bologna, Italy, March 1983.

Boon, Gerard K., 'The Diffusion of New Techniques', a paper presented at the General EADI Conference, Working Group Science and Technology, Madrid, September 1984.

Cardozo, Myriam and Redorta, Esthela (June 1984), *La política científica y tecnológica del Estado mexicano a partir de 1970*, in Series Estudios de Caso, no. 11, Centro de Investigación y Docencia Económica (CIDE), Mexico.

Center for Latin American Studies (May 1982), *Workshop on Strategies of Industrialization in Mexico*, University of California, Berkeley.

CEPAL (Comisión Económica para América Latina) (1985), *La crisis y desarrollo. Presente y futuro de América Latina y el Caribe*, Santiago, Chile.

CEPAL (1952), *El desequilibrio externo en el desarrollo latinoamericano: El caso de México*, México? D.F., 2 vol. (mimeo).

Cibotti, Ricardo and Lucángeli, Jorge (August 1980), 'El fenómeno tecnológico interno', in *Revista de la CEPAL*, no. 11, pp. 61-80.

CONACYT (Consejo Nacional de Ciencia y Tecnología) (1976), *Política Nacional de Ciencia y Tecnología: estrategias, lineamientos y metas*, Mexico.

CONACYT (1976), *Plan Nacional Indicativo de Ciencia y Tecnología*, Mexico.

CONACYT (October 1978), *Programa Nacional de Ciencia y Tecnología 1978-1982*, Mexico.

CONACYT (September 1984), *El CONACYT Hoy*, Mexico.

CONACYT (January 1985), *Ley para coordinar y promover el desarrollo científico y tecnológico*, Serie Documentos, no. 2, Mexico.

Cooper, Charles and Sercovitch, Francisco (1970), *The Mechanisms for Transfer of Technology from Advanced to Developing Countries*, SPRU, University of Sussex.

Daltabuit, Enrique; Colín, René Drucker; Guardiola, Augusto Fernández; Malo, Salvador; Peña, Antonio and Tapia, Ricardo (June 1977), 'Un análisis de la actitud del Gobierno respecto a la ciencia en México', in *Naturaleza*, vol. 8, no. 3.

Dilmus, James D. (March 1980), 'Mexico Recent Science and Technology Planning', in *Journal of Inter-American Studies and World Affairs*, Miami, FL.

Emmanuel, Arthiri (1981), *Technologie Appropiée ou Technologie Sous-Dévelopée*, P.U.F., France.

Fajnzylber, Fernando (1983), *La industrialización trunca de América Latina*, Nueva Imagen, Mexico.

Fajnzylber, Fernando and Tarragó, Trinidad Martínez, *Las empresas transnacionales: expansión internacional y proyección en la industria de México*, Fondo de Cultura Económica, Mexico.

Fitzgerald, E.V.K. (1979), *Patterns of Saving and Investment in Mexico: 1939-1976*, Cambridge, MA.

Fransman, Martin (July 1985), 'Conceptualizing Technical Change in the Third World in the 1980s: An Interpretative Survey', in *The Journal of Development Studies*, V. 21, University of Edinburgh, pp. 572-652.

García-Colín Scherer, Leopoldo (1979), 'La ciencia y tecnología del petróleo: situación actual y perspectivas futuras en México', in *Las perspectivas del petróleo mexicano*, Centro de Estudios Internacionales, El Colegio de México, pp. 65-82.

Green, Rosario (1976), *El endeudamiento externo de México 1940-1973*, El Colegio de México, Mexico.

Hodara, Joseph (June 1977), 'El intelectual científico mexicano: una tipología', CEPAL (mimeo).

Hodara, Joseph (July-September 1983), 'La planeación económica observada por un sociólogo', in *El Trimestre Económico*, vol. L (3), no. 199, Mexico, pp. 1425-35.

Hodara, Joseph (May-June 1984), 'La medición del avance científico en América Latina', in *Revista CONACYT*, Mexico, pp. 80-8.

Hodara, Joseph (1986), 'Reflexiones sobre en Programa Nacional de Desarrollo Tecnológico y Científico 1984/1988', El Colegio de México, (mimeo).

Hodara, Joseph (April 1986), *Políticas para la ciencia y la tecnología*, Coordinación de Humanidades, Universidad Nacional Autónoma de México.

Larralde, Carlos (et al.) (February 1978), 'Saber no es poder: temas de la ciencia aplicada en México', in *Nexos*, no. 2.

Lorentzen, Anne (February 1986), *Capital Goods and Technological Development in Mexico*, Centre for Development Research, Report no. 7, Copenhagen.

Malo, Salvador (December 1976), 'Cuando la leche es poca al niño le toca', in *Naturaleza*, vol. 7 no. 6 (58), Mexico.

Márquez, Miguel D. (1985), 'La cuestión tecnológica en América Latina e impacto de las nuevas tecnologías en la región', in Pedro Vuscović (ed.), *La crisis económica de América Latina, Antecedentes y Perspectivas*, Instituto de Estudios Económicos de América Latina, CIDE, Mexico.

Morito-Low, Hiroko (ed.) (1984), *Science and Technology Indicators for Development*, United Nations Science and Technology for Development Series, Westview Press, Boulder and London.

Muños, Izquierdo Carlos and Rodríguez, Pedro Gerardo (1980), 'La enseñanza técnica: canal de movilidad social para los trabajadores', in *Revista Latinoamericana de Estudios Educativos*, Centro de Estudios Educativos, Mexico.

Nadal, Alejandro (1977), *Instrumentos de política científica y tecnológica*, El Colegio de México.

NAFINSA (Nacional Financiera, S.A.) and CEPAL (1975), 'Condiciones de acceso de los bienes de capital al mercado de los países miembros', in *Mercado de Valores*, no. 37, Mexico.

NAFINSA and CEPAL (1977), Statistics on the Mexican Economy, Mexico, D.F.

Padua, Jorge (1984), *Educación, industrialización y progreso técnico en México*, El Colegio de México/UNESCO, Mexico.

Pérez Tamayo, Ruy (June 1978), 'La industrialización biomédica en México: espejismos y prioridades', in *Nexos*, no. 6.

Poder Ejecutivo Federal (May 1983), *Plan Nacional de Desarrollo 1983-1988*, Mexico; (August 1984), *Programa Nacional de Desarrollo Tecnológico y Científico 1984-1988*, Mexico.

Riveros, Miguel Angel (1986), *Crisis y reorganización del capitalismo mexicano*, ERA, Mexico.

Ros, Jaime and Alejandro Vásquez, Enríquez (1980), 'Industrialización y comercio exterior', in *Economía Mexicana*, no. 2, CIDE, Mexico.

Ruíz, Rogelio (forthcoming), *La capacidad tecnológica nacional y la dependencia tecnológica del exterior: el caso del sector de hidrocarburos*, Programa de Energéticos, El Colegio de México.

Sagasti, Francisco; Chaparro, Fernando; Paredes, Carlos and Jaramillo, Hernán (March 1983), *Un decenio de transición: ciencia y tecnología en América Latina y el Caribe durante los setenta*, GRADE, Lima.

Sagasti, Francisco and Cook, Cecilia (December 1985), *Tiempos difíciles: ciencia y tecnología en América Latina durante el decenio de 1980*, Grupo de Análisis para el Desarrollo (GRADE), Lima.

Solís, Leopoldo (1970), *La realidad económica mexicana: retrovisión y perspectivas*, Siglo Veintiuno Editores, Mexico, D.F.

Streeten, Paul, 'Self-Reliant Industrialisation', in Wilbur, Charles K. (ed.) (1985), *The Political Economy of Development and Underdevelopment*, London.

Unger, Kurt (1985), *Competencia monopólica y tecnología en la industria mexicana*, El Colegio de México.

UNIDO (United Nations Industrial Development Organisation) (May 1985), *Social Aspects of Industrialization*, working papers prepared by the Global and Conceptual Studies Branch Division for Industrial Studies, Vienna.

Urquidi, Víctor L., 'La necisidad de una política integral de ciencia y tecnología para el desarrollo', a paper prepared for the IEPES meeting on Science and Technology, San Luis Potosí, Mexico, March 1982.

Urquidi, Víctor L., 'La estrategia del desarrollo industrial mexicano frente al reto tecnológico', documento preparado para el Segundo Seminario Internacional 'Nueva Revolución Industrial y Estrategias del Desarrollo en América Latina', organizado por el CIDE, Oaxtepec, Mexico, December 1984.

Urquidi, Víctor L., 'Technology Transfer Between Mexico and the United States. Past experience and future prospects', paper prepared for the conference on 'Technology Transfer: US/Mexico Perspectives', Houston Area Research Center, The Woodlands, Texas, August 1985.

Urquidi, Víctor L., 'Tecnología y sociedad. Aspectos económicos en un país en desarrollo', documento presentado al Simposio Internacional sobre 'Las nuevas tecnologías y sus repercusiones en los países en desarrollo', organizado por la Academia Mexicana de Ingeniería, Mexico, April 1986.

Valenzuela, José Feijóo (October 1983), 'Sustitución de importaciones y desarrollo industrial en México', *Comercio Exterior*, vol. 33, no. 10, pp. 938-42.

Valenzuela, José Feijóo (1986), *El capitalismo mexicano en los ochenta*, ERA, Mexico.

Villarreal, René, 'La estrategia del desarrollo industrial mexicano frente al reto tecnológico', documento preparado por el Segundo Seminario Internacional 'Nueva Revolución Industrial y Estrategias del Desarrollo en América Latina', organizado por el CIDE, Oaxtepec, Mexico, December 1984.

Wionczek, Miguel S. (1976), 'El crecimiento latinoamericano y las estrategias de comercio internacional en la post-guerra', in Díaz Alejandro, Carlos F., Teitel, Simón and Tokman, Víctor E. (eds) *Política económica en centro y periferia*, Fondo de Cultura Económica, Lecturas 16, Mexico, pp. 234-74.

Wionczek, Miguel S. (July-September 1980), 'On the Viability of a Policy for Science and Technology in Mexico', in *Society and Science*, vol. 3, no. 3, New Delhi, pp. 1-24.

Wionczek, Miguel S. (1981), *Capital y tecnología en México y América Latina*, Miguel Angel Porrúa, Mexico.

Wionczek, Miguel S. (1982), 'The Roots of the Mexican Agricultural Crisis: Water Resources Development Policies (1920-1970)', in *Development and Change*, vol. 13, The Hague.

Wionczek, Miguel S. (January-March 1983), 'Obstáculos para la aplicación de la ciencia y la tecnología al desarrollo económico y social de los países menos desarrollados', in *Trimestre Económico*, vol. L (1), no. 197, Mexico, pp. 519-38.

Wionczek, Miguel S. (ed.) (1985), in collaboration with Luciano Tomassini, *Politics and Economics of External Debt Crisis. The Latin American Experience*, Westview Press, Boulder and London.

Wionczek, Miguel S. (April-June 1986), 'Industrialización, capital extranjero y transferencia de tecnología: la experiencia mexicana, 1930-1985', in *Foro Internacional*, vol. XXVI, no. 4, El Colegio de México, pp. 550-66.

Wionczek, Miguel S., Bueno, Gerardo M. and Navarrete, Jorge Eduardo (1974), *La transferencia internacional de tecnología. El caso de México*, Fondo de Cultura Económica, Mexico.

Puerto Rico

Sandor Boyson

Preface

Puerto Rico is an important laboratory for analyzing economic and technological change. As a late industrializer, its rapid rise from an agrarian economy to a 'knowledge economy' led by a dynamic information sector challenges conventional development theories about modernization, staged growth and the role of government in national transformation. As a hub of two fast changing US high-tech manufacturing branches - pharmaceuticals and computers - the island is also at the cutting edge of a worldwide production restructuring regime based on flexible manufacturing systems, telematics, multi-skilling of the work force, and new external strategic alliances.

A review of Puerto Rico's experience from both the macro and micro economic perspectives can perhaps provide some insights into mobilizing and managing an accelerated technological transformation process.

Our inquiry into the technological transformation of Puerto Rico takes the following approach: we begin with a macro assessment of the economic and social transformation since 1950. We then explore the discrete stages of this growth, starting with the early historical development of the industrialization strategy, and spanning the 1950-60 Operation Bootstrap period that culminated in the establishment of labour intensive manufacturing sector on the island. We continue with an analysis of the shift up the technology ladder to high-tech manufacturing in the late 1960s, a wave that carried the economy forward for the next two decades. Finally, we map the recent rise of the information sector, that bundle of goods and services comprised of education, R and D, the media of communication, information machines and information services.

In our Conclusions Chapter, we draw out the lessons learned from Puerto Rico's transformation experience, highlighting both the strengths and weaknesses built up by rapid development and government's pivotal yet often contradictory role in the entire process.

I Introduction and aims of the study

1 Introduction

The Commonwealth of Puerto Rico, an 'unincorporated' territory of the United States, is the smallest of four islands which comprise the Greater Antilles, a chain stretching towards the north coast of South America. Bounded by the Caribbean and Atlantic oceans, Puerto Rico has a land mass roughly 30 miles wide and 100 miles long. Over three fourths of the land mass is rugged mountainous terrain, with only a relatively narrow coastal plain varying from 2-13 miles in width amenable to cultivation. There are no known mineral deposits of any significance; no fuels available, except bagasse; very limited forest resources; and restricted fishing resources, due to the extreme depth of the waters surrounding the Island. Despite these constraining natural features, the island supports a population of 3.3 million.

Since the commencement of the industrialization campaign entitled 'Operation Bootstrap' in 1948, Puerto Rico has surmounted the twin burdens of resource deprivation and population density, and has engineered a rapid economic and social transformation. Between 1947 and 1959, Gross National Product doubled and per capita income reached the highest levels in Latin America. Over the longer period between 1950 and 1987, the structural changes in the economy of the island have been rapid: Gross Domestic Product rose 676 per cent from US$844 million to $5.705 billion (in constant 1954 dollars). This economic transformation has had profound social effects: Average life expectancy increased from 59.4 years in 1950 to 73.0 in 1980. The literacy rate reached over 90 per cent. Today over half of the youth aged 20-24 are enroled in higher education, the highest percentage in the world, and three times the average of Taiwan, S. Korea, Hong Kong and Singapore.

In large measure, this structural transformation has been fuelled by US direct investment. Attracted by special tax sparing incentives, unrestricted access to mainland markets, and a secure investment climate, US multinational corporations have funnelled massive investment flows to Puerto Rico. Between 1950 and 1960, the US private sector accounted for 60 per cent of fixed capital formation. By 1967, the annual US direct investment in manufacturing in Puerto Rico had reached $240 million, and accounted for almost 30 per cent of all US outward investment in developing country manufacture. By 1978, Puerto Rico accounted for 42 per cent of US corporate profits in the Latin American/Caribbean Region, and 30 per cent of accumulated investment in the region.

As a result of this investment, Puerto Rico today is home to 2,100 manufacturing operations, 28 per cent of which are engaged in high-technology production, including scientific precision instruments, pharmaceuticals and electronics. Over 35 per cent of the total worldwide assets of the US pharmaceutical industry, and over 11 per cent of the total assets of the US electronics/computer industry are located there. In 1987, the pharmaceutical industry alone exported $2.7 billion in pharmaceutical and medical products, and provided 70 per cent of all US imports.

Coincident with the rise and maturation of high-tech industrial production has been an expansion of the local information sector. The information sector, that bundle of goods and services comprised of education, research and development, media of communication, information machines and information services, has grown from 28.2 per cent of GNP in 1972 to 53.6 per cent of GNP in 1987. It is now the leading sector of the economy. The 'Telecommunications Revolution' has been a vital element of this expansion. By June 1989, the publicly owned Puerto Rico Telephone Company had completely digitalized the major telecommunications infrastructure, thus becoming the first country to do so in the world. By mid 1990, Puerto Rico will be at the centre of communications for the world's first completely digitalized *regional* telecommunications network. Such developments will further enhance the island's current position as the Caribbean Basin hub in Information Services, a position until now built largely on banking, computer, and advertising/communications sectors.

The magnitude, complexity, and pace of this overall technological transformation process - from agriculture to labour intensive manufacture to high-tech production to post-industrial services centre in the span of 35 years - has been both astonishing and bewildering. The fact that these stages of growth have unfolded in such a compressed manner on a small island has made Puerto Rico into a virtual laboratory for social scientists to analyze and debate the fundamental nature and contradictions of the transformation process.

2 Contradictions in the development process

Puerto Rico would seem, by preliminary indicators, to be part of a small circle of 'sprinters', along with the Four Tigers (Hong Kong, Taiwan, Singapore, South Korea), Brazil, and Finland, that have experienced a very fast rate of economic and structural transformation since 1950.

On the other hand, serious problems remain. Unemployment has remained high, despite emigration of one third of the populace to the US mainland in the 1950-60 decade and despite local economic development. between 1940 and 1988, unemployment fell only one percentage point, from 15 per cent to 14 per cent. *Local productive capital formation* seems also to have remained low, with only an estimated two per cent of the manufacturing profits going to local owners, and with a strong technological dualism emerging over time between the local sector and the externally owned sector.

Such distortions and imbalances in the economy have fuelled the debates between the dependency theorists and their critics, the modernization theorists.

Is Puerto Rico an 'enclave' economy, whose chief characteristics are a production structure imposed by external economic forces, with few linkages between the 'modern' sector and the rest of the economy? Has the Puerto Rican Government merely served as a handmaiden to US multinational corporations? So the dependency theorists would argue, calling into question the legitimacy of applying the very term 'modernization' to the Puerto Rico development experience.

Is Puerto Rico an outstanding example of 'planned' modernization, with technology and know-how transfers, social engineering and transformation itself proceeding on the basis of conscious policy and strategic decision making? So the modernization theorists would argue, pointing to the international renown of the Operation Bootstrap initiative. For these theorists, contradictions are inevitable given the very intensity of the transformation that has unfolded and represent 'growth pains', rather than chronic deficiencies.

Or does the truth lie somewhere in between these two positions?

II   The Puerto Rico case study: Overview of the transformation process

The WIDER Research Project on Development and Technological Transformation identified a set of criteria for measuring national technological transformation. These include the following:
1) Shifts in overall economic performance, highlighted by high and sustained rates of growth and intensive capital formation.
2) Shifts in sectoral output and productivity, including a reversal in shares of agriculture and industry.
3) Shifts in social structure, including a rural to urban shift, and an education/skills shift.

Set against all the above criteria, Puerto Rico has experienced a far reaching and dramatic transformation process in the period 1950-87:
1) There were massive shifts in overall economic performance:
-    GDP multiplied seven fold and per capita income five fold.
-    Growth rates averaged over seven per cent per annum even with adjustments for price movements.
2) There were shifts in sectoral output and productivity:
-    Agriculture's contribution to GDP fell from 18.2 per cent to 1.6 per cent; manufacture's contributions rose from 16.6 per cent to 39.7 per cent.
-    Agricultural work force dropped from 216,000 or 36.2 per cent of total employment to 38,000 or 5.1 per cent of total employment; manufacturing work force rose from 55,000 to 142,000.
-    Labour intensive industry gave way to high technology industry.

3) There were shifts in social indicators:
- The industrialization process produced a rapid expansion in basic physical infrastructure, and health and education facilities. The number of roads almost doubled. The number of telephones rose 20 fold. Electricity output multiplied 20 fold. Water service clients grew seven fold, and sewer service clients six fold.
- The result of such infrastructure improvements was an improvement in social welfare indicators. Life expectancy in the period increased from 61 years to 73 years, the level of developed countries.
- There was a revolution in skill formation. The percentage of management positions in manufacturing filled by Puerto Ricans increased from under 30 per cent to 94 per cent.
- There was a rural to urban shift, and in just sixteen years (1970-86) the rural population decreased from 60 per cent of a total population to just 27 per cent.

In the pages that follow, we will present a more in-depth statistical and analytic review of the overall magnitude and effects of the transformation process between 1950 and 1987.

1 Changes in real gross domestic product

Between 1950 and 1987, GDP multiplied almost seven fold, and GDP per head of economically active population multiplied almost five fold:

TABLE 2.1

CHANGES IN REAL GDP: 1950-87

Year	GDP (million US$ of constant 1954 dollars)	GDP per head of economically active population (in thousands of constant 1954 dollars)	Average annual growth rate (%)	
			GDP	Per head of economically active population
1950	844	1,234	-	-
1960	1,432	2,291	4.9	5.8
1970	3,068	4,016	7.2	5.2
1980	4,151	5,238	2.8	2.5
1987	5,779	5,705	3.1	0.8

Source: Puerto Rico Planning Board, Area of Economic and Social Planning, Bureau of Economic Analysis.

Note: Between 1950 and 1960, the active workforce decreased from 596,000 to 543,000, accounting for the fact that the GDP per head is higher than the GDP growth rate. For the decade as a whole, it is estimated 600,000 people emigrated to the United States from Puerto Rico.

This economic expansion, however, has not been of uniform strength over the long period. The phase from 1950 and 1974 was a time of feverish growth of GDP, with per annum growth averaging 0.2 per cent. Even with adjustments for price movements, a per annum GDP growth rate of over 7 per cent was achieved. These growth rates were substantially above those of the US, and provided evidence that the Puerto Rican economy was not so closely tied to the mainland economy during its period of rapid growth. However, the Energy Crisis and the resultant deep US recession in 1974-75, produced a mirror image slowdown in the Puerto Rican economy. The rise in federal transfer payments to the island, and the continuing development of the high-tech sector provided enough of a countervailing momentum to generate some positive growth during the last half of the decade.

For the long period 1965-80, the overall intensity of economic expansion in Puerto Rico was sufficient to place it fifth among the thirteen fastest growing economies. The next figure highlights the fact that between 1965-80, Puerto Rico was part of a small circle of 'sprinters' that included Singapore, South Korea, Brazil and Hong Kong.

During the expansionary long period, per capita incomes greatly benefited from rising hourly wages in industry. Between 1950 and 1970, average hourly earnings in production rose from US $0.42 to $1.76, a 319 per cent increase in contrast to a 133 per cent increase for the US production work force as a whole.[1]

The overall 1950-80 dynamic growth phase, characterized by overall high growth rates and rising per capita incomes, was to be followed by a plunge in economic activity. During the period 1980 and 1985, the average growth rate per annum plummeted to one per cent, as Puerto Rico suffered its worst recession in the modern era. For the first time, a recession was more severe in Puerto Rico than in the US, and the 1980 downturn was steeper and more long lasting than the mainland recession which began in the same year. This recession was aggravated by the threat of Federal funds cutoffs to the island as a result of the Federal budget deficit; and the threat of elimination of Section 936, which put a chill on US investment. Between 1985 and 1987, the island once again experienced a significant upturn in the economy. Its 1987 real growth rate of 5.1 per cent was more than double that of the US (5.1 per cent vs. 2.3 per cent); and almost double Japan's (5.1 per cent vs. 2.7 per cent). This upturn has been the result of multiple factors, including lower oil prices, low inflation and low interest rates, fast expansion in construction activity, recovery in the tourism sector, retention of Section 936 by Congress, and continued growth of the US economy.[2]

FIGURE 2.1

WORLD ECONOMIES SHOWING THE FASTEST RATES OF GROWTH: 1965-80

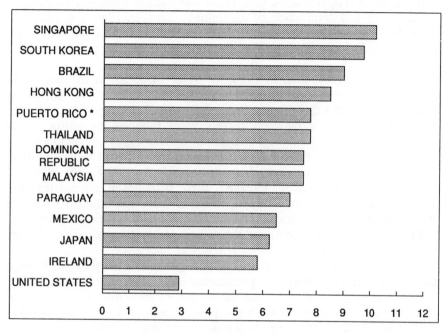

(percentage)

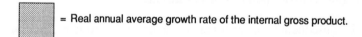

= Real annual average growth rate of the internal gross product.

Source: World Development Report, 1987.
* Puerto Rico Planning Board, Area of Economic and Social Planning, Bureau of
Economic Analysis.

2 Changes in sectoral output

The modernization of the economy has produced a vast shift in sectoral distribution of output and income. There was a simultaneous blossoming of manufacture and contraction of agriculture. Between 1950 and 1987, the agricultural sector's contribution to GDP declined from 18.2 per cent to 1.6 per cent; while manufacture's contribution rose from 16.6 per cent to 39.7 per cent.

Table 2.2 suggests that, in 1950, the value of output in manufacturing and agriculture was roughly equal. By 1987, the value of manufacturing output was 25 times that of agriculture.

These broad shifts between sectors were followed by shifts within sectors. Within manufacturing, changes in branch shares of manufacturing value added were dramatic. Table 2.3 demonstrates that in 1950, the food, beverage and tobacco branches accounted for 62.7 per cent of manufacturing value added; by 1987, these branches accounted for only 15.1 per cent. In the same period, manufacturing value added shares of intermediate goods, specifically chemicals and pharmaceuticals, leapt from 4.8 per cent to 41.5 per cent; and the capital goods share rose from 2.5 per cent to 29.1 per cent.

Thus, a major structural transformation has occurred, with high technology sectors moving to prominence and generating almost 70 per cent of manufacturing output on the island. In particular, the rise of the pharmaceutical industry has been phenomenal, and a more detailed explanation of its development will follow later in this analysis.

3 Changes in sectoral distribution of labour

A natural consequence of changes in sectoral investment, output, and production were changes in the sectoral distribution of labour.

In the 1950-84 period, as shown in Table 2.4, agriculture's work force dropped from 216,000 or 36.2 per cent of total employment, to 38,000, or 5.1 per cent of total employment; while manufacturing work force rose from 55,000 to 142,000.

This mass shift of labour into manufacturing employment had numerous benefits. The rising technological literacy and industrial skill levels of the work force had a considerable impact on raising overall productivity in the economy. In the Pharmaceutical Industry, for example, value of output increased from $630 million in 1978 to $2,751 million in 1986, a rise of 336 per cent, while employment increased only 51 per cent. This indicates both the rising technology intensity of the industry, and the abilities of the work force to master increasingly complex production processes.

With the rise of automated industries and the subsequent positive effects on work force skills and productivity, the great bulk of employment

TABLE 2.2

GDP BY ECONOMIC SECTORS - SELECTED YEARS
(IN MILLION US$ AT CURRENT PRICES)

Sector	1950	1960	1970	1980	1984	1987
Agriculture	132	164	161	394	343	372
Manufacturing	120	366	1,190	5,323	7,266	9,389
Construction and mining	30	101	379	370	306	408
Transportation and public utilities	61	156	439	1,235	1,660	1,872
Trade	144	319	898	2,277	2,785	3,503
Services	45	141	512	1,316	1,761	2,155
Finance, insurance, etc.	75	198	614	1,599	2,363	3,091
Government	75	187	610	1,897	2,173	2,629
Statistical discrepancy	42	60	231	70	-35.1	227
Total GDP	724	1,692	5,035	14,480	18,622	23,645
As per cent of total:						
Agriculture	18.2%	9.7%	3.2%	2.7%	1.8%	1.6%
Manufacturing	16.6%	21.6%	23.6%	36.8%	39.0%	39.7%
Construction and mining	4.1%	6.0%	7.5%	2.6%	1.6%	1.7%
Transportation and public utilities	0.0% / 8.4%	0.0% / 9.2%	0.0% / 8.7%	0.0% / 8.5%	0.0% / 8.9%	0.0% / 7.9%
Trade	19.9%	18.9%	17.8%	15.7%	15.0%	14.8%
Services	6.2%	8.3%	10.2%	9.1%	9.5%	9.1%
Finance, insurance, etc.	10.4%	11.7%	12.2%	11.0%	12.7%	13.1%
Government	10.4%	11.1%	12.1%	13.1%	11.7%	11.1%
Statistical discrepancy	5.8%	3.5%	4.6%	0.5%	-0.2%	1.0%
Total GDP	100.0%	100.0%	100.0%	100.0%	100.0%	100.0%

Source: Puerto Rico Planning Board (1985), 'Income and Product 1984', San Juan.

TABLE 2.3

CHANGES IN BRANCH SHARES OF MANUFACTURING VALUE ADDED: 1950-87
(PERCENTAGE BASED ON CURRENT PRICES)

Branch	SIC code	ISIC code	1950 shares %	1950 a) change %	1960 shares %	1960 change %	1970 shares %	1970 change %	1980 shares %	1980 change %	1987 shares %	1987 change %
Consumer goods		31-34-39										
Food, beverages and tobacco	20 Y 21	31	62.7	-8.0	37.8	-24.9	31.3	-6.5	17.6	-13.7	15.1	-2.5
Textiles, wearing apparel, leather	22, 23, Y 31	32	16.0	0.3	20.1	4.1	21.5	1.4	8.8	-12.7	6.2	-2.6
Wood products and furniture	24 Y 25	33	3.6	0.9	2.5	-1.1	2.3	-0.2	0.6	-1.7	0.5	-0.1
Paper, printing and publishing	26 Y 27	35	3.5	0.5	4.8	1.3	3.1	-1.7	1.7	-1.4	1.2	-0.5
Other	20, 30, 32, Y 39	39	6.9	2.6	15.8	8.9	14.5	-1.3	12.2	-2.3	6.4	-5.8
Intermediate goods		35-36										
Chemicals, petrochemical	28	35	4.8	2.6	3.4	-1.4	10.2	6.8	31.0	20.8	41.5	10.5
Non-metallic mineral products	36	36	-	-	-	-	-	-	-	-	-	-
Capital goods	33,34,35	37-38										
Basic metals		37										
Metal products and machinery	36, 37 Y 38	38	2.5	1.1	15.6	13.1	17.1	1.5	28.1	11.0	29.1	1.0
Total manufacturing		3	100		100		100		100		100	

Source: Puerto Rico Planning Board, Area of Economic and Social Planning, Bureau of Economic Analysis

Note: a) Based on 1947.

114

TABLE 2.4

SECTORAL DISTRIBUTION OF LABOUR

Sector	1950	1960	1970	1980	1984	1987
	(In thousands of persons)					
Agriculture	216	126	69	38	40	33
Manufacturing	55	81	132	143	142	152
Construction and mining	29	47	77	44	34	41
Transportation and						
public utilities	30	39	45	47	41	52
Trade	90	97	128	138	145	159
Services	77	75	116	135	140	167
Finance, insurance, etc.	3	6	13	21	22	30
Public administration	45	62	106	184	177	197
Home needlework	51	10	-	-	-	-
Total workforce						
(in thousands)	596	543	686	753	743	834
As per cent of total:						
Agriculture	36.2%	23.2%	10.1%	5.0%	5.4%	4.0%
Manufacturing	9.2%	14.9%	19.2%	19.0%	19.1%	18.2%
Construction and mining	4.9%	8.7%	11.2%	5.8%	4.6%	4.9%
Transportation and	0.0%	0.0%	0.0%	0.0%	0.0%	0.0%
public utilities	5.0%	7.2%	6.6%	6.2%	5.5%	6.2%
Trade	15.1%	17.9%	18.7%	18.3%	19.5%	19.1%
Services	12.9%	13.8%	16.9%	17.9%	18.8%	20.0%
Finance, insurance, etc.	0.5%	1.1%	1.9%	2.8%	3.0%	3.6%
Public administration	7.6%	11.4%	15.5%	24.4%	23.8%	23.6%
Home needlework	8.6%	1.8%	-	-	-	-
	100.0%	100.0%	100.0%	100.0%	100.0%	100.0%

Source: Puerto Rico Department of Labour and Human Resources, Bureau of Statistics, Household Survey.

generating opportunities still resided in the low-tech resource based manufacturing sectors.

It is interesting to note that, despite shifts in production investment and value added away from labour intensive and resource based activities, these sectors still accounted for much more significant employment generation than the capital and technology intensive sectors. In fact, the percentage of total manufacturing employment in the resource based sector represented by ISI Code #39 actually increased from 19.0 per cent in 1950 to 35.5 per cent in 1987.

Another salient feature of the change that occurred in employment distribution was the explosion of jobs created by government. Public administration employment nearly quadrupled between 1950 and 1984, from 45,000 to 177,000 jobs. This expansion of the public service sector was socially necessary to build an expanding infrastructure; to help offset the unemployment created by the contraction in the traditional agricultural and service sectors as industrialization accelerated; and to compensate for the effects of a capital intensive development strategy.

The magnitude of structural unemployment, however, has far outstripped the abilities of either government or the private sector to contain it within reasonable limits. Between 1940 and 1970, the unemployment rate in Puerto Rico fell from 15 per cent to 10 per cent; by 1986, the unemployment rate doubled back to 20 per cent thereby obliterating all previous employment gains.

Despite a recent drop in the unemployment rate to below 16 per cent in late 1987, over 200,000 workers are currently unemployed. As Dr. Surendra Patel has noted in his review of the Puerto Rican development experience: 'There is no country with a comparable experience of high growth combined with an equally high level of unemployment. In terms of output structure, Puerto Rico resembles a developed country. In terms of employment, it is like a poor third world country.'[3]

4 Changes in trade

a Exports

Along with technological transformation in production, came transformation in the structure of trade.

Between 1950 and 1977, the share of sugar, the primary agricultural commodity, in total exports dropped from 50 per cent to two per cent, while the share of manufacturing goods rose from 12 per cent to over 50 per cent. For the entire 1950-86 period, the percentage of primary goods in exports dropped from 52.5 to 20.1, while manufacturing goods reached 79.9 per cent of exports.

The extraordinary proportion of manufactured goods in the 1986 export basket placed Puerto Rico in fourth place (behind South Korea, Hong

TABLE 2.5

CHANGES IN BRANCH SHARES OF EMPLOYMENT IN MANUFACTURING INDUSTRY: 1961-87
(PERCENTAGE)

Branch	SIC code	ISIC code	1961 shares %	1961 change %	1970 shares %	1970 change %	1980 shares %	1980 change %	1987 shares %	1987 change %
Consumer goods		31-34-39								
Food, beverages and tobacco	20 Y 21	31	28.9	-	20.4	-8.5	16.5	-3.9	16.0	-0.5
Textiles, wearing apparel, leather	22, 23, Y 31	32	36.9	-	40.9	4.0	28.7	-12.2	26.3	-2.4
Wood products and furniture	24 Y 25	33	4.2	-	3.5	-0.7	2.5	-1.0	2.4	-0.1
Paper, printing and publishing	26 Y 27	35	3.2	-	2.9	-0.3	3.1	0.2	3.5	0.4
Other	20, 30, 32, Y 39	39	19.0	-	18.6	-0.4	32.5	13.9	35.5	3.0
Intermediate goods		35-36								
Chemicals, petrochemical	28	35	3.9	-	5.6	1.7	12.3	6.7	13.0	0.7
Non-metallic mineral products		36	-	-	-	-	-	-	-	-
Capital goods		37-38								
Basic metals	33, 34, 35	37	0.7	-	1.3	0.6	0.7	-0.6	0.4	-0.3
Metal products and machinery	36, 37 Y 38	38	3.2	-	6.8	3.6	3.7	-3.1	2.9	-0.8
Total manufacturing		3	100		100		100		100	

Source: Puerto Rico Planning Board, Area of Economic and Social Planning, Bureau of Economic Analysis

Kong, and the People's Republic of China), among the top less developed country exporters of manufacturers to developed country markets. Fully 92 per cent of Puerto Rico's exports went to developed country markets, mainly the US.[4]

Overall total value of exports soared from $329.5 million in 1950 to $11,555.9 million in 1986; and the value of exports as a per cent of GNP went from 43.7 per cent to 73.0 per cent.

b Imports

Between 1950 and 1983, total value of imports skyrocketed from $350.3 million to $8,523.8 million, indicating the degree of openness of the economy and the magnitude of the 'swamping' of local productive sectors that occurred as industrialization proceeded.

In the same period, the share of the island's food consumption met by local production fell from 55 per cent to 13 per cent, and food imports grew from $89.3 million to $1,131.1 million.

By 1984, Puerto Rico imported a total of $3,080 per capita, the highest in Latin America and almost double second place Panama's $1,412. Puerto Rico, in that year, bought more from abroad than Mexico, which had a population 20 times greater; and imported twice as much as Argentina. Put another way, Puerto Rico's imports market was equal in size to the combined import markets of Haiti, Paraguay, Honduras, Bolivia, Jamaica, Uruguay, Nicaragua, the Dominican Republic, El Salvador and Costa Rica.[5]

This propensity to import can be attributed to four factors:
1) Puerto Rico has the highest per capita income in the Caribbean/Latin America Region.
2) There has been an alarming reduction in lands under cultivation: by 1982, there was only 38 per cent of the cultivated land area of 1950.
3) Puerto Rico's current population density of 979 inhabitants per square miles is one of the highest in the world.
4) The industrial programme has increased the importation of intermediate goods, and raw materials for processing.

Thus, both export and import patterns have shifted substantially since 1950. These long term fluctuations in the trade profile are summarized in table 2.6.

5 Changes in social indicators

In the previous chapter, we focused on changes in production, in the sectoral distribution of GDP and employment, and in the trade profile. In this chapter, we will briefly review social infrastructure development.

The industrialization process produced a rapid expansion in basic physical infrastructure, and health and education facilities. The number of

118

TABLE 2.6

CHANGES IN TRADE AND ITS STRUCTURE: 1950-86

	1950	1970	1980	1986
I Exports				
Total value of exports (US$ million)	329.5	1,729.3	7,013.3	11,555.9
As per cent of GNP	43.7	36.9	63.3	73.0
Composition of exports (%):				
- Primary goods	52.5	29.8	27.7	20.1
- Manufactured goods	17.7	66.5	70.5	79.9
- Machinery & equipment	0.4	10.1	10.8	21.7
II Imports				
Total value of imports (US$ million)	434.3	2,555.6	8,638.3	10,098.9
As per cent of GNP	57.6	54.5	78.0	63.8
Composition of imports (%):				
- Primary goods	51.3	30.0	48.3	33.9
- Manufactured goods	53.3	70.0	51.7	66.1
- Machinery & equipment	13.5	24.0	14.3	22.3

Source: Statistical Yearbook Puerto Rico 1969; External Trade Statistics for 1960, 1970 and 1980; and Informe Economico al Gobernador 1987.

Notes: This classification follows as closely as possible the SITC, with the exception of Group 9, commodities and transactions not classified by type, which in the case of Puerto Rico are involved in manufactures, since they represent manufactured items. Returned merchandises and the re-export of motor vehicles are excluded from exports. In the case of exports, the primary products sector is concentrated on food and related products, which in the case of imports, they consist mainly in petroleum and related products.

roads almost doubled. The number of telephones rose 20 fold. Electricity output multiplied 25 fold. Water service clients grew seven fold, and sewer service clients six fold.

The result was an improvement in social welfare indicators. Life expectancy in the period increased from 61 years to 73 years, the level of developed countries.

Another outcome of this rapid industrialization and social infrastructure building period, was the rural to urban shift. Up until 1970, the countryside still contained over 60 per cent of the Island's total population. By 1986, this proportion had declined to 27 per cent. Thus, in a time span of only sixteen years, the process of Puerto Rico's economic and social transformation from a rural to a metropolitan society was completed.

6 Income distribution

Data on income distribution is scattered and not up to date. However, it is possible to piece together a composite picture for the years 1941, 1952, 1953, 1969, and 1977 based on various analyses.[6]

Between 1941 and 1977, the share of income represented by the lowest 40 per cent of families actually declined from 14.0 per cent to 10.7 per cent; while the richest 20 per cent maintained their share of total income at above 50 per cent. Thus, there was considerable erosion of income share at the lower income brackets, and some improvement for the middle groups.

The impression that local income distribution has not substantially shifted despite impressive growth rates is reinforced by comparing Puerto Rico with other countries in Latin America. Table 2.8 shows that the poorest 40 per cent of families fare better than their peers in Peru, Brazil, Mexico, Honduras, Panama, and Venezuela; but worse than their peer groups in Argentina, Chile, Trinidad-Tobago, and Costa Rica.

The economic and social tensions that could result from this skewed income distribution pattern have, in part, been redressed by increasing Federal transfers, including food stamps. Over 60 per cent of the population currently receive food stamps; such federal transfers account for over 17 per cent of personal income. Between 1950 and 1983, net federal transfers rose from 63.4 million dollars to 2,095 million dollars, an increase of 33 fold.

7 Development of technology embodying inputs and their utilization

In the preceding chapter, we traced the broad transition of the Puerto Rican production and employment base from agriculture to high technology. We also discussed the accompanying broad social transition that occurred. In this chapter, we provide a closer accounting of technology embodying inputs and their utilization as modernization unfolded; and take a more

TABLE 2.7

THE SOCIO-ECONOMIC INFRASTRUCTURE: SELECTED INDICATORS

Indicators	Unit	1950	1960	1970	1980
Transportation and communications:					
Road mileage	thousand km	3.6	4.7	5.9	6.9
Passenger vehicles	thousands	36.4	133.5	495.9	939.3
Shipping freight	million tons	2.3	8	19.1	-
Telephones	thousands	34.5	82.5	319.3	693.3
Electric energy:					
Production	million kwh	539	2,022	7,542	13,291
Number of clients	thousands	170	409	691	978
Water and sewer facilities:					
Water service clients	thousands	118	257	530	832
Sewer service clients	thousands	47	119	276	-
Health					
Life expectancy	years	61	69	70	73
Persons per doctor		-	1,130	758	534
Education:					
Literacy rate	%	75	83	89	9 a)
Number of teachers	thousands	9	13	22	31
School enrolment b)	thousands	488	738	926	1,028

Source: Puerto Rico Planning Board (1982), 'Socio-economic Statistics 1982', San Juan.

Cited in: Curet, E. (1986), 'Puerto Rico: Development by Integration to the U.S.', p. 88.

Notes: a)   Data for 1976.
b)   Including university level.

TABLE 2.8

INCOME SHARE OF POOREST 40% OF FAMILIES:
SELECTED LATIN AMERICAN COUNTRIES

Country	Year	Share of lower 40% of families
Argentina	1970	14.1
Chile	1968	13.4
Trinidad-Tobago	1976	13.3
Costa Rica	1971	12.0
Puerto Rico	1979	10.7
Venezuela	1970	10.3
Mexico	1977	9.9
Honduras	1967	7.3
Panama	1970	7.2
Brazil	1972	7.0
Peru	1972	7.0

Source: World Bank (1982), 'World Development Report 1982', New York, Oxford
University Press, Table 25; and U.S. Department of Commerce, Bureau
of the Census (1982), 'Census of the Population 1980', Washington, Government Printing Office, C-53.

Cited in: Curet, E. (1986), 'Puerto Rico: Development by Integration to the U.S.', p. 88.

detailed look at changes in capital formation, investment patterns and productivity sources in the economy.

To analyze long term changes in capital formation: i.e. physical technology embodied in the means of production, we must focus on three key features: its external control; its relative rise and fall as per cent of GNP; and change in input growth and productivity.

8 Capital formation and its external control

The weight of US corporate control of the economy in the whole period of lift-off and deepening of industrialization can best be appreciated by comparing the relative magnitudes of investment levels in Puerto Rico, Latin America and all developing countries.

By 1967, Puerto Rico received $240 million in US annual direct investment in manufacturing, while Latin America received $265 million, and all other developing countries $366 million. *Thus, by 1967 Puerto Rico was accounting for 28 per cent of all US direct manufacturing investments in developing countries*, as shown in tables 2.9 and 2.10.

By 1978, Puerto Rico accounted for 42 per cent of all US corporate profits and 30 per cent of all accumulated direct investment in the Latin American/Caribbean Region.

In the post World War II period, the economy was almost entirely dependent on such external capital and technology for industrial transformation. Between 1950 and 1978, imported capital as a percentage of total capital on the Island, rose from 43.3 per cent to 80 per cent.[7]

The logical result of this increasing external investment in Puerto Rico has been the increasing proportion of gross manufacturing income remitted off-island to corporate owners. Between 1950 and 1982 the proportion of the Island's gross manufacturing income paid out to US corporations rose from 12.4 per cent to 68.7 per cent, or $4.13 billion. These huge outflows account for the prominent GNP/GDP gap in Puerto Rico noted by so many analysts.

9 The relative stagnation of capital formation and its 'drag' effect on growth rates

Between 1950 and 1970, gross domestic fixed capital formation as a per cent of GNP rose from 14.8 per cent to 30 per cent. By 1980, fixed capital formation as a per cent of GNP had fallen to 18.5 per cent, and by 1987 it fell further to 16.9 per cent. This dramatic rise and decline in capital formation represented 'a very remarkable phenomena, (sic) without parallel in the experience of other countries.'[8]

As the rate of capital formation declined, the growth rate for the whole economy slowed drastically. As described previously, in the period 1965-

TABLE 2.9

A COMPARISON OF US ANNUAL DIRECT INVESTMENT IN MANUFACTURING IN PUERTO RICO, LATIN AMERICA AND ALL DEVELOPING COUNTRIES: 1953-69 (IN MILLION US$)

Year	US annual net direct investment in manufacturing: in Puerto Rico [1]	in Caribbean and Latin America, excluding Puerto Rico [2]	Total [3] = [1] + [2]	Shares of Puerto Rico in US annual net direct investment in manufacturing in Latin America and Caribbean [4] = [1] / [3]	US annual net direct investment in manufacturing in all developing countries outside of Caribbean and Latin American region [5]	Shares of Puerto Rico in total US annual net direct investment in manufacturing in developing countries [6] =([1] / ([1+5])
1953	14	(19)	(5)	-280.00%	(11)	466.67%
1954	10	89	99	10.10%	104	8.77%
1955	13	130	143	9.09%	140	8.50%
1956	42	178	220	19.09%	191	18.03%
1957	33	(251)	(218)	-15.14%	(245)	-15.57%
1958	83	54	137	60.58%	77	51.88%
1959	43	83	126	34.13%	107	28.67%
1960	62	104	166	37.35%	125	33.16%
1961	33	186	219	15.07%	202	14.04%
1962	82	237	319	25.71%	262	23.84%
1963	90	268	358	25.14%	325	21.69%
1964	107	295	402	26.62%	374	22.25%
1965	101	437	538	18.77%	510	16.53%
1966	125	29	154	81.17%	125	50.00%
1967	240	265	505	47.52%	366	39.60%
1968	152	485	637	23.86%	548	21.71%
1969	312	479	791	39.44%	608	33.91%

Source: Survey of Current Business, February 1981; and Bureau of Economic Analysis, unpublished data for Puerto Rico for 1955-69.

Note: US Direct Investment - The net book value of standing loans to, their foreign affiliates. It is sometimes confused with, and accordingly should be distinguished from, total assets of the affiliates themselves, which are the sum of total owners' equity held by, and total liabilities owned to, both US direct investors and all other persons.

TABLE 2.10

A COMPARISON OF US ACCUMULATED DIRECT INVESTMENT IN MANUFACTURING IN PUERTO RICO,
LATIN AMERICA AND ALL DEVELOPING COUNTRIES: 1953-69
(IN MILLION US$)

Year	US accumulated net direct investment in manufacturing: in Puerto Rico	in Caribbean and Latin America, excluding Puerto Rico	Total	Shares of Puerto Rico in US accumulated net direct investment in manufacturing in Latin America and Caribbean	US accumulated net direct investment in manufacturing in all developing countries outside of Caribbean and Latin American region	Shares of Puerto Rico in total US accumulated net direct investment in manufacturing in all developing countries
	[1]	[2]	[3] = [1] + [2]	[4] = [1] / [3]	[5]	[6] =([1] / [1+5])
			[3]	[4]	[5]	[6]
1953	82	1,134	1,216	6.74%	1,228	6.26%
1954	92	1,223	1,315	7.00%	1,332	6.46%
1955	105	1,353	1,458	7.20%	1,472	6.66%
1956	147	1,531	1,678	8.76%	1,663	8.12%
1957	180	1,280	1,460	12.33%	1,418	11.26%
1958	263	1,334	1,597	16.47%	1,495	14.96%
1959	306	1,417	1,723	17.76%	1,602	16.04%
1960	368	1,521	1,889	19.48%	1,727	17.57%
1961	401	1,707	2,108	19.02%	1,929	17.21%
1962	483	1,944	2,427	19.90%	2,191	18.06%
1963	573	2,212	2,785	20.57%	2,516	18.55%
1964	680	2,507	3,187	21.34%	2,890	19.05%
1965	781	2,944	3,725	20.97%	3,400	18.68%
1966	906	2,973	3,879	23.36%	3,525	20.45%
1967	1,146	3,238	4,384	26.14%	3,891	22.75%
1968	1,298	3,723	5,021	25.85%	4,439	22.63%
1969	1,610	4,202	5,812	27.70%	5,047	24.19%

Source: Survey of Current Business, February 1981; and Bureau of Economic Analysis, unpublished data for Puerto Rico for 1955-69.

Note: US Direct Investment - The net book value of standing loans to, their foreign affiliates. It is sometimes confused with, and accordingly should be distinguished from, total assets of the affiliates themselves, which are the sum of total owners' equity held by, and total liabilities owed to, both US direct investors and all other persons.

80 the growth rate was among the fastest in the world, averaging over seven per cent per annum. Then the plunge occurred. The growth rate fell to only one per cent per annum during the 1980-85 period, and the investment rate per annum averaged a negative four per cent. Despite the recent upturn in the economy, the level of investment and capital formation has still remained well below the historical heights attained previously.

The close (but not absolute) link between investment, capital formation and growth rates is shown in the next graph, which compares GDP and investment rates in the 1980-85 period for selected countries. This graph shows that Puerto Rico had a negative growth of investment and a low rate of GDP growth as well.

10 Input growth and productivity

When we review long term changes in manufacturing productivity on a subsectoral basis, we find a predictable trend towards higher value added and greater capital accumulation in the new technology and capital intensive externally owned industries, and relatively stagnant accumulation and value added trends in local resource based industries. For example, in 1952, ISIC category #39, stone, glass, clay, concrete, petroleum, refining, and rubber and plastics industries had a per employee participation in manufacturing value added of $115,095. By 1987, the per employee contribution in the resource based sector had fallen off to $25,204. In contrast, in the intermediate goods sector, a category dominated by the high-tech pharmaceutical industry, value added per employee rose from $6,067 in 1952 to $157,529 in 1987. Similarly, in the capital goods sector, value added per employee leapt from $2,845 to $87,489. Although these dollar values are all in current prices, and are lower when adjusted for price rises, the actual rise in productivity has still been very impressive.

Within the *services* sector, there were also dramatic changes in branch shares of value added, and per employee participation in value added. In 1952, trade had by far the greatest share in services value added, followed by public administration, finance, insurance and real estate. By 1987, the lagging finance, insurance, real estate, and public administration sectors had expanded dramatically, and almost equalled the branch shares of value added of the trade sector.

These changes in the manufacturing and services sectors are shown in the tables in the Appendix.

Thus, in every area of the economy and the social structure, there has been intense transformation since 1950. This overall transformation appears to fit the classic pattern described by Kuznets, Chenery and Patel, et al, involving large scale shifts in overall economic performance; in sectoral output and productivity; and in social indicators. We will now explore the critical, discrete stages in this transformation process.

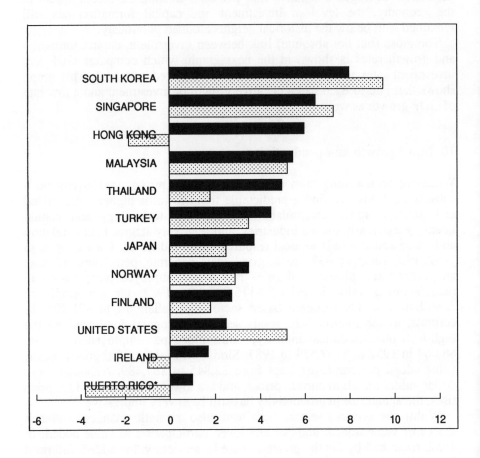

FIGURE 2.2

COMPARISON BETWEEN GROSS DOMESTIC PRODUCT AND INVESTMENT: 1980-85

   GDP growth rate.

Investment growth rate.

Source: World Development Report, 1987.
* Puerto Rico Planning Board, Area of Economic and Social Planning,
Bureau of Economic Analysis.

11 Stages in the transformation process

In any survey of the literature on national technological transformation, a staged development process for newly industrialized countries would be identified as a constant theme by analysts and researchers. A synthesis of findings in the field would produce a coherent model of national transformation based on an unfolding succession of stages in the economy - from agriculture, to primary commodity production, to labour intensive manufacturing, to capital and/or technology intensive manufacturing. This sequence of phases has indeed unfolded in Puerto Rico.

Up until the late 1940s, agriculture and primary processing of raw materials were the predominant sectors of the economy. Throughout the 1950s and until the mid 1960s, labour intensive manufacturing was the driving force of industrial expansion. Then came the great wave of capital and technology intensive manufacturing in the late 1960s that has run through to the present day, a wave that has lifted the industrial and economic structure to new heights.

Under conventional typologies of the development process, Puerto Rico has reached its ultimate growth stage, completed the full circle of available possibilities as a newly industrialized, middle-income economy. But conventional development typologies cannot account for what has happened in Puerto Rico. No existing development typology can account for the rise to dominance of the information sector - that bundle of goods and services composed of education, media of communications, R and D, information machines and information services. Between 1973 and 1987, the information sector grew so rapidly that, according to our analysis, it has become the leading sector of the economy, contributing 53.6 per cent of GNP. *In fact, Puerto Rico is the only documented case we have been able to find of a backward, agricultural society that has leapt into a 'post-industrial knowledge society' in the short span of only 40 years.*

In each of the successive stages of the economic transition, government has played a leading role as industrial entrepreneur, as architect and engineer of social infrastructure, as a catalytic agent for development of a local 'business environment' conducive to private sector capital accumulation.

In the early 1940s, the island's government built and operated factories for primary processing of raw materials and acted as the industrial entrepreneur in vital areas where the private sector hesitated to invest. In the late 1940s and on through the 1950s, local government mobilized an industrialization campaign, and under the programmatic umbrella of Operation Bootstrap, organized massive flows of off-shore capital and technology which led to the establishment of labour intensive industry on the island. In the 1960s and 1970s, local government targeted and energized the development of a set of capital and technology intensive industries, including electronics, computers, and pharmaceuticals. In addition, it brilliantly leveraged the competing economic interests of the Federal

Government and US multinational companies to forge a grand compromise, a tax incentive programme (Section 936) that became a premier incentive and lure for high-tech companies. Finally, government's acquisition and modernization of the island's telecommunications network, and its huge investments in public education during the mid 1970s and 1980s, laid the critical foundations for today's explosion of the information sector.

In the chapters that follow, we will explore in greater detail both the rapid unfolding of stages of growth, and the specific policies and actions by the Commonwealth Government that facilitated the economy's moving through these successive stages. This inquiry is divided into three chapters: (1) Overcoming technological stagnation: Operation Bootstrap and the rise of the industrialization strategy; (2) The rise of high technology manufacturing; and (3) The rise of the information sector.

III Overcoming technological stagnation: Operation Bootstrap and the rise of the industrialization strategy

In this chapter, we will establish the *economic and technological setting* for Puerto Rico's transformation experience. Our review will span the early history of the island and the first decades of United States control; the emergence of a nationalist party, the Popular Democratic Party in the 1940s; the Party's formulation and execution of the Operation Bootstrap development campaign; and the resulting economic 'liftoff' stage which unfolded throughout the 1950-67 period.

1 The early history

'The Caribbean was the ear in which all the first sounds of our history echoed. Crime and glory were born there together.' - German Archiniegas

In two successive days in May, 1493, Pope Alexander VI issued edicts which empowered the Catholic Kings of Spain and their heirs to claim sovereignty over all the countries and islands their envoys discovered. On a map of the Atlantic, the Pope drew a line running north and south, and he gave a monopoly on all lands west of that line to Spain, making the Caribbean Sea a Spanish lake. In November, 1493, Christopher Columbus landed on the west coast of Borinquen (as Puerto Rico was then called by the Taíno Indian inhabitants of the period) and claimed the island for Spain. Thus began a historical process of annexation by outside powers that has run uninterrupted for 500 years.

It fell to the legendary Conquistador, Ponce de León, to begin the real work of colonization. He quickly established a fort beside the Bay of San Juan. That safe port soon launched Spanish armadas throughout the New World. Puerto Rico, or 'Rich Port', was formally declared by the Spanish King as 'point of entry and key to all the Indies' and 'front and vanguard of the Empire in the Americas'.

The location of Puerto Rico converted the island into a key base to organize the defense of the Spanish galleons throughout the Americas, which were under constant attack by pirates. The island was duly fortified and whole garrisons were quartered there. To assist in the building of massive forts, African slaves were imported to supplement local labour. To pay for this construction and the upkeep of labour, a tax called 'El Situo' was placed on Mexico. For two hundred years, this subsidy formed the most important source of revenue for the island.

Throughout the 18th and early 19th centuries, Spain exerted a stifling hold on Puerto Rico's economic development, even forbidding the acquisition of technology and machinery, on the misled notion it could ensure monopoly rents over the import of manufactured goods.[9] The flow of technology was indirect: from England into Spain and then onward to Puerto Rico and the Caribbean. The finest reminder of this old technology trade route is the common machete, the island's long bladed cane-cutter's knife. The word itself, machete, is derived from Manchester, England where the steel and blades were produced. From 1815 on, Spain was so buffeted by the decline in her colonies and fortunes, she felt it necessary to change her colonial relationship and promote greater economic self-sufficiency in Puerto Rico. Spain's new attitude was expressed in the relaxation of tariffs on agricultural equipment. A great wave of immigration of risk-taking immigrants and new technologies from England, Italy, and other parts of the Caribbean and Latin American region all contributed to a surge in agricultural export commodity production namely sugar and coffee. Between 1828 and 1872, commodity exports increased in value from 5.5 million pesos to 22.5 million pesos per year.[10]

During this same period, the US became a large trade partner, a direct reflection of its growing power to control economic events in the region. By 1895, the ascendancy of the US as an economic and military power outside its own borders had become widely recognized by her regional partners. In that year, US Secretary of State, Richard Olney, stated the obvious: 'Today the United States is practically sovereign on this continent, and its fiat is law upon the subjects to which it confines its interposition.'[11] Its sovereignty included the sea lanes, and this meant gaining control over Puerto Rico and Cuba, and then moving forward on the establishment of the Panama Canal.

On April 25, 1898, the US Congress formerly declared war on Spain. US forces invaded Cuba and defeated the Spanish; and then formally annexed Puerto Rico as an 'unincorporated territory', its first overseas colony. 'The nascent US Empire, until then restricted in its expansion to is own continent, was making a bid for world power'.[12] The transition of Empires was now complete, and the unbroken line of outside control of Puerto Rico continued.

The US military governor took over governance of Puerto Rico. In 1899, he stated with scorn: 'So great is their poverty that they are always in debt to the proprietors or merchants. They live in huts made of straw. It is hard to believe that these pale, sallow and often emaciated beings are the direct descendants of the "conquistadors" who carried the flag of Spain to nearly all of South America and a third of North America.'[13]

By 1900, the military government in place was removed and, under the provisions of the Foraker Act, a civilian governor and senate were chosen by the US President. This form of government was replaced by a more representative version under the Jones Act of 1917, which created a bicameral popularly elected legislative assembly, but with the governor and key officials, including the Supreme Court, still approved by the US President. The Jones Act conferred citizenship on Puerto Ricans, and gradually allowed more local participation in self-government, with the US exerting veto power over all decisions.

2 The first wave of US capital and technology

With US control came US capital. The expansion of tariff protection to Puerto Rico and the creation of a fully integrated US/Puerto Rico trade territory, made sugar and tobacco production highly attractive to the US private sector. An initial development aid package of about $45,000,000 was granted to 'ready the ground' for private investment, and to build infrastructure - roads, utilities, irrigation.

During the first 30 years of US governance almost $120,000,000 in capital to modernize and commercialize agriculture and agro-processing poured into the island.

> 'Antiquated muscavado mills on individual estates gave way to modern sugar centralis, family properties merged into corporations, and others were bought out by corporations. Improved irrigation and cane varieties, and more efficient techniques of sugar extraction, resulted in a production leap: from 57,000 tons of sugar per year in 1898, to 200,000 in 1903, to 350,000 in 1913, to 900,000 tons in 1930.'[14]

US interests made sugar king in Puerto Rico, and, by 1934, just four US companies owned or leased 211,761 acres and produced 51 per cent of the processed sugar.

The increased flow of US investment funds and the rapidly growing production sector implied an expansion of the transactions sector, and a subsequent expansion of banking. Between 1898 and 1928, the banking sector increased from just four local banks with $1,830,000 in total deposits to 14 domestic banks and four US/Canadian banks with total deposits of $54 million.

Yet, the period of expansion of production and capital on the island did not translate into increased prosperity for the agricultural labour force, who earned an average of $3.00 a week in 1929. The 63 cents average daily wage in 1929 was then less than Cuba's $1.26 average, and Hawaii's 97 cents.[15]

Poverty, as reflected in health and infant mortality statistics, was appalling in the first three decades of US control. In 1930, the average life expectancy was 40.1 for men, and 41.5 for women. The infant mortality rate was 158 per 1,000 live births. Infections and parasitic diseases accounted for 1,238.5 deaths per 100,000 population, versus chronic and degenerative diseases which accounted for 209 deaths.[16]

This situation of a one-crop economy, dominated by large US plantations and mills, and a two class society, led Luis Muñoz Marín, the future governor and charismatic leader of the Puerto Rican Modernization Movement to write:

> 'By now the development of large absentee-owned sugar estates, the rapid curtailment in the planting of coffee and the concentration of sugar manufacture in the hands of the American trust, have combined to make Puerto Rico a land of beggars and millionaires, of flattering statistics and distressing realities. More and more, it becomes a factory worked by peons, fought over by lawyers, bossed by absentee industrialists, and clerked by politicians. It is now Uncle Sam's second largest sweatshop.'[17]

Yet worse was to come. Between 1928 and 1940, a series of disasters struck the Puerto Rican economy. A hurricane in 1928 devastated the coffee crop, and production dropped from 32 million pounds to 5 million pounds in one year. The Great Depression struck in 1929, and US import quotas were placed on sugar. In 1932, another hurricane hit.

The result was a contraction of production and exports fell from $107 million in 1926-27, to $75 million in 1932-33. Per capita incomes followed suit, plunging from $122 in 1929-30, to $88 in 1932-33. To compound these difficulties, the effects of overpopulation were becoming widespread. By 1932, 10,000 new labour force participants per year were coming onto the employment market.

As part of the larger federal New Deal and its Works Progress Administration Programme, a Puerto Rico Emergency Relief Programme was created in 1932 to help ease the widespread suffering. In 1935, this Relief Programme became the Puerto Rico Reconstruction Administration, a US federal agency. Its two fold purpose was to assist the unemployed, and to create a 'permanent employment' programme. This agency was the first attempt by the US Government and Congress to create a programme for economic development in a less-developed region.

In six years, the Puerto Rico Reconstruction Administration spent $72 million on school construction, hydroelectric plants, housing, purchase and operation of sugar mills, industrial plants for cement and bugle alcohol, and a family farm resettlement programme. In addition to these expenditures, other federal agencies spent $58 million in a large relief effort directed at Puerto Rico. Despite these six year initiatives, misery still abounded.

By 1940, overpopulation had reached its peak. A doubling of the total population between 1890 and 1940, and a steadily decreasing death rate had produced a density of 546 persons per square mile. Coupled with this overpopulation, was a monopoly over available land by a small number of landlord/farmers. The 1940 census revealed that six tenths of one per cent of all farmers held 31 per cent of all land, and 44 per cent of all capital assets. The result of the converging trends of overpopulation and land monopoly by a few was massive landlessness and poverty. Though the census listed only 54,200 farmers, 229,000 people claimed they made their full living from the land.

For the island as a whole, the average annual income was $341, less than one fifth of the US. The top 2.9 per cent of all families received 27 per cent of total income, while the lower 86 per cent of families received only 29 per cent of total income. In 1940, of 354,000 families examined by Works Progress Administration Caseworkers, 140,000, or as many as 40 per cent of the total, were certified as needy.[18]

3 The idea of planned development takes hold

The failure of the federally initiated reconstruction efforts during the 1930s to meaningfully address the problems of the island had a strong impact on both the island's political process and the thinking of a small group of high level Puerto Rican planners in government. The future architect of the Operation Bootstrap Development Campaign, Teodoro Moscoso, recalled the perceptions that pervaded his peer group in 1940:

> 'The Federal efforts were not cohesive - nor did they have accurately targeted programmes. It was left up to the Puerto Rican Group to try to develop their programme as they went along, and the Federal legislation merely provided the funds for the attempt. We began to think in terms of development directed by Puerto Rico, utilizing Puerto Rican-controlled resources as much as possible in order to prevent a stop and go type of development which, in reality, is non-development.'

The first major policy approach in the Industrial Campaign therefore had an emphasis on national mobilization, and the generation and popularization of a development ethos. This first phase resulted in a series of well conceived initiatives that attempted to lay the island's technical and economic foundation.

With the support of Rex Tugwell, the progressive Washington appointed governor, both Moscoso, as Tugwell's Chief Special Assistant, and Muñoz Marín, the head of the Puerto Rican Senate and leader of the Popular Democratic Party, began putting forward selected comprehensive programmes. The first programme was 'Bread and Land': The Land Reform and Agricultural Diversification Act of 1941, which limited ownership of land to 500 acres, and which created a land authority to buy back and redistribute land and capital to cooperatives of farmers. This programme 'satisfied a need for land reform and the retention of the efficiency of large scale operations in the competitive sugar industry.' As a result of this Act, over ninety thousand parcels of land were redistributed to cooperatives of farmers. This changed forever the social relations in the countryside, and overthrew the feudal order.

The Land Reform initiative was followed, in short order, by the creation of a Planning, Urbanizing and Zoning Board in 1942 to coordinate and guide new public enterprises and capital expenditure and to establish six year budgets that would match revenues to forward planning objectives of the government. Simultaneously, an Industrial Development Corporation and Development Bank were established to target and finance industries which 'offered greatest possibilities for the broadest utilization of the island's economic resources', and 'to point the way' for private enterprise. To appease conservative opponents of this piece of legislation, which included the Chamber of Commerce and sugar producers, the Development Bank was created with a Board composed of four executives of private banks. More initiatives followed. In 1945, an Agricultural Development Corporation, to develop pilot plant scale new and improved crops; and a Public Utilities Corporation, which included Water Resources, Aqueducts and Sewerage, Transportation and Communications Authorities, were all brought into existence.

Thus, in a very short period of time, between 1940 and 1945, the basic apparatus for planning and implementing a development campaign was put into place.

4 The development campaign begins in earnest

'Puerto Ricans had never taken their own destiny in their hands before, and no one had ever brought about the industrialization of an overpopulated tropical agricultural island yet on the world scene.'[19]

Establishing a basic set of governmental instruments for change does not necessarily lead to a coherent reality based development strategy. Sometimes the very act of putting into place this fundamental infrastructure exhausts the strength of the leadership and requires a period of calm and rethinking to target those instruments towards clearer goals, more realistic objectives. Such was the case for the Puerto Rican policy leaders, who created a set of instruments for one purpose and then redirected them towards an entirely different purpose shortly thereafter.

The 1942 Development Company Act and its subsequent modification is the key example of the fundamental policy shifts that occurred in the early years. The Development Company Act gave the Company 'broad powers to conduct programmes of all types to discover and develop to the fullest possible extent the human and economic resources of the island.' As Ross has noted, this Act was clearly intended to promote industrial self-sufficiency and local resource based development. The legislation specified that The Company 'was to promote industries based on a specified list of raw materials, including silica sands, clays, fibres of all classes, agricultural products, animals, forests, mining, fishing, and any other by-product, derived therefrom and any waste thereof.' The Company was also assigned the promotion of 'industrial enterprises and capital owned by Residents of Puerto Rico and to avoid the evils of absentee ownership of large scale capital.'[20]

To some extent, this strong orientation towards development directed from within and palpable suspicion of outside control reflected the deep conviction of Governor Rexford Tugwell, who had been US Secretary of Agriculture. He knew agriculture, and wanted local agricultural and resource based development to serve as the basis for Puerto Rican modernization. But the facts would not serve his vision.

5 Fomento takes the lead in a resource based development strategy

At the beginning of the modernization struggle, there were little local skills in strategy and programme planning.

Lacking these skills, the very first step in analyzing options and directing the overall development path could not be taken. The still small circle of political and governmental leadership was acutely aware of its own knowledge limitations, and so began a knowledge and technology transfer initiative that would serve as its first coherent act.

An immediate and critical result of this initiative was the recruitment by Fomento of Arthur D. Little Inc., the leading US technology and business planning consultant firm, as senior adviser to the development strategy formulation process. At that time, the President of Arthur D. Little, Earl Stevenson, served as Science Adviser to US President Franklin D. Roosevelt. His decision to assist Puerto Rico was a milestone in both Arthur D. Little's history and in the history of its sister institution, the Massachusetts Institute of Technology. This was the first time Arthur D. Little Inc. had agreed to undertake an area development study for a government; the first time the company had agreed to undertake a project that did not conduct specific technology related research for a private industry client; and the first time either the company or MIT confronted the reality of the Third World.

This relationship, which was to last for 20 years, provided Puerto Rico's emerging leaders with the best thinking of a superb group of scientists and managers. 'We have been under the eye of the purveyors of the highest technology in the US.'[21] Through this interaction, the proposed profile of the economic and technology development initiative came into focus.

Fomento began to implement the industrial strategy that had been prepared with the help of Arthur D. Little and MIT. This strategy was an 'opportunistic' one, which undertook short term actions to exploit existing natural resources and linkage opportunities.

Fomento initiated the following early actions:
- Advanced geographic and geophysical mapping systems were organized, and a Resource Inventory was initiated with the assistance of the US Geologic Survey.
- Factories to exploit available natural resources and linkage opportunities were established, such as a bottling plant to supply the rum industry.
- A product and technology scanning programme was established 'to conduct book research' on developments and trends elsewhere.
- A Research and Development Laboratory was created to conduct investigations into diversified uses of natural resources.
- An accelerated Industrial Engineering Master's Programme was started at MIT for Puerto Rican engineers.
- An Industrial Services Division was established to provide technical assistance to industry.

Yet, despite this movement, Fomento eventually came up against a brick wall.

To carry out its local resource based development mandate, The Development Company had initiated a comprehensive geologic survey of the island, in cooperation with the US Geological Survey. Teodoro Moscoso, by then Director of the Development Company, described the results of the survey: 'It took years to do. It's a very complete map ... to find nothing. Some minor copper ore, some silica ... no oil.'[22]

The original strategy, of an economic drive based on processing native materials for worldwide distribution, was challenged by the discoveries of the geologic survey, which identified only silica and some minor clay deposits. Industrial cement, glass containers and paper board plants were, as noted, built to exploit such limited natural resources as did exist.

By 1945, a growing realization was taking hold that a new strategy was needed. The need for such a strategy was made evident not only by the initial results of the resource survey, but also by the following additional fiscal and economic facts:
- At the cost of $10,000 per job in 1945 in government run factories, it would have taken $300,000,000 to create employment for the ranks of the 125,000 unemployed that year, even if the capital per worker was halved and one additional non-manufacturing job resulted from each factory job.[23]

- The grim possibilities for locally generated resource based manufacturing were matched by the grim possibilities for agricultural expansion. By 1945, the limits of arable land cultivation had almost been reached. In contrast, Puerto Rico's neighbour, Cuba, had only about 25 per cent of its land under cultivation, with 5,500,000 arable acres unused.[24] Productivity and yields steadily declined in Puerto Rico between 1940 and 1945, as agriculture's share of the island's net income dropped from 31 per cent to 25 per cent, and agricultural employment fell off by 10 per cent.

- By 1949, it had also become painfully obvious that the Puerto Rican Government could not continue to finance the national development effort from the receding windfall income of the World War II rum trade; a $275 million windfall roughly equal in magnitude to the amount that had accrued in the same period to Venezuela from exploitation of its primary resources.[25]

The need for major modifications in strategy produced a running conflict between two schools of policy thought: the progressive welfare oriented school, which wanted to continue a focus on funding housing, schools, etc., and the capital development school.

Capital development advocates argued that insular government agencies had spent less than 20 per cent of appropriations during the forties on economic development per se, and the government needed to back away from a welfare policy, and promote more intense capital accumulation.[26] Furthermore, these advocates argued that the local resource based programme had failed to provide the spark necessary for economic 'liftoff'. More emphasis on external capital and technology recruitment was needed to generate economic momentum. In 1952, investment statistics were marshalled to show that the US firms which had established operations on the island had average capital per worker levels of between three and four thousand dollars, well above the capital per worker levels of local industries. US plants also had far higher wage levels. The accumulation theorists insisted that greater capital formation and income enhancement could only come from more and more emphasis on recruitment of such US firms. Their winning logic increasingly refocussed the island's development strategy.

6 A new strategy emerges

'Let me brief you on the main facts of Puerto Rico. Puerto Rico is very densely populated. There are 650 of us to each square mile of territory. Half of the land can be cultivated, so there are 1,300 of us to each cultivated mile. The size of this problem can best be gauged by thinking of it this way: Suppose the population of all the continents and islands of the world should move into the United States, then the United States would have about 650 inhabitants per square mile, as Puerto Rico has now. But if we are to make a proper comparison, we must suppose further. Suppose that, with all the population of the world within its territory, the United States should find themselves lacking in practically all natural resources - no coal, no oil, no metals. Suppose further that with all the people of the world inside its boundaries American industry should be only beginning to develop. If you can imagine all these things together, you have a fair picture of what the people of the United States would be facing under such circumstances, and of what the people of Puerto Rico are facing today.'[27]

In 1947 and again in 1948, with the triumphant election of Muñoz Marín as the first local governor, an election that shattered further the legislature strongholds of conservative landowners and merchants, the Popular Democratic Party announced a change in tactics. An all-out 'Battle for Production' was launched, signalling the growing ascendancy of the capital accumulation advocates and the turning point in strategy.

Henceforth, there would be an operational shift in development policies and programmes, away from an emphasis on local resources and government control of industry and toward an open, capital and technology intensive strategy fuelled by the increasing recruitment of production know-how and industrial finance capital from the US private sector. 'So we turned from managers into promoters.'[28]

In reaction to a first stage failure to build the economy on local resources, a new campaign for industrialization would be based on 'capital accumulation and private enterprise, free factor movements, an export engine of growth and technological innovation.'[29] The name 'Manos a la Obra', or 'Hands at Work' was given to the campaign. The Anglicized and popularized version of the initiative was 'Operation Bootstrap'. The Operation was to be executed through the creation of a set of aids, such as rental buildings, long term loans at favourable rates of interest, and other fiscal incentives.

This policy departure had been greatly facilitated by the passage of the 1947 Industrial Tax Exemption Act. This Act completely exempted new industries, including tourism, and selected old industries from Puerto Rican income tax, property taxes, and municipal income taxes from twelve year periods. Since Puerto Rico had been already exempted from Federal Internal Revenue taxes, this Act essentially created a completely tax free zone for US industries.

To centralize the institutional and operational base for the new strategy, the Economic Development Administration (EDA) was created in 1949 as an umbrella organization containing the Development Company, an Industrial Services Branch, and an Industrial Research and Development Centre. EDA's Stateside promotions increased in intensity and sophistication. The trickle of EDA promoted factories increased: 9 in 1947; 16 in 1948; 32 in 1949, 74 in 1952. By 1955, new factories in garments, shoes, tobacco processing, etc., were putting in a half a million dollars a week in wages and employing 28,000 workers, five per cent of the work force. The technological transformation of Puerto Rico was underway.

7 The lift-off phase

'This, then, is the model: Traditional agriculture collapses under pressure from imports. The modern sector is built with foreign capital, the production of this sector is exported. Profits are exported, too. Not enough jobs are created. And the people are also exported.'

Weiskopf, T., *Factories and Food Stamps*
John Hopkins University Press, 1986.

The lift-off of the economy had an irresistible momentum. In the first five years of the Industrial Promotions Campaign, 361 US manufacturing firms established themselves on the island. Between 1950 and 1954, manufacturing employment rose by 12,000, and it was estimated that one government dollar invested in manufacturing was yielding $30 in Commonwealth Net Income. The multiplier effects gained strength; construction employment rose by 6,000, transport and public services by 3,000.

The island's 'social technology' sphere also grew rapidly in this period. In 1953, a Food Advisory Committee, headed by J.K. Galbraith, had recommended government acquisition and development of sites for food distribution: i.e., supermarkets, and recruitment of private sector managers. The recommendations were widely implemented. The success of food supermarkets started a revolution in distribution of goods to consumers. Show windows, prepackaging of goods, self-service - all these innovations came to Puerto Rico as US department store and pharmacy chains, and Puerto Rican entrepreneurs established operations in the retail services sector. Consumer credit networks formed to fuel the newly emerging middle class consumption desires. Public housing was built throughout the urban areas to accommodate the burgeoning work force. Educational facilities proliferated. Accelerated vocational training graduates rose 20 times, from 423 to 9,000 in the first five years of takeoff.[30]

With this frantic pace of industrialization came the rapid disintegration of the old leading sectors. Between 1951 and 1954, so many jobs were lost in agriculture and commerce and services, that total employment actually declined in the three year period when the island's net income rose a total of $224 million. In recognition of these disturbing trends, the 1954 Economic Report to the Governor revised its estimate of the time period needed to bring down unemployment from 6 to 30 years.

This was indicative of the decade of the 1950s as a whole: employment in agriculture fell by 90,000; and in the home needlework trades by 41,000, as 'the sponge of submarginal employment was being squeezed dry.'[31]

As a whole, the liftoff decade 1950-60 was a time of serious structural imbalance. In the most dynamic decade of industrialization, with a blossoming manufacturing base and a contracting labour force brought about the out-migration of 600,000 of the poorest, most unskilled Puerto Ricans to the US mainland (almost one third of the entire population), an official unemployment rate of 13 per cent still prevailed.

It could be argued that the dislocations and imbalances of the liftoff period were natural consequences of the explosive growth of externally owned manufacture, and the fact that most investment and production decisions were totally outside the control of local decision makers. While obviously containing a strong element of truth, this argument does not satisfactorily describe the full complexity of the massive transition Puerto Rico experienced during lift-off. The rise of manufacturing under the programmatic umbrella of Operation Bootstrap was, in fact, the driving force of a much larger and long overdue transition from a backward agrarian society to a modern industrial culture. Manufacturing acted as motor to rapidly increase social capital accumulation and consumer income, and also unleashed a disruptive series of economic and socio-political changes that broke the dominant feudal order of society forever.

8 The midterm challenge of readjusting the industrial structure

Within manufacture, one industry in particular provided an extraordinary spark to the entire liftoff stage, and closely fit Rostow's concept of a leading sector: the Apparel Industry.

In the 1950s, Puerto Rico was able to capitalize on its low wages and tax incentives to lure a wave of offshore investment in labour intensive industry. The Apparel Industry played a major role during the whole liftoff stage of Operation Bootstrap.

From the perspective of governmental planners, the Apparel Industry was a natural target for industrial promotion. Reports prepared by Arthur D. Little, Inc. and the Planning Board in the 1950-51 period emphasized the benefits of such promotion and the comparative advantages of the island as a host site. These benefits included the absorption of a large number of workers at low capitalization; the stimulation of local industry in areas such as cartons and containers; and the minimal infrastructure demands of production. The comparative advantages of the island were low cost labour; duty free import of raw materials from the US; and tax incentives. At the same time, the planners recognized and explicitly stated that the long term outlook for the industry was not particularly favourable, and 'the potential contribution of a large apparel industry to the island's standard of living is primarily one of absorbing cheap unskilled labour as an *intermediate step on the road to the creation of labour skills.*'[32] Thus, Operation Bootstrap executives had a great deal of foresight and an awareness of the limitations of the path ahead. Despite this awareness, the case for Apparel Industry development was too compelling to ignore in the impoverished circumstances of the time.

By the mid 1950s, however, their midterm track record of attracting mostly labour intensive apparel/textile production had greatly concerned Fomento's planners. Partly, their concern was based on observing rapidly rising wage levels, a rise which had been encouraged by a Tripartite Wage Commission. They understood rising wages would quickly eliminate Puerto Rico's labour cost advantages. Over a longer period of years, their concern would be seen to be fully justified. Between 1950 and 1961, average hourly earnings leapt 210 per cent to $1.03, and shot up from 29 per cent to 64 per cent of the US average.[33]

As a result of such concerns, an ambitious programme for industrial restructuring was undertaken and a highly targeted recruitment campaign was initiated in hopes of attracting 'externally integrated export industries.' The core of this programme was 'The Feasibility Study Approach'. This approach utilized three main weapons: sophisticated market opportunities studies; identification of integrated production areas for promotional emphasis; and targeted recruitment campaigns, utilizing direct mail, face-to-face contact, and on-site tours to attract the firms necessary to implement relevant production strategies.

Writings of a key development planner of the period, Hugh Barton, Director of Fomento's Office on Economic Studies, can give us insights into the mechanics of this approach:

> 'As a guide for the promotion of plants in other metalworking lines an analysis has been made of the processes performed by 20 of the most successful metalworking factories already in operation. Among the 20, the products produced were quite varied, including for example household appliances, costume jewellery, small power tools, electronic components and others. But there were found to be eleven processes common to at least two of the successful plants and in most instances to the majority of them. It was then found that these "successful processes" are also common to the manufacture of 160 other products not now being made in Puerto Rico. Here then is a "family of new industrial opportunities", toward which a pointed promotional effort can be directed in the interest of both expanding and strengthening the structure of industry.'[34]

Combined with generous producer tax incentives, this targeted approach helped in the identification and recruitment of new industrial opportunities; in the establishment of the petro-chemical, pharmaceutical and computer sectors in later years; and in speeding the overall transition of the economy from one based on cheap labour to one based on capital and technology intensive industries.

In retrospect, we can say that the success of Operation Bootstrap was a direct result of the assertiveness of the capital accumulation advocates in policy making circles of government.

The dominance of their policy model, based on recruitment of external capital and technology, persisted all through the 1950s and on through to the present day. But their model would never have succeeded had it conflicted with the external strategic environment. In fact, their model was directly dependent on a unique set of circumstances born from a special relationship with the United States in the immediate post war period.

9 Operation bootstrap: a special case in the annals of technological 'liftoff'

The uniqueness of Puerto Rico's transformation experience in the 1950-67 period was a direct result of its external relationship with the United States. The historic alliance between a small country and a world power, and the dynamics born from that relationship, constitute the basis for Operation Bootstrap's treatment as a special case in the annals of technological transformation.

> 'I know that our people, if it persists in creating solutions, will create solutions rather than feel it is forever enslaved by a banal dilemma, under the terms of which it is obliged to believe that there are only two doors through which it can go out to meet the future, even it both are mined with destruction. To this it could be said by a habitually superficial school of thought that it is better to go out one of the two doors, even though they are mined, than not to go out at all. The answer to this is that nobody speaks of not going out. Is it not man's duty to himself to look for ways of opening new doors, when those that there are may be mined for his destruction? And if intelligence multiplies the alternatives, is it not in that way widening liberty?'
>
> Governor Luis Muñoz Marín
> from his Inaugural Speech, 1948

One door led out to a future where nationalism fully prevailed and Puerto Rico would become an independent nation. This door would certainly lead to a continuation of severe poverty, due to extreme overpopulation and a limited natural resource base. The second door opened directly to a future where Puerto Rico was completely absorbed into the metropolitan economy and culture of the US. This door would lead to cultural and social destruction. A third door, an alternate path, started taking shape in the public imagination of the late 1930s. The national election victory of the Popular Democratic Party (PDP) in 1940 confirmed its existence and power.

'Bread, Land, and Liberty' was not only the symbol of the new party led by Muñoz Marín, but also accurately expressed the alternate path, sought by the jíbaros, the peasants, which were the PDP's base of support. The jíbaros wanted an end to their poverty, and the Third Door they had voted

142

to open would hopefully lead to a future where their practical, immediate economic concerns would be dominant over status issues.

This Third Door, in fact, led out to a mass development campaign, to pragmatic strategic alliances that mobilized human and social resources, capital and technology, and lifted the whole country in a decisive transformation.

Henceforth, we shall call this Third Door, and all that it held, the Great Compromise.[35]

The formal modification of US Public Law 600 in 1952, and the transition of Puerto Rican legal status to a self-governing Commonwealth only served to confirm the reality of this Great Compromise. The broad significance of this Compromise was that it represented an accommodation between Puerto Rican political leadership and the US government and private sector. Under the terms of this accommodation, Puerto Rico would provide a stable offshore low cost labour market for expansion minded US firms, and continue to act as host to a large military presence. In exchange, US capital flows would increase and help spur economic advancement, and the US Government would cede authority in most other major governance issues to the Commonwealth Government.

The reasons and motives underlying this Great Compromise were manifold. However, it appears the key motives for an accommodation on the part of US interests were desires by the US Government to protect a critical strategic military location in an era of worldwide rising expectations and decolonization. There was a simultaneous desire on the part of US private enterprise to embark on an expansionary international search for both low cost factors of production and new markets in the immediate Post World War II period.

10 The military and strategic importance of Puerto Rico

The memory of 1942 cast a strong shadow over the delicate negotiations that led to the Great Compromise. This was a memory of the first months of 1942, a period when the US lost control of its Caribbean sea lanes, when German submarines sank 122 cargo ships and the US gross national product dropped 25 per cent. The US economy had merely reacted to the practical reality that imports of strategic fuels and raw materials were suddenly cut off.

Up until the present day, the US is wholly dependent on the free flow of Caribbean trade. Fifty per cent of all US trade; 50 per cent of imported petroleum; and 40 strategic materials are currently transported to the US through the Caribbean.[36]

In addition to the fact that Puerto Rico represents a vital command post for movements of trade and has the only deep water bay in the Caribbean capable of sustaining a large naval armada, it also is a strategic defense bastion against nuclear attack. The first and most important Puerto Rican contribution is so big and so vital, it cannot be measured.' The island has been a highly valuable offshore defense bastion since the day it was annexed to the US. With the advent of the nuclear age, Puerto Rico has moved into the American defense pattern as an outpost capable of sending warnings to the mainland that might save an incalculable number of US lives in case of an attack. *The United States existence could hinge on an island warning.*[37]

Therefore, US economic and military vulnerability in the Caribbean was a powerful incentive for the Federal Government in reaching for a Great Compromise with Puerto Rico.

11 Puerto Rico as a model for de-colonialism

In the post war period, the worldwide rise of nationalism in developing countries had a powerful impact on the minds of US decision makers. The Compact of Commonwealth was announced with a fanfare by President Truman on July 3, 1952, as a model in harmonious relations between a big power and a small country. Puerto Rico suddenly became the official centre of the US Point IV Programme, a programme of Third World development. In five years, 9,000 policy makers from the developing countries streamed to the island to see 'the showcase of democracy' in action.

For the Puerto Rican Popular Democratic Party leadership, who had defeated an electoral coalition composed of the Chamber of Commerce, US cane and tobacco growers, and the Latifundia just years before, universal hunger and a failing resource based industrialization effort were incentives enough to reach for an accommodation with the US that culminated in the concept of a permanent Commonwealth status.

Thus, all the partners in this Great Compromise would benefit. The Federal Government would have a new model for managing relations with developing countries, and its military bases would remain secure. The US private sector would have a secure host site for offshore industrialization and investment would yield higher than usual profits and dependable profit repatriation. In exchange, the Puerto Rican economy would have sufficient capital and technology inputs for structural transformation, and autonomy enough to preserve its culture.

This Great Compromise opened the way for rapid economic and social change, and the success and international popularization of the Operation Bootstrap model.

One essential fact stands out from all others in this broad review of the Great Compromise. That fact was the decisive role of the Popular Democratic Party (PDP) in mobilizing a development campaign. The presence of highly attractive tax incentives in Puerto Rico since 1919 was not, in and of itself, sufficient to produce social and economic advancement. The change in US attitude toward Puerto Rico during the New Deal did not produce sustained development. Nor had Puerto Rico been able to historically benefit from its strategic military location. Is was only with the election of a new populist leadership in 1940 that the big power/small country relationship was fully exploited. The Development Plan, the Battle for Production, and the Commonwealth Compact which gave Puerto Rico self-governance - all were the result of local PDP initiatives and mobilizations. It was the drive and determination of a populist party to modernize that sparked the Great Compromise and resulted, at a critical moment, in a partnership for industrialization with the US Government and private sector.

IV   Part one: The rise of high-tech manufacturing

Fully 60 per cent of fixed capital formation in the decade 1950-60 was accounted for by US multinational corporations. This tendency merely deepened as the 1960s progressed. Despite the distinct lessening of the island's appeal as a site for labour intensive industries such as Apparel, the already frenetic pace of US investment in the economy nevertheless picked up significantly in the post 1967 period. Between 1968 and 1978, US annual net direct investment grew six fold from $263 million to $1.7 billion, and total accumulated investment grew 10 fold from $1.2 billion to $11.4 billion. It was in this period that capital and technology intensive industries, particularly pharmaceuticals and electronics, replaced the textile and food processing industries as the dominant factors in production.

In large measure, this shift in production occurred as a result of tax changes made by the US Government that increased Puerto Rico's value as an offshore tax haven. In January, 1968, the Federal Reserve, under the 'Foreign Investment Programme Act', had put forward a series of restrictions on the 'transfer abroad of net direct investment finances from US sources by non-financial organizations.'[38] Through Puerto Rico, corporate assets could be readily funnelled to Eurodollar markets and elsewhere. This attractiveness of Puerto Rico as a tax haven was further increased by the 1976 revision of the US Treasury Department's Possessions Corporation System of Taxation, and the creation of Section 936 of the Internal Revenue Code.

1 Section 936: the catalyst of the transition to high-tech manufacturing

In 1948, the Commonwealth Industrial Tax Exemption Act had completely exempted offshore industry investors from all income, property and municipal taxes for a 10 year period. Coupled with an earlier US Federal Possessions Tax Exemption, this Act meant that Puerto Rico had literally become a 'tax holiday' zone during a time period of intense production activity and tight labour markets in the post war US: 'Investors dreaming of paradise might visualize a place where a factory owner doesn't have to pay any taxes or rent. Actually there is no reason for such dreaming - for such a place, Puerto Rico, exists in reality.'[39]

In 1954, the US Congress approved a new Section of the US Tax Code (Section 931), which enabled US corporations operating in Puerto Rico to avoid paying taxes not only on Puerto Rico manufacturing earnings but also on *indirect earnings derived from reinvestment in other activities on the island, or in foreign countries*. This established the precedent for the island to become a major launching pad for international transfer of retained corporate profits, a position that only accelerated as the internationalization of labour intensive industries from the US unfolded. Thus, Puerto Rico was in the ironic position of drawing in tremendous capital flows into labour intensive industry in the 1950s and early 1960s, only to see the profits generated by these US companies being re-routed to establish the same industries in even lower cost zones in the Far East and elsewhere.[40]

Another, greater irony of Section 931 was that US corporations could derive 'little or no overall benefit from Puerto Rican tax exemption if profits on Puerto Rican operations were repatriated on a *current* basis; significant benefits could only be obtained and repatriated without taxable gain or loss when the Puerto Rican operating company was liquidated into the US parent firm.'[41] This meant that dividends (i.e. repatriated profits) paid by a Puerto Rican subsidiary directly to a US parent were fully taxable at a 48 per cent federal income tax rate. The typical result of this restriction was that a Puerto Rican subsidiary simply accumulated earnings from its operations until its exemption period expired and then it liquidated into its parent in a tax free merger; or it reinvested its locally generated profits abroad as described earlier. The practical effect of the tax scheme was 'a doubling of the after tax rate of return on investment by US corporations through a 931 subsidiary on the island.'[42] Between 1948-77, the operating period of this specific exemption in the island's industrial programme, the accumulated value to corporations of the tax exemption totalled $3.3 billion.[43]

For Puerto Rico, the practical effects of this exemption were twofold: it created a 'context for capital accumulation', which triggered the Industrial Revolution on the island; yet it also created instability in the industrial base, particularly in labour intensive industries that were more mobile and had less capital directly invested on the island. The exemption resulted in a continuous foment of plant closings, which were reliable proxies for corporate profit taking activities.

By 1967, with the rapid internationalization of US capital well underway, reformers in the US Congress sought ways to limit the transfer of net direct investment funds abroad by non-financial organizations. The passage of the 'Foreign Investment Programme Act' in 1968 placed restrictions on multinationals but left Puerto Rico untouched; and for the next eight years, the island served as a magnet for high profit high-tech companies, and as a transfer point for large scale corporate manufacturing profits that were routed into Eurodollar investments and other direct investments on a worldwide basis.

Between 1973 and 1975, US Congressional reformers sought to eliminate Section 931 and close down this conduit for untaxed funds transfer. It was within this strategic environment - of hostility to untaxed, deferred income outside the mainland US by multinationals, of congressional reformers bearing down to extinguish Section 931, the catalyst of Puerto Rican economic development - that the island's leadership devised a simple yet elegant counter-argument. Three Commonwealth officials - then Treasury Secretary Salvador Casellas, Fomento Administrator Teodoro Moscoso and Puerto Rico's Resident Commissioner in Washington Jaime Benítez - were entrusted by Governor Hernández Colón (serving his first term) with crafting an initiative to blunt the Congressional attack. In a series of Congressional testimonies between 1974 and 1975, they argued the following key points:

- That billions of dollars in US corporate profits were indeed 'floating' outside the US and revenue from capturing those dollars could be considerable.
- That there was a great opportunity to 'harness the windfall' that had been generated in and shipped out of Puerto Rico for conversion into Eurodollars.
- That the Commonwealth Government had sought to lure that pool of money back to the island for reinvestment by passing laws in 1973 and 1974 that had: (a) exempted 931 corporate interest income on bank deposits, and (b) called on companies to voluntarily reinvest their profits locally.
- That these provisions had failed and the companies were still keeping the funds outside Puerto Rico and the US.
- That the Federal Government needed to help Puerto Rico 'bring those dollars back under the US flag, under the dollar system and help the balance of trade.'
- That the only way to do this was to have the Federal Government tax income from all foreign sources outside Puerto Rico and to provide incentives for profits generated in Puerto Rico to be remitted directly to the US rather than being sent abroad.

These arguments persuaded Congress. The Puerto Rican delegation, in collaboration with the Congress, fashioned and submitted a revised Section 931 draft that had these critical features:
- Complete *100 per cent tax free repatriation of current profits* by a US subsidiary in Puerto Rico to its parent company, thereby eliminating the volatile effects of manufacturing profit repatriation by liquidation. This would apply only to income generated in Puerto Rico and/or income from the investment of funds in Puerto Rico.
- *Mandatory reinvestment of corporate retained earnings in Puerto Rico*, thereby eliminating the ability of companies to funnel profits generated on the island into Eurodollars.

These features were codified and approved by Congress under Section 936 of the Possessions Taxation System of the Internal Revenue Code in 1976. To maximize the economic development benefits of this revised tax code, the Commonwealth Government simultaneously approved a 10 per cent Commonwealth Tollgate Tax, with the purpose of taxing repatriated profits from subsidiaries to parents. This tax was bitterly opposed by organized business interests on the island; legislative veterans claimed it was the most vehemently fought battle in recent memory.[44] However, without this tollgate tax, two billion dollars in accumulated earnings could have been sent out of Puerto Rico without taxation. As a 'sweetener', corporations were given a one per cent reduction in the Tollgate Tax for every year that retained earnings were left in the local banking system earning competitive interest rates.

Section 936 and its sister Tollgate Tax represented a brilliant strategic victory for the Commonwealth Government. The local government had leveraged the full force of the Federal Government in extracting maximum economic benefits from the operations and retained earnings of the large multinational corporations in Puerto Rico. Suddenly, the Commonwealth captured a pool of '936' funds for the banking system that kept expanding at an annual rate of 12.5 per cent between 1976 and 1984; and that rose to $9.5 billion in 1988, or 41 per cent of all commercial bank deposits.[45] These 936 funds have primarily been used by banking intermediaries for commercial and industrial purposes; for mortgages and for consumer financing. In addition, 30 per cent of total 936 bank funds were required to be reinvested in government and put on deposit with the Commonwealth Government Development Bank, which has increased its capital base from $75 million in 1975 to $400 million in 1989 as the result of its arbitrage of 936 redeposits. The huge pool of 936 funds left on deposit has also served to lessen the needs of the banking system to borrow expensive short term funds from the Federal Reserve, and has lowered the general interest rates on capital in Puerto Rico by two to three percentage points.[46]

For corporations, the opportunity for direct tax free repatriation of profits from Puerto Rican subsidiaries to the US mainland - at a time when tax exemptions were suddenly being pulled back worldwide by the US Government - seemed an irresistible attraction. Puerto Rico, under the same rigourous patent and trademark laws as the mainland, instantly became a unique and favoured global tax haven location for US high-technology manufacture, with its heavy emphasis on 'intangibles', i.e. innovative, brand name, limited patent, high profit products. Between 1975 and 1988, 'virtually all of Puerto Rico's manufacturing employment growth occurred in the high-tech fabrication sector.'[47]

Today, Section 936 is widely considered the driving force behind Puerto Rico's economic development, and accounts for up to 29 per cent of total employment. Two hundred thousand jobs are indirectly generated above and beyond the 80,000 direct jobs provided by 936 companies.

The sheer volume of high-tech investment by '936' companies has drastically changed the whole profile of the economy. In 1965, high-tech industries accounted for only 10 per cent of total manufacturing employment; by 1986, the proportion had reached 40 per cent. Over 66 per cent of island exports come from this high-tech sector, and the share of national income from this sector is now 71 per cent, far higher than the 48 per cent share of US national income.

These changes are graphically represented in the set of figures in the Appendix.

Figure 7.1 shows that the manufacturing investment made by US multinationals in Puerto Rico under Section 936 was the highest in capital and technology intensity among the thirteen top offshore locations for the reference year 1982.

Figure 7.2 shows the leap in local high-tech production employment generated by the passage of Section 936 in 1976, and the simultaneous decline of labour intensive industry work force.

Figures 7.3 and 7.4 show both the employment and export distribution shifts in favour of high-tech manufacturing since 1976.

Figure 7.5 shows the post-1975 leap in high-tech industries' contribution to national income viz-a-viz the US.

Section 936 has not only been a decisive factor in catalysing high-tech manufacturing and overall economic transformation in Puerto Rico, it has also well served its intended beneficiaries, the multinational corporations. The tax savings to these corporations have been enormous. Although no comprehensive data is available, a recent survey of sixteen leading 936 corporations found a total tax saving in the years 1981-88 of over seven billion dollars. Table 4.1 provides a breakdown of these tax savings by firm, by year, and shows the great benefits leading high-tech sectors, particularly pharmaceutical companies, have reaped from Section 936.

The expansion of the high-tech manufacturing sector, directly induced by the creation of Section 936, has been led by the Pharmaceutical Industry. Between 1977 and 1987, the net income of the Pharmaceutical Industry exploded - from $943.3 million to $3.74 billion, which represented 59.1 per cent of the total net income of the manufacturing sector in 1987.

A case study of the Pharmaceutical Industry presents a unique opportunity to explore the inner workings of a high-tech industry that has

TABLE 4.1

TAX SAVINGS FOR SIXTEEN COMPANIES RESULTING FROM 936 OPERATIONS
(IN MILLIONS US$)

Company	1988	1987	1986	1985	1984	1983	1982	1981	Total 1981-88
SmithKline Beckman a)	$75.20	$112.40	$143.10	$132.90	$130.80	$104.00	$101.00	$117.00	$916.40
Pfizer a)	95.00	127.00	144.00	117.00	109.10	115.60	88.60	68.60	864.90
Westinghouse	79.90	84.80	97.50	88.30	102.00	107.80	74.90	95.10	730.30
Johnson & Johnson	99.00	103.00	101.00	98.50	74.20	58.90	53.30	n/a	587.90
Abbott Laboratories a)	76.00	78.00	92.00	86.00	72.00	53.00	53.80	48.40	559.20
Baxter International b)	73.00	79.00	108.00	64.00	44.00	67.80	62.30	44.30	542.40
Upjohn	46.00	66.70	71.20	43.50	52.40	60.60	58.80	60.50	459.70
Merck & Co.	69.20	88.50	70.80	59.10	29.90	30.50	22.10	30.50	400.60
Eli Lilly & Co.	49.00	64.00	78.00	63.70	49.30	38.50	26.70	24.50	393.70
Squibb	71.00	94.00	62.00	29.00	24.00	40.00	40.00	29.00	389.00
Schering-Plough a)	49.00	53.00	58.00	40.00	32.50	40.00	36.80	45.40	354.70
Pepsi Co a)	35.30	69.10	70.70	37.80	52.50	24.70	4.80	11.20	306.10
Digital	45.30	57.40	33.40	24.10	22.90	20.60	22.20	12.50	238.40
Hewlett-Packard a)	57.00	43.00	40.00	37.00	n/a	n/a	n/a	n/a	177.00
Becton-Dickinson	14.00	18.60	15.40	18.10	12.10	5.50	11.00	9.00	103.70
AMP	4.80	4.30	4.70	5.40	5.40	4.70	5.60	6.00	40.90
Totals	$938.70	$1,142.80	$1,189.80	$944.40	$813.10	$772.20	$661.90	$602.00	$7,064.90
No. of companies	16	16	16	16	15	15	15	14	
Average tax break:	$58.67	$71.43	$74.36	$59.03	$54.21	$51.48	$44.13	$43.00	$456.30

Source: Citizens for Tax Justice, compiled from corporate annual repo Cited in 'Caribbean Business', November 16, 1989, p. 32.

Notes: Since 1981, 16 major companies have reported more than $7 billion in federal tax savings as a result of their Section 936 operations, mostly in Puerto Rico. The above chart details these tax savings year-by-year and cumulatively for the eight-year period.
a) Includes Puerto Rico and Ireland.
b) Includes Puerto Rico and other low or no-tax jurisdictions.
n/a Not available.

built up a critical local mass of production and human assets. The complex interplay between the local government, acting as a catalytic agent and facilitator of industrial accumulation, and industry itself with its own market driven dynamic provides us with an opportunity to understand better the process of technological transformation. For its part, government has promoted the industry relentlessly - through its tax incentive programmes, industrial infrastructure aids, etc., while at the same time attempting to gently 'guide' the ensuing expansion of the industry into more undeveloped areas of the island, into a socially productive island wide decentralization. We explore these issues in the case study that follows.

IV Part two: The pharmaceutical industry: A driving force in the rise of high-tech manufacturing

1 The pharmaceutical industry in Puerto Rico: a historical perspective

The presence of pharmaceutical companies in Puerto Rico can be traced as far back as 1947. In that year, a local entrepreneur, John Padilla García established 'Laboratorios Terrier, Inc.', a firm specializing in injectable products. It is not coincidental that the first wave of US pharmaceutical industries came to the Island in the 1953-63 period, a period when Fomento was refining its Targeted Feasibility Approach, and seeking to promote 'externally integrated export industries'. Early on, Fomento planners had recognized the dynamic linkage possibilities represented by the complex production cycles of the pharmaceutical sector, possibilities only recently coming to fruition.[48]

The initial formulation of a sectoral development strategy for the Chemical Industry as a whole was contained in the 1951 'Ten Year Industrial Plan' prepared by Arthur D. Little, Inc. for Fomento. The promotion of chemicals production, particularly sugar based chemicals production, was prioritized under the category of 'industries for special attention'. This prioritization was based on a host of favourable industry characteristics, including the fact that products could be made from raw materials of local origin and that ocean shipping costs were relatively low in relation to the total cost of production. This initial policy formulation was followed by a detailed market analysis, 'Opportunities In The Chemical Industry in Puerto Rico', submitted by Arthur D. Little to Fomento in January, 1961. This report analyzed 40 branches of the chemical industry, and recommended the intensive development of pharmaceuticals production based on its scoring second in value added among all industry branches. Other factors favouring pharmaceuticals that were cited by the analysts included: the extremely high value per pound of materials which made these products quite insensitive to transportation costs; the large intermediate business the pharmaceutical industry branch could generate; and the scientific/technical nature of production, which represented a step up the technology ladder. Thus, a conscious sectoral strategy had been conceived and refined early on in the industrialization process, a strategy that Fomento sought to execute in its operations.

The first US pharmaceutical company to establish operations on the island was Sterling Products International in 1953. The firm's decision to establish an operation on the island was largely the result of the close, personal relationship between a top corporation officer and Teodoro Moscoso, then head of the Economic Development Administration, and a pharmacist by training. By demonstrating it could turn a profit in Puerto Rico, Sterling paved the way for an early influx of other US pharmaceutical companies who came in search of abundant labour and tax concessions. Between 1953 and 1963, Western Fher Labs, Eli Lilly and Company, Bectin-Dickinson Labs, Baxter Laboratories, Stiefel Labs, Endo Labs, Parke Davis, and Warner Lambert set up factories on the island. For the 10 year period, a total of 16 drug companies started up operations (including eight locally owned operations).[49] By 1963, the value of shipments of pharmaceutical products from Puerto Rico had reached $23.8 million, almost a four fold increase from the $6.6 million of only five years before. Between 1963 and 1967, value of shipments leapt again to $81.9 million.

As noted previously, the 1968 Federal Reserve 'Foreign Investment Programme Act', substantially increased the value of Puerto Rico as a production site. Profits generated on the island could be readily funnelled to Euro-dollar markets and elsewhere, circumventing tightened federal restrictions on foreign investment. This produced an intense wave of investment in new production capacity that resulted in yet another leap in value of shipments. Between 1967 and 1972, pharmaceutical exports soared from $81.9 million to $283.3 million. It was during this period, that the overall production efficiency and overall profitability coefficient of the industry in Puerto Rico reached .837 vs. .719 in the mainland industry.[50]

The creation of Section 936 in 1976 further enhanced the profitability of operations in Puerto Rico, and led to the explosive growth of the industry during the late 1970s and 1980s. Between 1978 and 1986, value of exports increased from 630.7 billion dollars to 2.75 billion dollars, a 336 per cent rise in value, and gross profit margins increased over the US average still further.

Today, the pharmaceutical industry in Puerto Rico is the largest in the Western Hemisphere, with 87 firms operating 110 manufacturing plants, employing 14,758 workers and providing 20 per cent of all personal labour income.[51] In 1987, the industry had $3.7 billion in exports; contributed 59.1 per cent of net income in manufacturing; and accounted for 34.3 per cent of total assets in equipment and machinery in the whole manufacturing sector. Virtually every major US drug company is represented on the Island including 23 Fortune 500 firms. Biological products, such as vaccines, toxoids, and serums; medicinal chemicals and botanical products; and pharmaceutical preparations are among the range of products turned out by the industry. As a whole, the industry is operating at a high level of profitability, with a profits to sales ratio of 47.93 and a profit to equity ratio of 28.72.

As the industry matures and continues to develop, two noticeable positive trends are emerging: a slow build-up of Research and Development (R and D) activities; and an increasing vertical integration of operations on the Island. These trends shall be briefly discussed.

2 Research and Development

Between 1982 and 1985 (the latest year data is available), the number of US pharmaceutical firms claiming R and D expenses on their tax returns to the Commonwealth and US Treasury Departments rose from 17 to 24. During this same period, the dollar value of expenses claimed soared from $36.55 million to $108.75 million; and the ratio of R and D expenditures to net sales increased from 2.34 per cent to 8.48 per cent.[52]

It would be easy to dismiss these R and D tax claims as merely over valuations and distortions based on the inclusion of technical service and quality control expenses. Yet, sufficient case study material exists to support the contention that R and D activity in this sector is indeed on the rise. For example, Lederle Corporation (Puerto Rico) has locally developed two new products; has six more pending approval at the US Food and Drug Administration (FDA), and has eight other new products in development.[53] Though Lederle has focused on new formulations of old drugs, on copying and modifying compounds that can gain quick FDA approvals, its R and D effort is nevertheless an advance over simple product manufacture. There are quite a few more examples that could be added as evidence for the argument that R and D is slowly evolving.

Another indicator has been industry encouragement of university based research. To support R and D in the pharmaceutical industry, the National Science Foundation and the University of Puerto Rico established a University/Industry Research Centre (UIRC) in Pharmaceutical/Chemical Science. Since its inception in 1987, the Centre has recruited 16 industrial sponsors and sponsored eight research projects, totalling $140,000, in areas related to new drug discovery, process development, and polymers.

It would be erroneous, however, to assume that there is an unlimited capacity for expansion of R and D by US companies in Puerto Rico. From a corporate accounting perspective, it makes little sense to relocate 'strategic' R and D activities to Puerto Rico from the mainland. Corporate logic dictates that such activities remain in a high tax zone, where they can be claimed as deductions, rather than situated in the low tax environment of Puerto Rico.[54]

3 Vertical integration

Early attempts by Fomento to promote vertical integration in the pharmaceutical industry were blunted by the economic realities of the emerging industry's insufficient size and limited demand for supplies. In 1964, for example, Fomento planners determined that only 69,625 dozen glass vials and ampules had been imported by the industry during the previous twelve months, 'a volume of shipments insufficient to justify local manufacture'.[55] Until recently, the industry had to import all of its production inputs - from cardboard to labels to capsules. The current size and dynamism of the sector, however, has encouraged market driven expansion of packaging companies and other supplier networks. Pharmaceutical companies have grown to understand that cost saving of up to 50-80 per cent can be generated by localizing supplier networks and purchase of components. Pharmaceutical companies have followed the trend in US industry pioneered by the automobile industry, and have encouraged their mainland suppliers to set up operations on the Island. In 1987 alone, five major contract packagers, capsule makers, folding box manufacturers, and label makers have begun operations on the Island. It is estimated that 3,000 to 5,000 people are now employed by supply companies that service the pharmaceutical industry. The contract packaging market, in particular, has shown dynamic growth in the eighteen months between 1986 and mid-1987, with local plants experiencing a rise in sales from $52 million to $72 million.[56]

4 Government's role in managing the dynamics of the pharmaceutical industry

The mechanisms utilized to encourage pharmaceutical industry development have been manifold, and are described below in their most current form.

a Commonwealth Tax Incentives that Augment Section 936 Tax Benefits

i Tax exemption programme based on targeted development zones In response to pressures from elected officials representing rural constituencies, Fomento initiated a policy of encouraging industries to locate in targeted underdeveloped zones. Since the mid-1960s, a programme of special tax exemptions has been in operation that bases the length of exemptions on locational factors:

Zone	Time Period
High Development	10 years
Intermediate Development	15 years
Low Development	20 years
Vieques and Culebra (Offshore islands)	25 years

The new Tax Incentives Act of 1987 provides 90 per cent exemption on industrial development income (IDI) and property taxes for the entire exemption period to new exempted business. The length of the period may vary from 10 to 25 years, depending on the zone in which the exempted business is located.

The success of this long standing programme in achieving a geographic spread in the pharmaceutical industry is shown in Table 4.2.

ii Other local tax incentives Sixty per cent exemption municipal gross receipts tax All companies coming under the exemption programme are granted a 60 per cent exemption from the municipal license fees, excise and all other municipal license taxes for the duration of their tax exemption grants.

Fifteen per cent production worker payroll deduction The law provides for a 15 per cent payroll deduction based on the industrial development income of the exempted business that generates less than $20,000 in net industrial development income per production employee before taxes. This deduction is limited to 50 per cent of the net industrial development income.

First $100,000 net income total exemption incentive All manufacturing plants under the programme that have industrial development income of not more than $500,000 and employ not less than 15 persons are allowed 100 per cent tax exemption on the first $100,000 of such income annually. (Note that any firm having industrial development income of $100,000 or less is totally exempt.) This will assist smaller firms in accumulating capital for expansion and will increase their return on investment computations.

b Locational incentives

Special locational incentives in the form of negotiable cash grants are available for establishing manufacturing facilities in areas of high unemployment in Puerto Rico. The incentives, which are administered by the Puerto Rico Industrial Development Company (PRIDCO), can be applied toward the following:
1) Training of supervisory personnel.
2) Salaries for instructors and technical personnel while training production workers.

TABLE 4.2

DISTRIBUTION OF FOMENTO PLANTS OPERATING BY MUNICIPALITY
AND TAX EXEMPTION PERIOD

Municipality	Number of plants	Exemption zone
Aguadilla	2	15
Arecibo	5	15
Barceloneta	11	15
Caguas	4	10
Carolina	10	10
Cayey	2	15
Cidra	1	15
Dorado	2	10
Fajardo	1	20
Guayama	3	15
Gurabo	1	15
Hormigueros	2	10
Humacao	11	15
Jayuya	3	20
Manatí	14	15
Mayagüez	5	10
Ponce	5	10
San Germán	1	15
San Juan	3	10
Vega Baja	1	15

Source: Economic Development Administration (1982), 'The Drug and Pharmaceutical
Industry in Puerto Rico', April.

3) Payment of rent on PRIDCO buildings during the initial start-up period of operations.

4) Full or partial payment of freight charges on machinery and equipment from point of origin to the plan in Puerto Rico.

5) Other purposes, subject to the approval of PRIDCO's Investment Committee. The amount of the grant for which a firm is eligible depends on the employment opportunities created, the location and size of investment.

c Sites and buildings

A unique feature of the Fomento effort to promote industrialization has been its involvement in industrial real estate and the management of industrial parks.

Since its inception in 1942, the Puerto Rico Industrial Development Corporation (PRIDCO) has operated as the financial and real estate arm of Fomento, providing the necessary physical facilities for new industrial plants. During the last 45 years, PRIDCO has provided 50 per cent of all new plants that have been required by companies establishing themselves on the island. The construction of general purpose factory buildings, ranging in size from 4,000 to 100,000 square feet, and the construction of specialized structures to suit particular clients have been the central tasks of PRIDCO. In the first six months of 1988 alone, PRIDCO has invested $38.3 million dollars in 57 industrial buildings totalling 1.3 million square feet.[57]

d Other Fomento support services to the pharmaceutical industry

Technical assistance Helps industries in the selection of machinery and equipment, selection and use of new materials, estimates of production costs, studies on time and motion, site plans, plant layout and inventory control.

Environmental Advice Programme Provides information to industrialists about laws and regulations concerning environmental protection.

Quality control Assists industrialists with the design and installation of quality control systems. There is also assistance for the financing of equipment and the training of personnel.

Managerial and supervisory personnel development Offers development and training programmes by means of seminars, courses, and conferences for managerial, technical and supervisory personnel.

e The twin plant initiative

As a result of Amendments to Section 936, made in 1986 at the request of the governor of Puerto Rico, a 'Twin plant' initiative has been established to encourage production sharing arrangements between the island and other Caribbean Basin Initiative (CBI) countries. This programme extends the tax sparing provisions of Section 936 to encompass labour intensive activities conducted in other CBI countries by US industries based in Puerto Rico. The goal of this programme is to enable a corporation to capture the efficiencies generated by combining high-technology intensive activities performed on the island with the labour intensive activities performed in outlying low labour cost islands.

In addition to extending preferential tax treatment to production sharing arrangements, low cost financing and investment capital for development project loans, bond purchases of equity shares, and debt/equity swaps are all being made available by Puerto Rico to CBI countries that provide tax information to the US Treasury. The source of this new low cost financing is the pool of 936 funds on deposit in financial institutions in Puerto Rico.

The Twin Plant Initiative was conceived and developed by Puerto Rico as 'a clever bargaining chip' to both fend off ferocious attacks on Section 936 in Congress, and to strengthen an ineffective Caribbean Basin Initiative (CBI). The CBI had been put forward as the premier private sector oriented development and trade initiative of the Reagan Administration. Despite its promise, the CBI programme had never delivered results, as evidenced by the fact that between 1983 and 1987, exports to the US from CBI participating countries actually declined from $9.2 billion to $6.1 billion.[58] Therefore, the Twin Plant Initiative was Puerto Rico's response to immediate threats against its own economic welfare, and threats to the welfare of the region stemming from a political backlash to the failures of CBI.

From a longer run perspective, the Twin Plant Initiative was conceived of as an 'insurance policy' that protected Puerto Rico against an exodus of industries to lower labour cost islands by extending its spatial sphere of tax exemption, enabling it to coordinate and manage the growth of an integrated system of production throughout the Caribbean, and establishing a new, broader 'context' for capital accumulation.

From a corporate perspective, the twin plant option made solid financial sense, allowing for greater cost efficiencies and income after taxes than other available manufacturing strategic alternatives. The financial calculations, presented in Table 4.3 by the General Manager of Westinghouse in Puerto Rico, illustrate the superior benefits of a twin plant operation versus other production options for a generic 'base case'.[59]

For pharmaceutical companies, the 'blending' of competitive advantages through complementary production facilities provides additional incentives to retain operations in Puerto Rico that might otherwise have had to move to the Far East. These companies have started to exploit the Twin plant Programme and have established twin plants in Costa Rica (Pharmaseal, Abbot Labs, Eli Lily and Co., Upjohn); Grenada (Abbot Labs, Smith Kline), and the Dominican Republic (Warner Lambert, American Cyanamide, Eli Lily, Bristol Myers). Between January 1, 1986 and November 30, 1987, $6.5 million had been invested in pharmaceutical industry twin plants, an amount that is expected to increase significantly as

TABLE 4.3

MANUFACTURING STRATEGIC ALTERNATIVES - FINANCIAL COMPARISONS
(DOLLAR/PRODUCTIVE HOUR)

	Base case	A Domestic plant	B Offshore plant	C Puerto Rico	D Twin plant
Sales billed	150.0	150.0	150.0	150.0	150.0
Domestic costs:					
Direct labour	15.0	10.0	-	-	-
Direct support	10.0	6.7	-	-	-
Base case all other	110.0	110.0	110.0	110.0	110.0
Sub-total	135.0	126.7	110.0	110.0	110.0
Offshore costs					
Direct labour	-	-	0.8	8.5	2.4
Freight and duty	-	-	3.0	3.0	4.0
All other	-	-	3.2	5.7	3.5
Sub-total	-	-	7.0	17.2	9.9
Total costs	135.0	126.7	117.0	127.2	119.9
Memo:					
Cost improvement $/hour	-	-8.3	-18.0	-7.8	-15.1
Income before taxes	15.0	23.3	33.0	22.8	30.1
% Sales billed	10.0%	15.5%	22.0%	15.2%	20.1%
Income taxes	5.7	8.9	12.5	4.4	5.1
$I.B.T.	38%	38%	38%	19.3%	16.9%
Income after taxes	9.3	14.4	20.5	18.4	25.0
% Sales billed	6.2%	9.6%	13.6%	12.3%	16.7%

Source: Author's estimates based on official sources.

current projects under development move on-line. During the same period of time, over \$42.4 million in total investment in the CBI twin plant programme was made by Puerto Rico based manufacturers, generating 5,000 jobs in outlying islands.

Up until now, this case study has described the evolution of the Pharmaceutical Industry and the dynamics of managing its evolution. Market forces, and economies of agglomeration based on the growth of infrastructure and work force skills, have combined to produce prolonged industry expansion. As the industry has matured, vertical integration of the sector and corporate diversification into innovative new product/process research and development are beginning to emerge.

To encourage growth, local government management has attempted to provide: (a) core facilities and industrial parks; physical infrastructure, and technical support services to generate a critical mass of firms in this sector; (b) tax incentives and grants to help ensure the geographic distribution of production island-wide; and to maximize the spread effects of economic development, and (c) strategic regional production sharing alternatives to help offset rising local wages and to retain sectoral competitiveness, i.e. the Twin plant Initiative.

5 Prospects of the Puerto Rican pharmaceutical industry

Regulatory delays, and competition from generics and from international producers have become major factors in the strategies and operations of US pharmaceutical companies, factors which are strongly conditioning the Puerto Rico pharmaceutical industry's current and future development trajectory. Reacting to high product development, production, and marketing costs, and the squeeze of international competition, US companies are reaching out to form mergers and joint ventures. Smith Kline and Beckman with Beecham; Merck with Johnson and Johnson; Johnson and Johnson with Amgen: these examples are representative of the merger and strategic partnership wave hitting both the US pharmaceutical industry and the larger US health care sector, resulting in a tripling of mergers between 1981 and 1988.[60]

At the local level, this partnering wave is reflected in Merck/Puerto Rico's cost saving joint venture with Mova, a local contract manufacturing firm; and Smith Kline and Beckman's revenue enhancing contract manufacturing alliances. Nor are they, by any means, the only local companies engaged in such activities.

Lederle/Puerto Rico, a subsidiary of American Cyanamid, is another company actively engaged in establishing contract manufacturing, product licensing and marketing agreements. It has already introduced into production ten new drug applications, new generic formulations of old prescription drugs it has licensed, copied and modified in-house.

Another characteristic shared by US pharmaceutical companies and expressed by their local subsidiaries is the shift to advanced high technology production. Squibb, for example, has just installed a complete computer driven bulk chemical process facility; the entire building is run by one supervisor. By 1992, a second fully automated building will be on-line. In addition, Squibb just dedicated a technical services facilities for quality/process improvements, staffed by 22 professionals; including six Phd's in chemistry. In the case of Smith Kline Beecham/Puerto Rico, this shift has been expressed in 'total quality control' campaign and a joint venture with IBM to develop a prototype flexible manufacturing system. For Merck/Puerto Rico, the shift has been less dramatic, more incremental, the result of a concerted production improvement effort between headquarters and the Puerto Rican subsidiary that has gone on for a longer period of time. For Ortho Biotech/Puerto Rico, a division of Johnson and Johnson, the shift to advanced high-tech production has meant pioneering a unique biotechnology/mammalian cell culture production system, rather than extracting greater efficiencies from a conventional operation.

The general tendency to advanced production methods in the pharmaceutical sector is gaining momentum island-wide as the competitive environment intensifies. In recognition of this overall sectoral trend, IBM has recently established a centre on the island to develop and market pharmaceutical industry process control applications software.

Thus, it appears the entire pharmaceutical sector on the island is in the midst of a radical restructuring process. This process is characterized by the accelerated adoption of flexible manufacturing systems; by the multiskilling of work forces; and by increased external alliances. In essence, the local industry is reaching for the world frontier in production technology, and is seeking a new best practice regime in response to a changed competitive environment.

Local pharmaceutical subsidiaries - which are crucial centres of corporate profitability and competitiveness - can no longer afford the artificial sense of security provided by Section 936. They must increasingly strive for new production efficiencies and quicker responses to dynamic markets. Given their importance in long term corporate strategies, Puerto Rico's pharmaceutical subsidiaries are more and more having to become pioneers in the field testing of manufacturing and organizational innovations for wider intra-firm dissemination. The implementation of a national prototype computer integrated manufacturing plant by IBM and Smith-Kline Beecham on the island is but one example among many.

The experience of the island's pioneering pharmaceutical subsidiaries is more appropriately understood when seen from the perspective of a broader industrial game of 'catch-up' underway in the US. As a group, US manufacturers have lagged well behind their counterparts in Japan, Sweden, West Germany and elsewhere in the deployment of radical manufacturing innovations. For example, between 1981 and 1986, Japan spent twice as much on automation as the US; and 55 per cent of all machine tools introduced in that time period in Japan were computer numerically controlled machines (the building blocks of flexible manufacturing systems) versus only 18 per cent for the US.[61]

As a research intensive branch of US industry, whose world market power has largely been based on brand and patent exclusivity, the pharmaceutical sector has until quite recently been insulated from cost and price competition. As a result, the branch has not been subjected to extraordinary pressures to achieve rapid productivity gains. This has been particularly true for the one third of the US worldwide industry operating in Puerto Rico, where the tax incentive structure has served to maintain high levels of profitability virtually detached from real production efficiencies. Surging competitors and a subsequent saturation effect in certain product lines; diminishing long term rents on research activities; expiring top brand name drugs patent; and the rising generics industry - these have all been key factors in a renewed emphasis on production technology as a weapon in a war based increasingly on cost and price competition, product differentiation and market segmentation.

This war must be fought with flexible, multi-product manufacturing plants capable of rapid response times and with tighter coordination between corporate R and D, scale up, production and marketing units. This war must be fought by aggressively searching for, acquiring, and commercializing technologies and products regardless of the source; and by entering into a diversity of strategic external alliances to reduce overall transaction costs and conserve capital. In other words, we are witnessing nothing less than an entire paradigm shift in the pharmaceutical industry.

What are the economic and social implications of this paradigm shift for Puerto Rico?

Clearly, the most worrying implication is for employment given the enormous role of the pharmaceutical industry in the manufacturing sector. In 1986, the industry employed 14,758 workers, provided 9.7 per cent of all manufacturing income on the island and 20 per cent of all personnel labour income. Prima facie, it might seem reasonable to assume there would be a concurrence between rising automation in the pharmaceutical industry and rising displacement of work force.

However, the emerging reality is more complex. In fact, what we have seen is a relatively stagnant growth in work force during a time period in which a massive expansion of output occurred. Between 1978 and 1987, employment increased only 52 per cent, while the value of production increased from $630.7 million to $3.01 billion, a 478 per cent rise. Even discounting for price inflation, this strongly suggests that productivity gains accruing to technology and capital are far outstripping gains to labour, and that future growth of output in the industry will be biased more and more in favour of these inputs to production at the expense of labour. This merely confirms the trends identified in our case study. Yet, until now, we have not seen the widespread displacement of work force that might be anticipated as automation takes hold. Rather, we are seeing a relatively stagnant level of employment in relation to the size of output expansion. This could change dramatically as current investments in computer driven manufacturing comes on-stream in the years ahead. We suspect, however, that this will not be the case; rather, we anticipate internal shifts of work force from direct production tasks - i.e. formulation, assembly and packaging - into more indirect tasks, such as warehousing and shipping, and technical/administrative support.

A more important tendency in employment is towards higher skill requirements. As flexible manufacturing systems spread throughout the sector, and as alternative biotechnology production processes such as mammalian cell-culture proliferate, important and radical changes in the skill profile will follow. The diffusion of more and more programmable computer numerical control tools across the factory floor will mean that responsibility for their operations will tend to move to lower levels of the organizational hierarchy. Technicians will increasingly replace engineers and assume lead responsibilities for real-time production-line programming adjustments, and will have to acquire sophisticated programming skills. New quality control techniques will require a production work force with high skills in statistics and math. The increased flexibility of production will require an increasing flexibility in work force tasks. Multi-skilling will become imperative as work teams will be formed more fluidly, and assigned and reassigned according to the demands of a dynamic product mix. Thus, a premium will be placed on critical thinking and problem solving skills.

As new biologically engineered processes advance and begin to replace chemically engineered processes, effects on the skill profile will also be substantial. The nature of a biological substance is far different than a chemical one, exhibiting wider variability and instability in response to environmental changes. This will mandate a greater commitment to testing start point materials and to 'in-process' control.[62] A more multi-disciplinary production line work force will be required than in conventional pharmaceutical industry processes, uniting biologists, chemists, process engineers, and technicians in all phases of production.

The net effects of these technology induced changes will be the need for continuous re-skilling of the work force in the more conventional bulk chemical segment of the industry; and the creation of a wholly new multi-disciplinary work force in the emerging, biologically based segment. This will require a tremendous commitment on the part of industry managers, government training programmes and universities, and a closer communication between them in assuring the availability of skills. A major step in this direction has been the establishment in 1989 of an Advanced Pharmaceutical Manufacturing Technician Training Centre, which represents a consortium of twelve companies, the Pharmaceutical Department of the Medical Sciences Campus (University of Puerto Rico), and the Commonwealth Right to Work Administration. This Centre, the

165

first of its kind in the US, is providing intensive training for current and future industry work force in all aspects of pharmaceutical production.

Another implication of the paradigm shift in the local Pharmaceutical Industry relates to effects on suppliers and the intermediate sector. The increasing adoption of just-in-time and total quality control systems will tend to build increasing economies of agglomeration. A key factor in the future success of quick response systems, and in the achievement of further reductions in inventory and stock carrying costs will be greater availability of proximate suppliers of material inputs into production. The isolated island geography and long lead times in shipping of materials seems to mandate a continuing trend to re location of mainland suppliers to the island to service the industry.

In addition, tighter controls will be placed on suppliers by the industry. Vendor certification programmes that screen, select, and train long term strategic supply partners (such as the programme Smith-Kline has initiated locally) will probably expand exponentially as industry total quality control initiatives gather momentum. In this way, the pioneer pharmaceutical firms will spread advanced techniques through their demands on suppliers and the intermediates sector.

The diffusion of automation in the industry will also require a greater critical mass of associated software engineering firms that can customize and integrate automation systems. The recent initiation of a Pharmaceutical Industry Software Centre by IBM highlights this emerging need. In the future, more local firms will probably arise to service niche markets; for example, we are already seeing small consulting firms being created that specialize in optical disk technology to meet the information/documentation storage needs of the industry.

The further build-up of a technologically advanced supplier/intermediate sector in support of pharmaceutical production could have important spread effects. These include widening the high skills base of the economy; and giving suppliers the opportunity to gain new proficiencies needed to expand into new export markets for goods and services throughout the region.

Thus, as the Pharmaceutical Industry in Puerto Rico reaches for the cutting edge of world production technology, it can act as a powerful catalyst for yet another technological shift upstream in the whole manufacturing sector.

Finally, from an economy-wide perspective, we would state that maturation and restructuring of the Pharmaceutical Industry in Puerto Rico is part of a deeper, often disguised overall structural transition phase.

The spectacular growth of the high-tech manufacturing sector since the mid-1970s has served to provide not only direct income and employment effects but also to feed the growth of an associated information sector. This information sector, nurtured by both industry and government expenditures on services and education, is in a powerful upswing. As the high-tech manufacturing sector continues to mature, to reach near the top of its growth curve, a new lead sector - the information sector - rises up with fresh energy, with wide expansion potential. We will now turn our attention to this information sector.

V   The rise of the information sector

This is the first comprehensive attempt to map the rise of the information sector in Puerto Rico, and to assess its overall contribution to the island's economic growth in the period 1972 to 1987.

For the purposes of executing this study, we have employed the methodology originally developed by Fritz Machlup in the 'Production and Distribution of Knowledge in the US' (1962)[63] and later refined by Rubin and Huber ('The Knowledge Industry in the US, 1960-80').[64] This methodology identifies five basic economic categories subsumed under the general heading of an information sector: (1) education; (2) media of communication; (3) information machines; (4) information services; and (5) other information activities, including research and development. Machlup utilized final demand, or 'total sales' of each industry branch to measure its contribution to gross national product; and produced a set of national income accounts that demonstrated an aggregate knowledge industry contribution of 29 per cent of US GNP in 1958. Machlup's methodology was applied by Michael Rubin and Mary Taylor Huber in their growth accounting exercise 'The Knowledge Industry in the United States, 1960-80' (1986). Rubin and Huber found that the contribution of knowledge production to US GNP had risen from 29 per cent in 1958 to 34 per cent in 1980.

Utilizing this same approach, we have grouped SIC (Standard Industrial Classification) data together to compile a set of accounts for that composite bundle of goods and services which represents the local information sector. Our findings show that the information sector in Puerto Rico is now the leading sector of the economy. Education, Research and Development, the media of communication, information machines and information services collectively account for over nine billion dollars in gross sales receipts per annum and represent 53.6 per cent of total Gross National Product (1987).

The performance of the island's information sector has outpaced the growth of the economy as a whole. Between 1972 and 1987, Gross National Product expanded 295 per cent, a 7.5 per cent average annual growth rate. In this same period, the information sector expanded 561 per cent, a 12.2 per cent average annual growth rate. Its individual industry branches grew more rapidly than other manufacturing and services branches. For example, between 1972 and 1987, information services had an 11.7 per cent average annual growth rate; all other services had only a 1.8 per cent average annual growth rate.

The findings of this study are clear: trade in information intensive goods and services, or 'intellectual commerce' is now the driving force of economic development. Thus, in a matter of four short decades, Puerto Rico has gone through the full spectrum of development stages - from an agrarian society dominated by sugar and tobacco production; to a labour intensive manufacturing economy based on textile and needle-craft production; to a technology intensive manufacturing economy; and more recently to a knowledge economy, driven by the quick pace of expansion of information related goods and services.

We will now proceed to highlight the growth pattern of the branches that comprise the information sector.

1 Education

'Whatever may be the natural resources of developing areas, the ultimate and decisive factor is the human element. Developing the human element is not only the critical challenge in developing countries, it is also one which holds prospects of rewards as never before. For new horizons in technology are now working an important change in the potential relations of areas and economies. In the technology prior to World War II, industrial raw materials seemed the *sine qua non* for economic progress, and usually for social progress as well. But, today one of the great underlying changes of our times is that once more the human element is becoming decisive in the affairs of men. No longer is iron King; but the human mind.'

> Muñoz Marín, Governor of Puerto Rico, from an address entitled, 'The Will to Develop', presented at the 6th World Conference of the Society for International Development, Washington, D.C., March 15, 1964.

A revolution in education has unfolded in Puerto Rico over the past thirty-five years. During this period, the total enrolment for second level education (high school) rose from 57,390 to 220,447, representing a rise in the enrolment rate per 1,000 of population from 25.9 to 69.0. The number of college graduates rose from 14,839 to 148,020, a rise in enrolment per 1,000 population from 6.7 to 45.3. The number of scientists and engineers expanded two and one/half times, from 2,383 to 6,704. The percentage of management positions in manufacturing filled by Puerto Ricans increased from under 30 per cent to 94 per cent.

Puerto Rico today has the world's highest proportion of youth aged 18 to 22 enrolled in institutions of higher learning, as shown in Figure 5.1.

This expansion has been fuelled by Commonwealth Government expenditures. By law, seven per cent of the annual Commonwealth budget must be allocated to public education. If training and private education monies are factored in, then the total expenditures on education and training may account for 8.6 per cent of national output.

'Nowhere in the whole world are such vast sums spent on education. This includes even countries as highly developed as the US, Soviet Union and Japan. The comparable share in Third World countries varies between 2 to 3.5 per cent.'[65]

Figure 5.2 highlights the fact that Puerto Rico spends a greater percentage of its government receipts on education than other countries in the world at similar levels of development.

Apart from wide social impacts on the skill profile of the island, the education industry has made a positive contribution in terms of direct employment and in indirect multiplier effects associated with its rising expenditures. The top five universities alone have a work force of 16,642 and spend over $380 million a year. To these totals, we must add the employment and expenditures of a second tier of private and technical school whose ranks have grown from 264 in 1975 to 1,066 in 1989. If we add up all the expenditures on education made by public and private institutions, libraries and governmental training programmes, we find over $1.4 billion injected into the economy per annum (1987). This level of expenditure makes the Education Industry a dynamic source of growth in the economy in its own right, above and beyond the intrinsic social value of its products.

2 Research and Development

Research and development, as used, is a term that encompasses a complete spectrum of technology activities: basic research, applied research, development and commercialization of new products and processes, and operations or trouble-shooting production research. In Puerto Rico, universities and the private sector are the two primary participants in these

FIGURE 5.1

UNIVERSITY ENROLMENT AS A PERCENTAGE OF THE 18-22 AGE BRACKET

1965

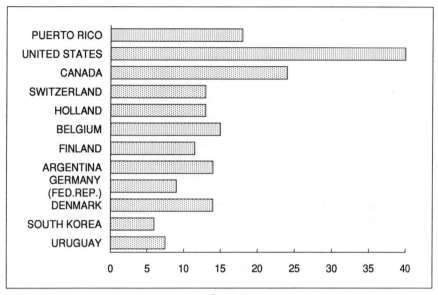

Per cent

1984

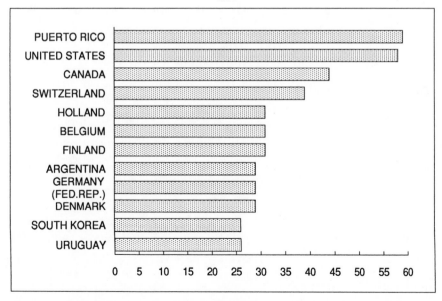

Per cent

Source: World Bank Atlas

171

FIGURE 5.2

PUBLIC INVESTMENT IN EDUCATION AS A PER CENT OF TOTAL
EXPENDITURES BY THE CENTRAL GOVERNMENT: 1985

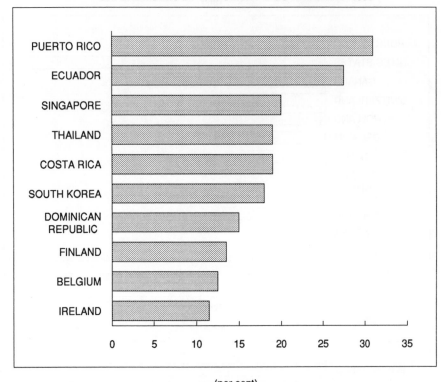

(per cent)

Source: World Bank Atlas.

TABLE 5.1

EXPENDITURES ON EDUCATION AND TRAINING: 1972-87

	1972	1977	1982	1987
Public education:				
Primary and secondary				
schools	190,751,334	285,435,098	431,540,815	518,449,095
Vocational schools	34,944,832	32,948,565	50,297,356	48,427,404
Universities	102,571,772	173,174,093	288,215,738	406,152,199
Private education:				
(all levels)	43,095,000	131,028,000	240,008,000	384,081,000
Libraries:				
Public	1,703,083	2,127,163	2,405,740	2,669,965
In-school	2,992,142	3,781,467	6,624,651	8,540,320
Other a)	n/a	n/a	3,897,548	n/a
Training b) c)	14,915,894	78,007,735	65,388,105	95,682,951
Totals	$390,974,057	$706,502,121	$1,088,377,953	$1,464,002,934
Percentage of increase from base year: 1972-1987:		374.5%		

Source: Budget of Puerto Rico 1972, 1977, and 1982. The Commonwealth's Office of Managment and Budget; Puerto Rico Planning Board; The Statistics Office of the following universities: Interamerican University, University of Puerto Rico, Sacred Heart University and the Anna Mendez Foundation.

Notes: a) This includes grants to libraries, library and learning resources and education information centre expenditures.
b) Training includes training and retraining of employees, the CETA programme, and training of veterans.
c) This total is much lower in 1972 due to the fact that the CETA programme was not started until 1973.

activities, with each sector focusing on different stages of innovation based on their specific capability.

a University Research

Scientific research is currently underway in all major university institutions on the island. In 1986-87, $18,310,860 in research expenditures were made by the University of Puerto Rico (UPR), Inter American University, Catholic University and Anna Mendez Foundation. Of this amount, UPR accounted for $16,844,633 or 82 per cent.[66]

In comparative terms, however, university research in Puerto Rico is lagging behind its US and regional competitors.

In the most recent comparisons within the US, Puerto Rico is last in university R and D expenditures behind all 50 states.[67] In the latest available comparison with Latin America, it also appears Puerto Rico is trailing its key competitors. For example, in 1978 Venezuela spent $56 million on university research, Mexico $67 million and Brazil $307 million, versus Puerto Rico's $5.4 million in 1980 and $18.3 million in 1986-87.

b Industry Research

There seems to be a recent movement in Puerto Rico's industries towards research and development. It appears that industries are moving from an early stage exclusive emphasis on production related technical activities to more innovative product and process development. This shift has been revealed in three ways: (a) through case presentations made at conferences by industry managers, such as the presentations on Research and Development initiatives at SK and F and Lederle during the April, 1988 Fomento Conference on Pharmaceutical Industry R and D, (b) through survey research, and (c) through reviews of R and D expenses listed on tax returns.

In a 1988 Industrial R and D Survey, conducted by the Governor's Advisory Council of Science and Technology, a sample of 108 firms reported expenditures on R and D totalling $10,890,000. This technical activity encompassed the full range of developmental tasks, from basic research to applied research on products and processes. Eight firms reported basic research activity. Twenty firms reported applied research on current products. Fifteen firms reported activities in the experimental development of new products. Sixteen firms reported applied research on current processes; and eleven on new processes.

A preliminary projection of survey findings to the total universe of firms on the island leads to a tentative estimate that approximately $82 million is being spent on R and D by Puerto Rico's industries. This projection represents a very conservative definition and valuation of R and D activity, in comparison with industry's own definition and valuation.

The actual Research and Development expenses claimed by tax exempt 936 corporations on their income tax returns to the Commonwealth and US Departments of Treasury are far larger than the figures cited above. In 1982, 34 firms claimed $83.09 million in R and D expenses; in 1985, 92 firms claimed $248.96 million. Thus, in three years, there was almost a tripling of both total numbers of firms claiming R and D expenses, and total R and D dollar values claimed. It is quite likely that these companies are considerably widening their tax return definition of R and D and R and D related expenses to include both the costs of operation of technical services and quality control units. Despite this overvaluation of R and D, it would appear that there indeed has been recent industry movement in this direction.

Utilizing the most conservative available estimates, the estimated island-wide total of both *university and industry R and D investment* reached $98,844,633 in 1986-87. This estimated total R and D expenditure represented 0.41 of Gross Domestic Product, putting Puerto Rico on a par with such national economies as India (0.36); Argentina (0.36); and Venezuela (0.35), in the latest year cross-comparative data could be obtained (1983). However, Puerto Rico was far behind the US as a whole (0.41 vs 2.71); and other world leaders, such as Japan (2.93) and Israel (2.47).[68]

TABLE 5.2

RESEARCH AND DEVELOPMENT IN INDUSTRY: 1982-87   a)
(R AND D EXPENSES CLAIMED IN TAX FILINGS BY
MANUFACTURING FIRMS)

Year	Number of firms claiming R and D expenses	R and D expenses (millions US$)
1982	34	$82.09
1983	78	$207.14
1984	96	$250.28
1985	92	$248.96
1986	62	$221.35
1987	61	$292.01

Source: Commonwealth Department of the Treasury; Government Development Bank-Office of Economic Studies.

Note: a) Because the term research and development is not fully defined by the IRS, it is likely the definition of R and D expenses used by companies includes aspects of technical services, process-engineering and production trouble shooting.

175

TABLE 5.3

TOTAL UNIVERSITY RESEARCH EXPENDITURES: 1979-87

Year	University of Puerto Rico	InterAmerican	Catholic University	Anna Mendez	Caribbean/ Central University	Ponce School of Medicine	University R and O totals
1979-80	5,139,519	0	0	0	0	0	5,139,519
1980-81	5,424,623	0	335,274	0	0	0	5,759,897
1981-82	6,232,363	0	378,505	0	0	0	6,610,868
1982-83	14,366,033	0	381,961	0	50,000	0	14,797,994
1983-84	14,352,871	0	536,784	0	40,000	27,696	15,546,717
1984-85	10,346,883	488,552	594,070	0	564,800	143,336	12,137,641
1985-86	14,381,831	440,337	128,031	0	0	n/a	14,950,199
1986-87	16,844,633	423,476	408,919	633,832	0	n/a	18,310,860

Source: Accounting Section, University of Puerto Rico, Central Administration; Epscor Program Office, UPR Rio Piedras Campus; Offices of External Resources, InterAmerican, Catholic University, Anna Mendez, Caribbean Central University.

3 Media of Communications

Puerto Rico today has as modern a communications infrastructure as anywhere in the Caribbean and Latin America. There are 112 radio stations on the island, the largest concentration of stations for any similarly sized geographic area in the US. There are eight commercial television stations serving the 891,000 households - 99 per cent of all households with television sets. Additionally, ten cable television stations have on offer thirty-five channels of programming and reach almost 20 per cent of all households. San Juan, the capital of the island, has four daily newspapers with a combined circulation of 586,257, more dailies than any city of similar size in the US.[69]

Puerto Rico's telecommunications infrastructure is world class. There are two publicly owned telecommunications networks - the Puerto Rico Telephone Company (PRTC) which serves 66 of the island's 78 towns; and the Puerto Rico Communications Authority (PRCA). PRTC is the linear descendant of the multinational International Telephone and Telegraph (ITT), which was founded in Puerto Rico in 1914 by Sosthenes Behn, an island resident. Since PRTC was first acquired by the Commonwealth Government in 1974, it has invested $790 million in completely digitalizing the island's carrier networks and access lines.

PRTC and PRCA, along with thirty-three private interconnect companies, sell home telephones, telephone switchboard (PBX) and key systems for offices, and microwave and earth satellite stations. PRTC dominates this interconnect market, claiming almost 70 per cent of market share.

AT&T has been an aggressive player in the long distance market, and is currently completing a fibre optic cable from Florida to Puerto Rico that will make Puerto Rico into a hub/distribution link to Jamaica, Colombia and the Dominican Republic.

The overall explosion of the communications sector in Puerto Rico in the period 1972-87 has been remarkable. In this period, total gross income of the communications sector grew 664.9 per cent, from $113,908,000 to $871,318,000, and it is the driving force, the lead industry in information sector expansion.

In Tables 5.4 and 5.5 we chart the growth of this sector for the years under study.

4 Information machines

The long term growth of the electronic and electrical industry (SIC Code #36), and the more recent development of the computer and related products industry (SIC code #3573) have been important aspects of Puerto Rico's manufacturing vitality.

TABLE 5.4

THE RISE OF THE COMMUNICATIONS SERVICES SECTOR: 1972-87
(SALES IN DOLLAR AMOUNTS)

	1972	1977	1982	1987	Change from base year: 1972-87
Telephone and telegraph	70,243,000	184,439,000	342,252,000	554,944,000	790.0%
- Private	62,303,000	32,650,000	41,205,000	85,957,000	138.0%
- Public a)	7,940,000	151,789,000	301,047,000	468,987,000	309.0%
Radio and television a) b)	n/a	44,463,000	85,176,000	137,899,000	310.1%
Cable television c)	n/a	n/a	9,752,000	31,703,000	325.1%
Media advertising (commissions on sales)	13,645,000	27,407,000	47,572,000	86,228,000	631.9%
Television, radio and theatre production	4,560,000	6,618,000	10,590,000	11,000,000	241.2%
Motion pictures (production and distribution)	8,590,000	14,145,000	21,590,000	30,992,000	360.8%
Motion pictures (theatres and moviehouses)	16,870,000	26,008,000	22,169,000	18,552,000	111.0%
Total	113,908,000	303,080,000	539,101,000	871,318,000	764.9%

Source: The Puerto Rico Planning Board (unpublished data) and the 1972 PRTC/ITT Annual Report.

Notes: a) The per cent of change is for the years 1977-87.
        b) For the year 1977 this figure includes cable television.
        c) The per cent of change is for the years 1982-87.

TABLE 5.5

THE COMMUNICATIONS SECTOR
INDICES OF MARKET PENETRATION: 1988

	No. of firms	Audience size	In-home penetration
Television a)	8	891,000 households	99%
Cable tv b)	10	166,815 households	19%
VCR's c)			44%
Faxes d)		10,000	59% e)
Radio a)	112	3,847,000 (weekly)	
Newspapers a)	4 (daily)	543,257	
	3 (weekly)	43,000	
		586,257	65%

Source: a) Caribbean Business to Business Guide, 1989 (compiled from various tables).
b) Public Service Commission, Division of Diversified Enterprises, December 1987.
c) Caribbean Business, Thursday June 8, 1989, p. 28.
d) Caribbean Business, Thursday, June 8, 1989, p. 35 and Puerto Rico Department of Revenue, 1989 (figures are for 1987).

Note: e) An estimation of all island businesses.

In 1953, there were only 14 electrical/electronics plants on the island manufacturing $3,805,002 worth of products, such as fluorescent lamps and radio tubes. Only seven years later (1960), there were 63 plants producing $62,000,000 worth of output. Today, 145 plants produce $905,500,000 worth of products, including electrical switches, relays, plugs and sockets (40 per cent of total value of output); radio, telephone and T.V. components (15 per cent); carbon and graphite products (14 per cent); transistors (6 per cent); and motors and generators (4 per cent).[70] The evolution of this sector is shown in Table 5.6.

The largest employer in this sector is Westinghouse of Puerto Rico, with $600 million of sales in 1987, 11,700 employees, and 23 factory sites. Motorola is the second largest employer, with 1987 sales of $545 million, 2,300 employees, and six factory sites.

The explosive long term growth of this sector is starting to slow, as rising labour costs in Puerto Rico take their toll. In 1988, the local average hourly wage for electrical assembly workers was $5.76 hour, whereas in Brazil, Mexico and the Dominican Republic the wage bill came to $3 a day.

Puerto Rico's Computer and Related Products Industry, on the other hand, has managed to withstand a general shake-out in the US industry, and has maintained its dynamic growth. Nineteen manufacturers, including nine Fortune 500 companies, are operating 26 plants island-wide, as shown in Figure 5.3, a map of production units.

These companies are manufacturing a wide range of products, including:
- diskettes
- computer interfaces
- magnetic recording heads
- mini-computers
- modular systems
- digital circuit modules
- computer peripherals
- memory systems
- printed circuit boards
- input matrix print-heads[71]

In addition, two software companies, Lotus Development Corporation and Ashton-Tate Corporation are in operation on the island, producing the Lotus 1-2-3 Spreadsheet programme and the DBase III programme respectively.

As a whole, the Computer Industry currently employs 7,000 people and has a sales volume that has grown from $132 million in 1977 to $1.14 billion ten years later (1988).

For the purposes of our study on the information sector, we have followed Machlup's protocol and have selected out the growth in sales of these categories of information machines: communications equipment; measurement and control instruments; and electronic computing equipment. Unlike Machlup, we have not included 'signaling devices', which have not been tracked as a separate four digit SIC category since 1958; nor did we

TABLE 5.6

THE GROWTH OF THE ELECTRONICS SECTOR - SIC MAJOR GROUP 36

Year	No. of plants	No. of employees	Total value of production	Total value of exports	Product lines
1948	1	16	-	-	
1953	14	860	$3,805,002	$3,000,000	Flourescent lamps; phonographic records; mica parts for electronic tubes; telephone switch-boards; carbon resistors; radio tubes; transistors and diodes.
1960	63	4,502	$62,000,000	$56,000,000	Resistors; precision wire wound resistors; magne-tic relays; pulse trans-formers.
1966	97	8,020	$142,400,000	$92,000,000	Telephone and electric equipment; radio trans-mission receiving equip-ment; circuits; switches; printed circuits; pulse transformers; tv, radio, phonographic, tape recorder and camera units.
1972	137	12,000	$243,000,000	$158,000,000	Digital circuits; electric measuring instruments; power transformers; motors; electrical household pro-ducts; photoelectric cells; magnetic tape; core memories; ultrasonic intru-sion alarms, transducers.
1977	141	14,069	$284,000,000	$190,000,000	High speed printers; colour gun mounts; semi-conductors; digital circuit modules; pacemakers.
1982	159	17,200	-	$671,300,000	Videocassettes and circuitboards.
1986	140	21,634	-	$860,860,000	
1987	145	20,200	-	$905,500,000	

Source: Puerto Rico Development Administration; Office of Economic Research; Electronics Industries Profiles 1953, 1960, 1972, 1977, 1982 and 1986.

FIGURE 5.3

FORTUNE 500 COMPANIES - MANUFACTURING IN PUERTO RICO (S.I.C. 3573)

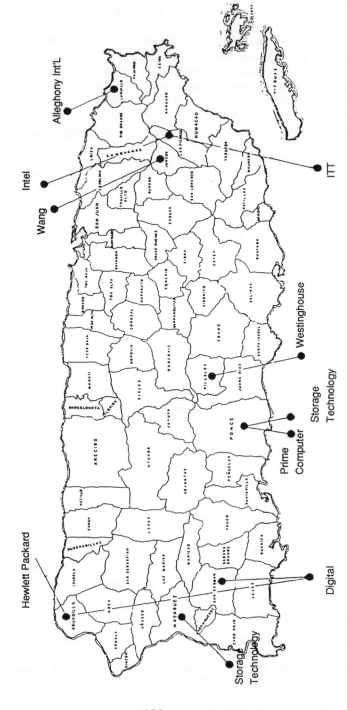

TABLE 5.7

IMPORT/EXPORT PROFILE OF THE TELEMATICS INDUSTRY

Code	Description	Total 1980		Total 1987		Total import ave. yearly growth rate	Total export ave. yearly growth rate
		Imports	Exports	Imports	Exports		
	Accounting and computing equipment						
3573	Electronic computation equipment	776,668	114,179,980	162,446,069	1,021,668,784	114.53%	36.76%
3574	Calculators and adding machines	1,555,383	1,053,278	1,815,293	1,115,431	2.23%	0.82%
366	Communications equipment	2,630,304	21,706,984	63,850,145	80,166,504	57.72%	20.52%
3661	Telephone and telegraph devices	2,144,114	1,956,474	33,191,829	25,989,595	47.90%	44.70%
3663	Radio and television transmission equipment	-	-	-	-	-	-
3669	Communications equipment, n.e.c.	-	-	-	-	-	-
	Total	7,106,469	138,896,716	261,303,336	1,128,940,314	67.36%	33.01%

Code	Description	US 1980		US 1987		US import ave. yearly growth rate	US export ave. yearly growth rate
		Imports	Exports	Imports	Exports		
	Accounting and computing equipment						
3573	Electronic computation equipment	-	110,362,658	146,636,906	912,129,847	-	35.22%
3574	Calculators and adding machines	-	365,345	1,333,432	834,095	-	12.52%
366	Communications equipment	-	18,340,653	49,013,929	69,157,448	-	20.88%
3661	Telephone and telegraph devices	-	207,602	21,552,780	23,490,673	-	96.51%
3663	Radio and television transmission equipment	-	-	-	-	-	-
3669	Communications equipment, n.e.c.	-	-	-	-	-	-
	Total	-	129,276,258	218,537,047	1,005,612,063	-	34.05%

table continued....

TABLE 5.7 (CONTINUED)

		V.I. 1980		V.I. 1987		V.I. import ave. yearly growth rate	Total export ave. yearly growth rate
Code	Description	Imports	Exports	Imports	Exports		
	Accounting and computing equipment						
3573	Electronic computation equipment	-	871,974	-	1,659,416	-	9.63%
3574	Calculators and adding machines	-	314,962	-	34,790	-	-27.00%
366	Communications equipment	-	1,053,731	-	668,968	-	-6.28%
3661	Telephone and telegraph devices	-	825,794	-	251,424	-	-15.62%
3663	Radio and television transmission equipment	-	-	-	-	-	-
3669	Communications equipment, n.e.c.	-	-	-	-	-	-
	Total		3,066,461		2,614,598		-2.25%

		Foreign countries F.C. 1980		F.C. 1987		F.C. import ave. yearly growth rate	Total export ave. yearly growth rate
Code	Description	Imports	Exports	Imports	Exports		
	Accounting and computing equipment						
3573	Electronic computation equipment	776,668	2,945,348	15,809,163	107,879,521	53.80%	67.26%
3574	Calculators and adding machines	1,555,383	372,971	481,861	246,546	-15.41%	-5.74%
366	Communications equipment	2,630,304	2,312,600	14,836,216	10,340,088	28.04%	23.86%
3661	Telephone and telegraph devices	2,144,114	923,078	11,639,049	2,247,498	27.34%	13.56%
3663	Radio and television transmission equipment	-	-	-	-	-	-
3669	Communications equipment, n.e.c.	-	-	-	-	-	-
	Total	7,106,469	6,553,997	42,766,289	120,713,653	29.23%	51.62%

Source: Puerto Rico Planning Board, Bureau of Economic Analysis.

Note: Part of all of the data is missing, therefore we cannot determine the rate of growth. The growth rates correspond to the years 1980-87.

use the newer category of 'inter-connection equipment' because of local data limitations.

5 Information services

The services sector in Puerto Rico is the largest employment sector. In 1988, the Commonwealth Department of Labour reported that 867,000 people were working in the services sector, as compared to 196,000 people in the government sector and 158,000 people in manufacturing.

The services sector encompasses a vast variety of business activities and skill levels, from restaurants to computer programming. Rubin and Huber, updating Machlup's original categorization of professional knowledge services have added new sub-sectors arising from technological change, such as data-processing. We closely follow their measurement procedures, and have charted the growth of the following information services:
- legal services
- engineering and architectural services
- accounting and auditing services
- real-estate services
- insurance services
- wholesale trade (value of intelligence services of traders)
- data-processing and computer programming
- demand-deposits (costs of processing)
- credit cards (costs of processing)
- miscellaneous commercial services (management consulting, commercial photography, etc.)

We have been unable to follow Rubin and Huber's lead in charting the growth of Security and Commodity Brokers, Dealers and Exchanges. This information is simply not available in Puerto Rico; nor does the US Security and Exchange Commission disaggregate their reporting by geographical area.

We have also been unable to chart the expenditures of the Commonwealth Government on information activities in the manner prescribed by Machlup and Rubin and Huber. The budgetary reporting formats of the US Federal Government and Commonwealth Central Government are simply incompatible. Therefore, we have taken the simple, yet, we believe, effective expedient of substituting the large Commonwealth Government budgetary reporting category of 'Expenditures on Management and Control.' This category certainly represents the most information intensive tier of government operations.

In the tables that follow, we track the phenomenal growth of information services sector.

TABLE 5.8

THE GROWTH OF SELECTED 'KNOWLEDGE INTENSIVE' SERVICES: 1972-87

Category of services:	1972	1977	1982	1987
Engineering and architectural	42,489,000	50,611,000	61,907,000	81,131,000
Legal	49,444,000	73,639,000	119,132,000	186,209,000
Medical - total	133,201,000	334,115,000	653,518,000	983,453,000
- Dentists	12,004,000	22,513,000	40,345,000	69,292,000
- Doctors	69,439,000	133,736,000	274,579,000	412,292,000
- Hospitals	39,400,000	154,094,000	290,784,000	424,542,000
- Laboratories	8,235,000	12,193,000	30,515,000	53,533,000
- Miscellaneous	4,123,000	11,579,000	17,295,000	23,794,000
Accounting and auditing	25,117,000	31,127,000	66,135,000	105,056,000
Miscellaneous commercial services	99,439,000	177,986,000	298,845,000	446,041,000
Total	349,690,000	667,478,000	1,199,537,000	1,801,890,000

Source: The Puerto Rico Planning Board (unpublished data).

TABLE 5.9

THE GROWTH OF THE COMPUTING SERVICES INDUSTRY: 1977-87

	Data processing/ computer programming services: (sales)	Wholesale computer (sales)	Total in the computer services industry
1977	$12,768,000	$124,558,000 a)	$137,326,000
1982	$19,815,000	$203,253,000 a)	$223,068,000
1987	$34,400,000	$283,445,000 a)	$317,845,000

Source: Puerto Rico Planning Board (unpublished data).

Note: a) These are estimates of sectoral sales based on a sample of the seven largest computer wholesale companies in Puerto Rico including Wang, IBM, Honeywell, Burroughs Sperry and Xerox.

6 Total knowledge production in the economy: 1972-87

In the preceding chapters, we have reviewed the growth trends in each of the five sub-sectors that comprise the composite information sector in Puerto Rico. By compiling total sales and expenditure information for education; research and development; media of communication; information machines; and information services, we are able to present a comprehensive set of national income accounts for the Information Section for the years 1972, 1977, 1982 and 1987.

Total Knowledge production grew from $1,625,163,040 in 1972 to $9,129,260,274 in 1987 - a 561.7 per cent rise in value from the base year. The average annual growth rate of the total information sector - 12.2 per cent per annum over the fifteen year period - was far higher than the 7.5 per cent average annual growth rate of total Gross National Product. The average annual growth rates of both the information machines and information services sub-sectors were much higher than those for the Manufacturing and Service Sectors as a whole.

Between 1972 and 1987, total knowledge production claimed ever larger shares of Gross National Product - 28.2 per cent of conventional GNP in 1972; 39.0 per cent in 1977; 43.7 per cent in 1982; and 53.6 per cent in 1987.

These results seem to provide compelling evidence that the information sector is the driving force of the local economy, and that Puerto Rico is moving forward rapidly towards a destiny as a high-skills knowledge intensive society.

7 Issues raised by our findings on the information sector in Puerto Rico

Does the rise of the information sector to a dominant position in the production structure of a newly industrialized society like Puerto Rico's mandate a rethinking of conventional wisdom in development economics?

Many development economists have supported the idea that industrialization produces a series of progressive stages in the economy. Kuznets, Chenery, et al, have provided ample statistical evidence that societies undergoing rapid transformation typically experience a reversal in shares of agriculture and manufacturing in GNP: i.e. manufacturing replaces agriculture as the driving force of the economy. Other development economists have taken the theory of stages still further, to define a sequence of progressive changes that unfold in the manufacturing sector itself as it matures: from an early primary raw material and labour intensive phase to a capital and technology intensive later phase. More recently, some economists have sought to bring the role of the services sector into this conception of a staged growth process.

TABLE 5.10

KNOWLEDGE PRODUCTION

	1972	1977	1982	1987
I. Education				
Public				
- Primary and secondary	190,751,334	285,435,098	431,540,815	518,449,095
- Vocational	34,944,832	32,948,565	50,297,356	48,427,404
- Colleges & universities	102,571,772	173,174,093	288,215,738	406,152,199
Public libraries	4,695,225	5,908,630	9,030,391	11,210,285
Training	14,915,894	78,007,735	65,388,105	95,682,951
Private (all levels)	43,095,000	131,028,000	240,008,000	384,081,000
Total education	390,974,057	706,502,121	1,084,480,405	1,464,002,934
% of GNP	6.8%	8.6%	8.6%	8.6%
% of adjusted GNP	6.7%	8.0%	8.0%	8.0%
II. Research & Development a)				
Public	n/a	n/a	10,704,431	18,310,860
Private	n/a	n/a	82,090,000	292,010,000
Total R and D	n/a	n/a	92,794,431	310,320,860
% of GNP	n/a	n/a	0.7%	1.8%
% of adjusted GNP	n/a	n/a	0.7%	1.7%
III. Communications media				
Printing and publishing				
(includes books, periodicals,				
newspapers, stationery,				
and envelopes)	59,696,000	113,510,000	189,032,000	303,754,000
Photography	2,538,000	2,867,000	5,011,000	6,946,000
Phonography	990,000	n/a	2,442,000	n/a
Television and radio	n/a	44,463,000	85,176,000	137,899,000
Retail sale of radio, tv, and				
supplies, incl. music				
stores	15,620,000	19,092,000	28,571,000	58,777,000
Cable t.v.	n/a	n/a	9,752,000	31,703,000
Theatre production	4,560,000	6,618,000	10,590,000	11,000,000
Motion pictures:				
- Production/distribution	8,590,000	14,145,000	21,590,000	30,992,000
- Cinemas	16,870,000	26,008,000	22,169,000	18,552,000
- Total	25,460,000	40,153,000	43,759,000	49,544,000
Spectator sports	35,284,400	46,229,000	68,321,000	91,346,000
Media advertising				
(commission on sales)	13,645,000	27,407,000	47,572,000	86,228,000
Telephone and telegraph				
- Private	62,303,000	32,650,000	41,205,000	85,957,000
- Public	7,940,000	151,789,000	301,047,000	468,987,000
- Total	70,243,000	184,439,000	342,252,000	554,944,000
Total communications media	212,416,400	465,686,000	832,478,000	1,332,141,000
% of GNP	3.7%	5.7%	6.6%	7.8%
% of adjusted GNP	3.6%	5.3%	6.1%	7.2%

table continued...

TABLE 5.10 (CONTINUED)

	1972	1977	1982	1987
IV. Information machines				
Communications equipment	31,932,259	53,732,344	99,006,612	114,147,789
Measuring and controlling equipment	28,329,000	69,448,000	51,287,109	n/a
Electronic computing machines	26,600,000	132,100,000	402,431,131	1,021,668,784
Total information machines	86,861,259	255,280,344	552,724,852	1,135,816,573
% of GNP	1.5%	3.1%	4.4%	6.7%
% of adjusted GNP	1.5%	2.9%	4.1%	6.2%
V. Information services:				
Legal	49,444,000	73,639,000	119,132,000	186,209,000
Engineering and architectural	42,489,000	50,611,000	61,907,000	81,131,000
Accounting and auditing	25,117,000	31,127,000	66,135,000	105,056,000
Medical				
- Dentists	12,004,000	22,513,000	40,345,000	69,292,000
- Doctors	69,439,000	133,736,000	274,579,000	412,292,000
- Hospitals	39,400,000	154,094,000	290,784,000	424,542,000
- Laboratories	8,235,000	12,193,000	30,515,000	53,533,000
- Miscellaneous	4,123,000	11,579,000	17,295,000	23,794,000
Total medical	133,201,000	334,115,000	653,518,000	983,453,000
Demand deposit costs	18,085,000	33,282,860	52,624,050	74,194,200
Credit card costs	10,780,000	13,746,000	23,599,800	26,041,290
Real estate brokers	36,400,000	105,800,000	190,800,000	286,200,000
Insurance agents and brokers (Total subscribed premiums)	261,858,099	491,600,000	796,000,000	1,447,500,000
Wholesale agents (value of services) b)	80,425,800	202,225,175	236,020,050	338,500,000
Computer and data processing	n/a	12,768,000	22,415,000	34,400,000
Miscellaneous business services (including management consulting, professional photography, security and leasing equipment services)	99,439,000	177,986,000	298,845,000	446,041,000
Commonwealth government expenditures (including management and control)	177,672,425	231,198,932	434,862,204	878,253,417
Total information services	934,911,324	1,758,098,967	2,955,858,104	4,886,978,907
% of GNP	16.2%	21.5%	23.4%	28.7%
% of adjusted GNP	16.1%	19.9%	21.7%	26.6%

table continued...

TABLE 5.10 (CONTINUED)

	1972	1977	1982	1987
Total knowledge production	1,625,163,040	3,185,567,432	5,518,335,792	9,129,260,274
Total GNP	5,771,000,000	8,173,800,000	12,626,500,000	17,028,700,000
Total adjusted GNP	5,822,939,000	8,827,704,000	13,636,620,000	18,390,996,000
Knowledge production as % of GNP	28.2%	39.0%	43.7%	53.6%
Knowledge production as % of adjusted GNP	27.9%	36.1%	40.5%	49.6%
Other than education	21.4%	30.3%	35.1%	45.0%

Source: Section I - All public education, public libraries and training figures are from the Commonwealth budgets for the years 1974, 1979, 1984 and 1989; private education figure is from the Puerto Rico Planning Board (unpublished data).

Section II - Public R and D is from the Office of External Resources at the following universities: U.P.R., InterAmerican University, The Anna Mendez Foundation, and the Sacred Heart University. Private R and D is from the Government Development Bank-Office of Economic Studies.

Section III - All are from the Puerto Rico Planning Board (unpublished data) except for 1972 figure for public telephone/telegraph, which came from the ITT/PRTC 1972 Annual Report Revenue Figures.

Section IV - Communication equipment came from the Economic Development Profiles, Electronic Sector Analysis for the years 1972, 1977, 1982 and 1987; measuring and controlling devices came from the Census of Manufacturing, US Bureau of the Census for the years 1972, 1977 and 1982; Electronic computing equipment came from the Government Development Bank-Office of Economic Studies and Fomento Profiles of the Computer Industry.

Section V - All services up until direct deposits are from the Puerto Rico Planning Board (unpublished data), direct deposits and credit card costs are from the Puerto Rico Planning Board and the US Federal Reserve System Functional Costs Analysis Annual Editions; real estate, insurance, wholesale, computer and data processing, and miscellanous business services are from the Puerto Rico Planning Board (unpublished data), and government expenditures are from the Commonwealth budgets for the years: 1972, 1977, 1982 and 1987.

Notes: a) R and D includes basic, applied, and development.
b) The wholesale agent figures for 1982 and 1987 are estimates.

TABLE 5.11

THE RELATIVE GROWTH OF THE INFORMATION SECTOR
VIZ-A-VIZ THE REST OF THE ECONOMY

	Percentage of increase over base year: 1972-87	Average annual rate of growth: 1972-87
A. THE INFORMATION SECTOR		
I Education	374.5%	9.2%
II Research and development a)	334.4%	27.3%
III Media of communication	627.1%	13.0%
IV Information machines	1307.6%	18.7%
V Information services	522.7%	11.7%
VI Total information sector	561.7%	12.2%
B. THE WHOLE ECONOMY		
I Total services	350.9%	8.7%
II Services (except information services)	130.2%	1.8%
III Total manufacturing	685.2%	13.7%
IV Manufacturing (except information machines)	646.8%	13.3%
V Total GNP	295.1%	7.5%

Source: The same as for Table 5.10.

Note: a) Both rates of growth for R and D are for the period of 1982-87 because there is no information available for 1972 or 1977.

The relevance of the information sector to development theory has been far more contentious. It is interesting to note that a 1988 study on the contribution of the information sector in ten Pacific Counties (including the newly industrializing countries of Singapore, the Philippines, Taiwan, Malaysia, Indonesia and Thailand) concludes:

'The limited data does not support the belief that a rapid transformation from agrarian and industrial structures to information economies is already well underway in less advanced economies.'[72]

Yet, the evidence from the Puerto Rico study does indeed suggest that a new typology of stages needs to be defined, based on the emergence, growth and dominance of a boundary spanning information sector that encompasses the most advanced aspects of both the manufacturing and services sectors, and represents a next, higher synergistic stage of economic development.

Given the apparent idiosyncrasy of the Puerto Rican case, how can we forge a theoretical construct to accommodate and explain the rise to dominance of the information sector in the process of development?

Perhaps we can begin to clarify some of the critical issues if we refer to Beniger's definition of the information sector as a broad, multifaceted set of technologies, skills and organizational structures which are deeply rooted in the Industrial Revolution; and which represent the establishment and ongoing maturation of social control mechanisms in response to unprecedented change. In reviewing time series data from 1800 through 1980 compiled by Lebergolt, Fabricant, Porat and Bell, Beniger asserts that the timing of the information sector's emergence and development in the United States supports this definition:

'When the first railroads were built in the early 1830s, the information sector employed considerably less than one per cent of the US labour force; by the end of the decade it employed more than four per cent. Not until the rapid bureaucratization of the 1870s and 1880s, the period that marks the consolidation of control, did the information sector more than double to about one eighth of the work force. With the exception of these two great discontinuities, one occurring with the advent of railroads and the crisis of control in the 1850s, the other accompanying the consolidation of control in the 1870s and especially the 1880s (marked by the rise of bureaucracy), the information sector has grown steadily but only modestly over the past two centuries.'[73]

Beniger thus clearly associates the dramatic early acceleration of the information sector in the US with major discontinuity - a period when society was grappling with extreme rupture and change and seeking to exert a 'purposive influence' over events almost beyond control. Put another way, the birth of the Industrial Revolution in the United States created an unprecedented societal upheaval that directly led to a quantum leap in the size and sophistication of the information sector. (Of course, this line of argument invariably leads us to ask whether the present period is sufficiently disruptive to catalyse another quantum leap in the information sector?)

What might Beniger's premise imply for our theorizing about the remarkable rise of the information sector in Puerto Rico? First of all, that the industrialization process which took root on the island in the early 1950s set up the conditions of large scale disruption and discontinuity that Beniger associates with a quantum leap forward of the information sector. Secondly, during the wholesale disruption that accompanied the birth of the Industrial Revolution in Puerto Rico, the island's institutions and firms had virtually unlimited opportunities for transfer of technologies, practices and systems from the United States the pacesetter country in the development of the control revolution and its spinoff information sector. This combination of very early industrialization and unparalleled access to the innovator country - at its moment of greatest economic and technological strength - conferred advantages in the 'kick-starting of an information sector' not shared by any other less developed economy in the 1950s.

It was this favourable overall environment for information sector technology transfer that enabled Fomento's targeted promotional effort aimed at the US electronics industry, which had been triggered by another Arthur D. Little commissioned study in 1954, to ultimately succeed so spectacularly. It was this favourable environment that gave the 1958 Fomento promotions of the office machinery industry and the 1964 promotions of the computer/data-processing industry such terrific long term momentum. One could argue that the genius of the Operation Bootstrap architects lie in recognizing and seizing the special opportunities that such a favourable strategic environment for information sector development allowed.

Still another perspective on the question of why the information sector is dominant in Puerto Rico could be gained by applying the formulations of Perez and Freeman. They would assert that the key factor of the previous 'kondratiev' long-wave was energy. The organization of production was based on the seemingly unlimited supply of low cost oil, which 'together with petrochemicals and other energy intensive materials, drove the mass production paradigm - fully deployed after the Second World War, and now exhausted.'[74]

The OPEC boycott and skyrocketing oil prices in the early 1970s placed a premium on the conservation of energy and materials and spurred the growth and diffusion of microelectronics and information intensive process controls in the production sphere. Information Technology became the key factor of the new technoeconomic paradigm and its deployment became, in Perez' term, the new 'common sense' among engineers and managers.

Thus, the rapid and sustained rise of the information sector in the period between the oil shocks of the early 1970s and the present might well relate to the island's complete dependency on imported oil. It could be claimed that such a dependency has accelerated the shift of paradigms. The electronics industry on the island certainly benefited from this transition, as it found a suddenly enlarged market for its control products. The local pharmaceutical industry became a prime purchaser of these products. The construction industry sought design changes and new information systems to promote energy conservation. Management consultants were enlisted in large numbers to devise strategic changes in industry and government practices. In other words, an entire chain of responses was set up by the energy crisis that favoured the rapid promotion of the new key factor - microelectronics based technology - in industry and government and the household economy as a hedge against failing energy intensive practices.

The sustained growth of the information sector since 1973 might have been strongly accentuated by the vulnerability of firms and institutions on an island completely dependent on imported oil - the key factor of the previous technoeconomic paradigm. This vulnerability led to a pronounced, dramatic readjustment - a micro level technological revolution across a spectrum of key firms and institutions.

Yet, the Oil Crisis in Puerto Rico does not fully explain why its information sector should have rose to dominance in the 1973 - 1987 period. After all, Singapore and Taiwan were no less dependent on imported oil given their island geographies. The answer, we believe, again lies in the unique relationship of Puerto Rico to the United States, where the microelectronics revolution was first engineered. The political association of Puerto Rico, and its inclusion under US trade and patent laws meant that companies and institutions on the mainland had no legal trepidations about transferring leading edge technologies and best practices to related or unrelated parties in the island's manufacturing and services spheres. In addition, in the post 1976 period, Section 936 investments resulted in a massive expansion of intra-corporate telecommunications and informatics networks between the island and the continental US. As the technoeconomic paradigm described by Perez and Freeman unfolded, closer integration between production units and headquarter research, engineering, marketing and planning units were required, and this gave another real impetus to the expansion of telematics on the island.

Thus, we have provided two complimentary rationales for the accelerated development and rise to dominance of the information sector in Puerto Rico. The first rationale - based on the Beniger model - attributes the *'kick-starting' of the information sector* to the impact of early industrialization and technological integration with the United States. The second rationale - based on the Perez/Freeman model - attributes the *sustained growth of the information sector* to excessive vulnerability to volatile imported oil prices. This vulnerability led to a radical readjustment process at the firm and institutional level, and the early widespread adoption of factor saving information technologies from the US, where the microelectronics revolution first emerged. Both rationales emphasize the special relationship between Puerto Rico and the United States. It was this close integration with a global technological pace setter that catalysed and supported the information sector in Puerto Rico.

What are the major policy implications of this conclusion for other newly industrializing countries? It would appear that a stable stream of technology and know-how from advanced technological centres over a long period of time is the fundamental prerequisite to an initial acceleration and a sustained expansion of the information sector. Obviously, few small countries would voluntarily wish to duplicate the status of a Commonwealth with the United States or any other large power for that matter. Stable conditions necessary for effective technology transfer, however, can be created through many other integrative vehicles, including long term strategic alliances between host country public and private institutions and pioneering companies on a world-wide basis.

Apart from challenging conventional development paradigms, and raising some general policy implications for newly industrializing counties, the specific policy implications for Puerto Rico are the following:

1) Until now, the high-technology manufacturing sector (pharmaceuticals, electronics and computers, professional instruments), which is largely owned and operated by US multinationals, has been regarded as the driving force of the economy by the island's decision makers. Yet, the education, media of communication and information services sectors - all sectors with a high degree of local ownership - now collectively represent 45.1 per cent of GNP (1987). The information machines sector, with its external ownership, only accounts for 6.7 per cent of 1987 GNP. Therefore, knowledge intensive development appears to have been concentrated in those sectors that are largely locally owned and operated.

2) The policy implications of this are profound. Since the Operation Bootstrap period of the late 1940s, the island's economic development strategy was aimed at attracting US multinationals through generous tax incentives. Tax policy has never been specifically directed at stimulating the locally owned knowledge sectors which have become so critical to sustained economic dynamism. Nor have formal user incentives been devised to encourage the diffusion of services and products emanating from these local knowledge sectors.

3) More generally, the concept of a distinct and dynamic information sector, culled from both the manufacturing and service sectors, allows for the creation of special strategies for further sectoral development, embracing technology policies, human resource and high skills training policies, trade and marketing policies and coherent infrastructural investment policies.

4) Finally, the quantification of the direct financial contributions of a distinct information sector makes more 'transparent' the effects of government expenditures in selected areas of the economy, and moves such expenditures out of the more ambiguous realm of 'social policy' and into the arena of economic advancement. This lends credence to the continued prioritization of education and information infrastructures in future

spending plans, and provides valuable supporting evidence for these expenditures in times of fiscal austerity.

VI   Conclusions

In comparative terms, Puerto Rico's industrialization process has been extraordinarily compressed. The percentage change in share of industry in GDP since 1950 in Puerto Rico appears to have been the greatest of any country covered in the WIDER study. The simultaneous contraction of agriculture has also, in relative terms, been unusually pronounced. Of all the countries in the WIDER study, Puerto Rico currently has the lowest percentage share of agriculture in GDP and employment, evidence of the intensity of agriculture's decline since 1950 and its rapid replacement by manufacturing as the driving force of the economy. Within manufacturing itself, we have seen a rapid evolution of the production structure and a succession of leading sectors. More recently, the information sector has risen up and has become the new leading sector for the 1990s and beyond.

1 The staged evolution of the industrial structure

On the *microeconomic* level, we would restate the conclusions of our analyses that Puerto Rico has moved through successive industrialization stages at a breakneck pace. In a 40 year period, agriculture was pushed aside by labour intensive manufacturing which, in turn, was supplanted by capital and technology intensive manufacturing. More recently, the information sector has risen up as the emerging new lead sector and now accounts for 53.6 per cent of Gross National Product. As a result of this staged expansion, Puerto Rico currently has three world class industries: pharmaceuticals (accounting for 35 per cent of US global production assets), electronics (accounting for 11 per cent of US global production assets), and telecommunications.

At each stage of development, Puerto Rico's leading sectors have operated much in the manner predicted by the Rostow paradigm, generating the linkages and spread effects that have provided momentum to economic takeoff and sustained national transformation. The macro level impacts of individual lead sectors have been amplified in Puerto Rico by the very small size of the island's economic and spatial geography. The 'lumpiness of investment' in successive lead sectors (i.e. the great relative weight of investment these sectors have attracted in relation to the island's total capital investment pool) has, in itself, led to an economy-wide structural shift from less productive uses of capital and technology and labour to higher productivity activities. Yet, as Fishlow notes in his analysis and reworking of Rostow's theories, such large relative weights of individual lead sectors can also result in a 'successful industrialization that is *unbalanced* in the sense that a single or limited number of industries, is the source from which an initial acceleration ramifies through the economy - there is a consequent discontinuity in production.'[75]

At first glance, Fishlow's comments appear to be rather tautological: a lead sector creates imbalance in the production structure precisely because it is the leading sector and other sectors are lagging behind. Such dualism between sectors will obviously occur if one sector is attracting a disproportionate share of investment and is more efficiently absorbing capital, technologies, and labour, than other sectors. This dualism will be further compounded if the lead sector is owned by foreigners and its profits by and large flow out of the country. We would argue however, that Fishlow's seemingly simplistic observation invariably leads to a much deeper theoretical question and concern. Why does one sector become a leading sector? What are the distinctive characteristics of an industry that denote a period of high growth, and why does a particular production site seem to energize that growth? It is the synergy between an industry and a host site, which results in explosive production expansion, that concerns us. This synergy not only leads to the emergence and sustained upward trajectory of a specific industry branch, but also interacts with and conditions the economy as a whole. The special characteristics of each lead sector thus conditions the development of the economy in unique ways, just as the environment in which the industry takes root will condition and help shape its production regime.

If we direct these questions and concerns to the Puerto Rico case, we find that the apparel, pharmaceutical and information industries have had widely divergent characteristics, markets and support needs. These industries were able to flourish in Puerto Rico based on available factors of production in the time periods in which they took hold; and, in turn, mobilized and molded those factors of production in ways that led to aggregate shifts in the local economy.

The *apparel industry* had the following key characteristics at the time it took hold in Puerto Rico:
- It was (and still is) subject to frequent cyclical movements.
- Despite this overall environment of instability, there was some differentiation between more stable, lower value, greater volume producers of 'non-style' items such as work clothes, house dresses, etc.; and more unstable, higher value 'styled goods' producers.
- The industry, as a whole, was highly mobile. The capitalization per worker was very low ($2,000 per worker in 1951); and the average apparel firm required only $25,000 in total start-up capital. Thus, firms did not have either high entry or exit barriers.
- The industry was extremely sensitive to labour costs due to its labour intensity.
- The industry was not infrastructure intensive, and did not require much beyond basic water, electrical and shipping services.[76]

Given these industry characteristics, Puerto Rico's large pool of cheap labour; its long tradition of home needlework skills that could be adapted to sewing machinery; its adequate water and electrical systems; and its tax incentives and duty-free imports of basic raw materials from the US were all host country conditions that created the 'right environment' for apparel industry expansion. In turn, industry expansion fuelled overall economic takeoff and provided the following direct and spinoff effects:
- The great majority of garment occupations were semi-skilled machine operators, jobs well suited to the rural work force. This not only raised the income levels of the work force, but provided a crucial entry point into industrial culture.
- The apparel manufacturing sector acted as an incubator for training workers for similar work in other industries. For example, cloth processing workers could shift over to canvas goods and automobile assembly production; sewing machine operators could shift to house furnishings manufacture; shipping and inventory control workers could shift to many other industries. In this way, the Apparel Industry served Puerto Rico as 'an intermediate step on the road to the creation of labour skills.'

Apart from the benefits of the industry to the economy during takeoff, other more negative effects have been:
- The very instability of the industry, and the fact that it has remained the largest employer in manufacturing until today, has contributed to turbulence in the labour market.
- The inability of the industry to adopt new technologies and new management practices has hindered its structural adjustment into a more competitive form. Its decline has been prolonged, not only because of shifting regional and international competitive advantages, but also because of this lack of structural adjustment. This has acted as a drag on overall economic development, a countervailing slowing trend.

The *pharmaceutical industry* represented a diametric opposite to the Apparel Industry, but was not less suited for the island at the time it took hold as the second stage lead sector:

- Unlike the apparel industry, the pharmaceutical industry has been characterized by high returns, high value added, high capital investment costs; and extremely low labour utilization, except in packaging and distribution.
- The industry is a highly technical one, with a high ratio of scientific and engineering personnel in total employment.
- Although companies tend to be fully integrated from raw materials forward to finished products, there is a large intermediate business in the pharmaceutical industry, and companies require a range of specialized inputs into production and an allied core industry (parts fabrication, vial and ampule makers, etc.) to service their needs.

Overall international market demand for pharmaceuticals is extremely stable and recession proof, and lead companies' success are based on patent exclusivity, and product differentiation.[77]

These industry characteristics synergized with a set of special factors in Puerto Rico that included:

- Tax and incentive structures that allowed for profit maximization and capital cost reductions (i.e. subsidized industrial building rents).
- Sufficient supply of technical personnel flowing out of the expanding university system in the 1960s.
- Adequate core industries, particularly a fabrication industry, had been built up in the 1950s and early 1960s.
- Adequate physical and communications infrastructure.

As Chappuis noted,

> 'from the P.R. Government's perspective, the large capital investments involved in pharmaceutical manufacturing created high exit costs and incentives to retain facilities for long periods of time in order to achieve an adequate return on investment, which made the industry a very stable "partner" for industrial promotion efforts.'[78]

Beyond the stability of the industry, additional direct and spinoff effects on national transformation have included: the large scale development of a highly trained local managerial and technical work force; the generation of massive surplus capital flows into the financial and government sectors, leading to an overall reduction in the costs of capital for development; and the creation of an industrial market for intermediate inputs and an array of services (accounting, computer, management, legal, public relations, communications, etc.). Thus, unlike the apparel industry in a previous stage, the pharmaceutical industry established more stable vertical and horizontal linkages, and facilitated the economies of agglomeration and the clustering of technology intensive activities that formed the basis for an aggregate shift upstream to a higher productivity economy. In this sense the industry has extended the spread of advanced technologies economy-wide.

However, the industry's sheer dominance in the industrial economy has also created problems, which include:
- The industry's high degree of external ownership has not lessened over time. Consequently, there is still a large leakage of profits from this sector back to the US mainland, and an aggravation of the GDP/GNP gap.
- The resistant, enclave nature of branch operations in the industry, with its strong intra-corporate backward and forward linkages, has taken a long time to wear down. As noted in our case study of the industry, for example, a critical mass of specialized contract packagers has been a relatively recent phenomenon. The industry's intrinsic enclave characteristic has been most persistent in the area of research. The inability of the island industry to build a research infrastructure for new product development has largely been the result of dependency on headquarter research facilities.

It is not a contradiction to state that, although the industry has profound spread effects economy-wide, direct industrial linkages have taken a long time to materialize. The creation of a vertically integrated local pharmaceutical production chain has taken over thirty years; the creation of an industry research base is still embryonic. This slow formation of direct linkages between the industry and other subsectors has aggravated the dualism within the manufacturing sphere.

In discussing the latest lead sector in the current stage of national technological transformation, the *information sector*, we have to be extremely cautious in defining industry characteristics and effects.

Unlike the two previous lead sectors we have analyzed, the information sector is not a specific branch of industry with readily identifiable, homogeneous characteristics covering a distinct set of firms. Our operating definition of the information sector embraces a diversity of manufacturing and service activities - education, R and D, information machines, information services, media of communications. Each sub-sector operates within its own parameters.

For example, the local telecom supplier industry is characterized by an expanding market and a set of well established competitor firms. The preservation of market share is often based on new product introductions and second and third generations of existing products. The island's higher education industry, on the other hand, is characterized by a declining market due to demographic shifts and the aging of the population, and by a highly stratified supplier profile with a few large public universities and many smaller technical colleges.

With this heterogeneity between sub-sectors, it does not seem fruitful to talk about the information sector as if it had one distinct set of characteristics. Rather, we must focus on the synergy between sub-sectors that results in an expanded critical mass of entrepreneurial, technical and managerial skills in the economy, and a heightened flexibility and market responsiveness in the whole techno-industrial structure.

This information sector embraces subsectors that are mobilizing a whole new range of technological trajectories, from increased automation and just-in-time practices in the computer manufacturing sphere; to strategic telematics networking in the financial services sphere. Yet, the information sector also embraces a set of sub-sectors where technical and organizational change have been more incremental, such as education and public relations. This diversity encourages us to believe that the potential for a wide diffusion of new technologies and high-skills on an inter-sectoral basis is ever present.

From a long term historical perspective, we can say that the apparel lead sector created an embryonic industrial culture and a set of basic manufacturing skills in the work force that had transferability and relevance in building other industries. The pharmaceutical lead sector created a techno-industrial elite of pace setter firms and associated suppliers, and built up a critical mass of technology intensive activities in the economy. The information sector might well represent a more mature phase of growth - a wider and deeper phase - further spreading advanced technologies and skills throughout the economy, and further diversifying the industrial structure.

Thus, we have described the evolution of the industrial structure from one in which a single, unstable industry provided the initial source of acceleration and growth in the economy; to the present 'multipolar' structure in which diverse sources of growth co-exist and interact. This dynamic interactivity enables us to hope that a sharp dualism between foreign owned firms and local firms in the economy might begin to lessen. Such a 'closing of the gap' would have positive impacts on the aggregate growth pattern of the island.

2 Deficiencies in the growth pattern

In the past 40 years, many strengths have been built up in the economy of the island as a consequence of rapid industrialization. The establishment of capital and skill structures; the development of the most advanced high-tech industries; a great rise in output and productivity; and a general increase in the health and welfare of the citizenry have all been outcomes of this massive change. In general, we can say the change of the last 40 years has left the legacy of a diverse set of installed physical technologies and an array of social technology spinoffs.

However, many countervailing weaknesses have also been built up in the economy and these, too, represent the legacy of the frenzied pace of transformation. These weaknesses include an extreme 'openness', as evidenced by the almost complete trade dependency of the island and large capital leakages; and the crowding out and retarded development of local productive capital in an economy with so large a concentration of externally owned industries. Let us examine each of these weaknesses in turn.

3 Extreme economic openness

With the decline in agriculture and the shift to an export oriented high-tech manufacturing economy, Puerto Rico's openness to external trade escalated. Puerto Rico today is one of the most 'open' economies in the world, almost completely dependent on international trade for its continuing survival. *Of all the countries in the WIDER study, Puerto Rico has the highest percentage of foreign trade as a share of GDP.*

High levels of economic integration with the United States has allowed Puerto Rico to mobilize a much greater amount of capital than would have been possible through domestic savings alone, and thereby to considerably accelerate economic development. It has also enabled the island to tap a treasure house of proprietary multinational corporation technology and a vast export market.

On the other hand, integration has meant Puerto Rico cannot establish independent monetary and trade policies. With the exception of excise taxes on imported goods and tollgate taxes on exported capital, Puerto Rico does not have, nor can it effectively develop policy levers for import or export regulation (such as tariffs, quotas and exchange controls). The regulatory membrane separating the local economy from the international economy is thus extremely permeable. Products and capital go in and out of the island with great ease of mobility. Unlike many industrializing countries, Puerto Rico cannot build or protect infant industries as part of a coherent import substitution strategy.

The economy is thus continually being 'swamped' by imports. Today, the island imports over 70 per cent of the value of its foodstuffs and 87 per cent of its non-durable and durable goods purchases. This import swamping has been certainly compounded by the rapid disintegration of agriculture. In 1987 alone over $281 million worth of fish, $213 million of fresh meat; $185 million of wood products, $24 million of potatoes, and $10 million of tomatoes had to be imported.

Puerto Rico, given its trade reliance and its lack of barriers, has been particularly vulnerable to shifts in the overall trade policies of the United States. Since the 1970s, the relaxation of US trade barriers and the reduction of effective rates of protection through successive rounds of the General Agreement on Tariffs and Trade (GATT) have served to further erode the price competitiveness of local products viz-a-viz those from lower labour cost countries - in both home and US markets. For example, Puerto Rico retailers directly import, or re-import from the US, apparel products from low cost labour countries, driving down the domestic market share of local producers. The same is also true in agriculture. Puerto Rico's immediate neighbour, the Dominican Republic, with its large arable land area, extensive production, and low cost surplus labour has cornered the Puerto Rican market for items ranging from pigeon-peas to mangos.

If we move from the imports side of the trade equation to exports, we find *unrestricted capital exports, or leakages, from the economy have also been detrimental*. One measure of the magnitude of such leakages is the GDP/GNP gap. As the manufacturing profile of the island shifted upstream to higher value added technology intensive industries, and as Section 936's direct profit repatriation effects took hold in the mid-1970s, the greater profits generated by leading production sectors flowed more rapidly out of the island to mainland owners. Assuming GDP is the total revenue accruing from all economic activities on the island, while GNP represents only those revenues that actually accrue to local owners, we would therefore expect to see a widening of the GDP/GNP gap over time as more revenues flowed to outside owners. That, in fact, is what happened - the excess of GDP over GNP has grown from 11 per cent in 1973 to 33 per cent in 1986. The following table highlights the fact that Puerto Rico has an unusually severe gap, even when compared to other counties that have embarked upon a similarly 'open' economic development course:

Ratio of GDP to GNP - 1985[79]

Portugal	94.8%
Singapore	100.5%
Greece	100.8%
Italy	100.9%
Spain	101.5%
South Korea	103.7%
Israel	105.1%
Ireland	113.1%
Puerto Rico	132.9%

Along with the great outflow of profits to offshore investors reflected in the GDP/GNP gap, there has also been the increased placement of capital assets owned by Puerto Ricans abroad. Economic integration has meant that island investors have the same ability as mainland investors to invest capital in diverse financial instruments or in business opportunities far afield that command the highest rates of return. The ingrained logic of seeking maximum rates of return on capital has led island residents to place 19 per cent of the $64 billion local reproducible capital pool outside the island (1984). Between 1976 and 1984, these overseas assets rose from 10 per cent to 19 per cent of the total pool of locally owned financial capital and grew at an average annual rate of 35 per cent. Thus, not only US multinationals but local individual and institutional investors have increasingly transferred financial assets off-island.

One major structural result of this heightened total outflow of capital from the island since the mid-1970s has been a decreasing proportion of gross domestic fixed capital formation as a per cent of GNP. Between 1950 and 1970, fixed capital formation rose from 14.6 per cent of GNP to 30 per cent (in constant 1954 dollars), one of the highest rates in the world. By

1980, fixed formation had been halved to 15.1 per cent (in constant 1954 dollars). This dramatic rise and decline in capital formation represented a 'very remarkable phenomena, without parallel in the experience of other countries'.[80]

The worsening of the island's resource balance: the increase in capital outflows and the decline in fixed capital formation has led to a fall-off in overall growth rates. From an average annual growth rate of 7.2 per cent in the decade 1960-70, growth fell sharply to a 2.8 per cent average annual growth rate in the decade 1970-80. Although growth rates and gross domestic fixed investment have picked up in the post-1985 period, they are still well below their historical highs.

Thus, Puerto Rico's economic openness, an outgrowth of its integration into an advanced industrial economy, has had negative as well as positive impacts on local development.

4 The retarded development of local productive capital

Given the extreme openness of the economy, local productive forces on the island are subject to the full brunt of international competitive pressures. There are no assurances that domestic firms will have any innate competitive advantages over off-island firms even in the competition for local markets.

The case of *agriculture* and the swamping of the economy with agricultural imports from lower cost producers illustrates this point succinctly. Even in those agricultural sub-sectors where government has elected to subsidize the costs of local production as a way to maintain home market product price competitiveness, the external competition has been so keen that more and more subsidies are required merely to keep the local price at comparable levels with the international price. For example, in 1988, the failing sugar industry alone received over $100 million to maintain a network of price supports. As a whole, Commonwealth subsidies to agriculture reached $352.2 million in 1988, or the equivalent of $8,802 per employee in the agricultural work force.[81] Despite such enormous subsidies, local agriculture has not been able to either capture significant local market share or to restructure itself though modernization initiatives to be able to compete successfully. There are only a few exceptions: the poultry industry, for example, being one of the only bright spots in the overall sectoral picture.

When we turn to *manufacturing*, we find a similar degeneration of local productive forces. Only an estimated 2 per cent of manufacturing profits and 20 per cent of manufacturing employment accrue to the local sector. This deficiency could well be attributed to the overall thrust of the industrial development initiative since Operation Bootstrap began, which has resulted in uneven technology development in the economy.

During the past three decades, US corporations have brought technology and know-how to Puerto Rico in an impressive migration of manufacturing offshore. Yet the existence of externally owned capital and consumer goods industries does not mean that these industries necessarily serve the needs of the local economy, or that production know-how and technology automatically diffuse to other sectors.

This conclusion is supported by survey research. A 1988 inventory of industrial users of computer numerical control tools in Puerto Rico, conducted by the Governor's Advisory Council on Science and Technology, revealed only nine local firms among the thirty-six firms identified as using CNC tools; and that none of the 136 CNC tools currently in use were deployed within the critical local textile, apparel or furniture sub-sectors. Thus, the revolution in manufacturing production technologies has not yet seemed to touch the sample of firms from Puerto Rico's leading local sectors. Compare this situation to the textile industry on the US mainland which, according to the US Department of Commerce, had over 9,500 CNC machines in use in 1988; or to the US furniture industry, which had 7,000 CNC machines in use. A recent survey of CNC users in the local furniture industry in North Carolina identified over 1,400 CNCs installed in that one state alone.[82]

In the face of fierce economic competition from abroad, local manufacturing industries have simply been unable to effectively absorb new technologies in a technology transfer/modernization process and have been unable to bolster competitive efficiencies. The primary reason for this inability is a lack of adequate fiscal resources. The Economic Development Bank, the Government Development Bank, and commercial lenders are all engaged in portfolio lending to the private sector. These loans, however, are not providing targeted modernization capital for island industries to acquire and install new technologies and management systems to help them remain competitive. The need for loans specifically directed at technology modernization has been consistently affirmed by survey research. A 1978 survey by Clapp and Mayne of 400 small and medium scale local businesses for Fomento revealed that 47 per cent had difficulties in finding capital for upgrading operations. Ten years later, an industrial R and D survey of 108 businesses by the Governor's Advisory Council on Science and Technology reported that 63 per cent of the local respondents rated the creation of a 'Modernization Loan Programme' as a high or very high priority.[83]

The benefits of such targeted loan programmes are revealed by the results of state supported technology modernization programmes around the US. A recent study of such a publicly supported programme found that, in small furniture subcontractors in North Carolina who had undertaken major production technology conversions to CNC tool use, high enough profits were generated to enable 50 per cent of the sample firms to repay mortgages on machinery within seven years, rather than the fifteen years specified in the mortgage contract.[84] But the costs, as well as the benefits of adapting new technologies in small firms can be very high. For example, a small furniture operation employing 25 persons, might need three computer-numerical control tools, software and training to completely modernize production. Although such technology adoption would lower costs of production between 25-30 per cent, the initial outlay of capital would be approximately $300,000. Initial outlays in the Apparel/Textile Industry can also be steep. The installation of a single automated production line, including cutters, stitchers, bonders and boxers can cost $750,000.[85]

Unlike Puerto Rico's 936 manufacturing firms, who are actively involved in a massive modernization effort involving new production technology, the reorganization of work practices, and new telecommunication links to end-markets, local manufacturing firms simply do not have adequate current levels of profitability to support such large investments in the future.

Another problem, intimately related to inadequate profitability, is the deficiency of in-house research resources for new product/process development in the local manufacturing sector. At the firm level, off-shore firms perform significantly more research and development than their local counterparts. In the aforementioned 1986 survey of industrial R and D in Puerto Rico, conducted by the Governor's Advisory Council on Science and Technology, it was found that the average off-shore firm in the sample had a total R and D budget eight times the total R and D budget of the average local firm. Although 25 per cent of local firms in the sample reported some form of R and D, ranging from problem solving engineering research to new product development, the level of effort is still quite low, and is quite poorly funded.

At the same time, there is a lack of publicly supported industrial R and D infrastructure to compensate for these in-firm weaknesses. This lack was clearly recognized by local firms in the industrial survey: only 16.0 per cent of the sample rated government as 'an important source of industrial technology'; and only 7-8 per cent of the sample rated universities as 'an important source of industrial technology.' Within the island's university system, scientific research agendas have not been concerned with industrial applied research. Limited university research funds have traditionally been expended on *basic research* in the life sciences, primarily human health and medicine; in agriculture; biology and environmental sciences; and in physical, chemical and earth sciences. Of the 309 scientific publications by Puerto Rican researchers in 1987, only 8 were in engineering, technology and applied science fields.[86]

The overall result of scarce in-firm research resources in the local sector and a basic research orientation in the university sector has been a lack of commercial development of technologies, products, and processes. Of the 2,509 Small Business Innovation Research Grants awarded by the Federal Government in 1986, Puerto Rico received none.[87] Only 318 patents and 42 trademarks have been registered by island innovators in the past two

decades.[88] Puerto Rico does not compare favourably in this regard with its neighbour:
- In 1978, Puerto Rico registered 19 patents vs. 114 patents registered by Venezuela.
- In 1980, Puerto Rico registered 13 patents vs. 71 for Chile, 174 for Mexico, and 590 for Argentina.[89]

Thus, the problems of low levels of meaningful technology transfer and inadequate applied research and commercialization initiatives are all contributing to the retarded development of the local manufacturing sector, and a serious dualism in the whole manufacturing sphere. The advanced externally owned industries, such as pharmaceutical and electronics, have achieved extraordinary productivity increases over time that have not been shared by lagging, locally owned industries, such as apparel, food processing and furniture. There has been a widening of the technological gap over time, rather than a closing of the gap. This has certainly contributed to an overall intensification of the dualism in the economy.

In conclusion: Puerto Rico's economic and technological transformation, fuelled largely by the import of capital and technology from the US mainland, has produced a positive expansion of the productive base and has generated an array of social technology spinoffs in a short period of time. Yet, at the same time, transformation has also resulted in countervailing weaknesses. While allowing mass inflows of direct investment, extreme openness of the economy has simultaneously led to the swamping of the economy with imports, and the wholesale outflow of profits and capital. As a result, local productive forces have been subjected to both extreme international competition and investment shortfalls due to the migration of capital to the US mainland and elsewhere. Public financial and technical support infrastructures have not substantially eased the plight of local productive sectors, nor effectively compensated for these overall weaknesses in the economy.

Thus, in Puerto Rico today we see a profound dualism - in financial and technological terms - between externally owned modern production sectors and lagging locally owned production sectors. At the macroeconomic level, this dualism expresses itself most dramatically in the GDP/GNP gap, in the huge differential between the profits that are produced and the profits that actually remain on the island. An essential irony of the situation is the presence of high growth and investment rates side-by-side with high unemployment rates. Such contradictory growth has characterized the long period development of Puerto Rico, and has been a unique feature of its modernization. This is the irony alluded to in the independent observations of two economists, separated by 40 years, who arrived at strikingly similar conclusions about Puerto Rico's development experience:

> 'In the race for economic progress, the Island finds itself in an Alice in Wonderland situation where one has to run very fast merely to stay in the same place.' (Harvey Perloff, 1948.)[90]

'It seems like the story of Alice in Wonderland. The more the country moved ... in investment, in employment ... the more it stayed where it was.' (Dr. Surendra Patel, 1988.)[91]

5 The role of the Commonwealth Government in economic and technological transformation

Our analyses of the stages of growth in the transformation process have continuously confirmed the crucial role of the Commonwealth Government in catalysing change. In each successive phase of development - from pre-liftoff right on through economic maturity - the government has acted as pioneer and entrepreneur, providing strategic leadership through its policies and programming. This high-risk, high-impact behaviour has resulted in both spectacular successes and frustrating failures. In either case, the effects of government on the whole economic and social order have been profound, indeed determinant. Let us briefly summarize the critical successes and failures uncovered by our research.

6 The policy successes

Substantial credit for the rapid evolution of the industrial structure must go to the Commonwealth Government which, at every stage, has made important and far reaching strategic decisions.

In the liftoff phase of transformation, the formulation and execution of an export oriented industrialization strategy was the crowning achievement of the government. In his classic text, 'Development Planning' (1965) Meier described this achievement well:

> 'During the post war period, some countries have exhibited the most prodigious spurts of economic development ever recorded. Japan has been most outstanding; Puerto Rico comes very close. In Puerto Rico, the growth rate on a per capita basis ranged from 5 to 9 per cent per year. All income levels in the population benefited, so the growth has been even more balanced than in Japan. The sophistication of Puerto Rico appeared in certain unusual areas of government, such as planning, industrial promotion, tourism, and welfare administration. The government worked out an ingenious set of incentives for attracting entrepreneurial talent. It did its utmost not only to bring in new industry, but to see that high levels of worker productivity were achieved as quickly as possible.'[92]

Meier's comparison of Puerto Rico's liftoff phase with Japan seems particularly appropriate. In the international context of the 1950s, both the governments of Puerto Rico and Japan took brave steps in turning away from the then dominant strategy in newly industrializing countries of short term employment creation and labour intensive industrialization, toward a more competitive long term thrust. The similarities between the Puerto Rican liftoff strategy and that of Japan's were indeed striking:

In both cases, government acted as economic and industrial pioneer.

- Both governments emphasized technology search and transfer policy instruments, and the adoption of advanced technologies in production.

- Both emphasized policies that allowed rapidly rising wages to force the move up-steam in industry.

- In both countries, information and service industries expanded in support of production, and caused a wide diffusion of technical knowledge.

We would assert that, at the most fundamental policy level, the leadership circles of post war Japan and Puerto Rico both shared a 'productionist conviction', and an overriding commitment to industrial development.

The firmness of the 'productionist' ethos showed itself most forcefully in the area of technology choice and the decision on wages. In support of government policy to install advanced technology 'even at the cost of jobs', the Tripartite Wage Commission, which had been created in the early 1950s to govern industrial relations, pursued a policy of allowing wages to rapidly rise, so as to provide an incentive for companies to install labour saving automation equipment.[93] This policy came at a time when Puerto Rico's comparative advantage was clearly in low cost labour. Given the island's large surplus of unemployed workers, the decision on wages and technology was deeply problematic. As the Chief Economist of the Planning Board observed at the time:

> 'In an expanding economy which is diversified and highly industrialized, workers displaced by mechanization in one industry can generally shift (after retraining) to other industries. In Puerto Rico, opportunities for absorbing displaced workers are extremely limited. Therefore, the problem of introducing labour saving devices is serious and complicated.'[94]

Yet, the architects of Operation Bootstrap understood that Puerto Rico's labour cost advantage was ultimately short lived, and that a longer lasting industrialization process would have to be built on more permanent competitive attributes - management and technology. For this reason, the decision to let wages rise and to encourage the technical substitution of labour was a brave and far-sighted approach. Wage policy helped accelerate overall economic evolution and pushed the industrial sector upstream, up the technology and product ladder. Along with its wage policy, the government actively promoted more advanced technology industries through Fomento's Industrial Targeting Programme, which began in 1954 to purposefully recruit off-shore capital intensive electronics, chemicals, plastics, metalworking and petrochemical companies to the island. The government's advocacy for and creation of a 'context for accumulation' - a tax and incentive structure conducive for capital investment and profitability - was a strong additional catalyst for development of technology intensive industry. Finally, the appropriation and modernization of the telecommunications infrastructure was a crucial spur to information sector development.

In our view, then, government's fundamental productionist conviction, which expressed itself in an array of industrial policy areas, was a critical component of success.

7 The policy failures

As a developmental state engaged in continuous negotiation with the largest US multinationals, the Commonwealth Government has often been placed in a precarious, contradictory role. On one hand, the State has sought to steer the economy in ways that promote greater social justice and more balanced overall development; on the other hand, the state has had to continually confront, and often accede to the organized bargaining demands of US multinationals.

Dependency theorists tend to stereotype this process, labelling it as a habitual submission by the State to corporate interests. We have shown repeatedly throughout this thesis that the reality is far more complex, and can be more accurately described as an intricate accommodation between conflicting interest groups in the governance of the economy. To maintain a stable social contract, the Commonwealth Government has had to shape and institutionalize divergent sets of policies to counter the simultaneous demands of its most powerful constituencies.

Thus, policy outputs in the industrial sphere were aimed at appeasing the demands of multinationals for unfettered mobility of capital and low, subsidized costs of operation; while policy outputs in the social sphere were aimed at appeasing the demands of organized labour for secure government employment and increased welfare benefits in the areas of education and health, as partial compensation for wage restraint.

This process of accommodation has built up long term patterns of resource allocation that directly undermine the overall economic and social stability sought by the state. Heightened dualism between offshore and local manufacturing interests; the over concentration of fiscal and human resources in the bureaucratic sector at the expense of more productive sectors - these have been the consequences of skewed decision making by the state and constitute the policy failures to which we now turn.

8 The historical lack of technological infrastructure to support entrepreneurial development

Early in the formulation of Operation Bootstrap, it had been assumed by Fomento strategists that local enterprise would be slow in joining forces with the development programme. This judgement had been based on the following realities of the period:

- Agriculture, as the Island's lead sector at that time, had been largely written off as a source of entrepreneurial talent and economic expansion potential by government planners. In Moscoso's view:

> 'Could we have increased our income through agriculture? If we could, it would have taken many years and many millions of dollars because we had to change the entire agricultural culture after the plantation system. Farmers were notoriously conservative. So were the agricultural workers associations, which were so powerful. The only way to get our local agriculture to be competitive would have been to mechanize it completely and that would have politically destroyed us at the time. So we decided that the way to raise income the fastest was through industrial diversification.'[95]

- Local entrepreneurial talent had been concentrated in small trade and retail businesses, and had focused on traditional 'low volume, high margin' transactions. There did not exist a local industrial bourgeoisie in Puerto Rico at the time of the development campaign. In 1954, Fomento was so desperate to enlist local participation in the Industrialization Campaign and to answer political criticism that its efforts were only geared to 'Americanos', it sent out an entire programme field force, a literal army, to scour the Island for local industrial prospects but 'all too often, came up with nothing.'[96] Fomento wound up settling for a strategy of trying to target and encourage competent local employees to take over ownership of manufacturing plants about to close down, and supplied some technical assistance and small amounts of funds to encourage the takeover process.[97] However, this strategy in itself tended to concentrate local ownership in more marginal, lower technology industries and further marginalized entrepreneurs as the Industrialization Programme unfolded.

These frustrating early experiences with entrepreneurial development had a deep impact on the thinking of Fomento planners and, in turn, the rest of the government's industrial promotion apparatus. The government industrial recruitment strategy would henceforth aim at attracting pioneer US firms and would show little concern or emphasis on stimulating the locally owned manufacturing sub-sector. One measure of this narrow policy thrust was the low volume of technology transfer transactions engineered by Fomento to improve the technical and managerial basis of local manufacturing. *Of the more than 1,200 Fomento promoted manufacturing start-ups since 1967, only seven have been joint ventures with local partners.* Compare this lack of policy emphasis on technology transfer to local sectors with India's strong emphasis on transfer. Out of a total 777 operating external direct investment projects sponsored by Fomento in 1987, there was not a single joint venture between external investors and local entrepreneurs.[98] In the same year, India, with 1,041 operating external direct investment projects, had 285 joint ventures.[99] The chronic failure of

212

government policy to take local production seriously has shown itself in the long period absence of direct technology transfer initiatives and also in the under development of the entire public science and technology support infrastructure. We have already described how the local industrial sector does not generally view government or university as important vehicles for technology information or research and development assistance. This perception has been fed by government's historic reluctance to give policy recognition or fiscal support to explicit science and technology programming. Between the early 1960s and up until 1988, 11 major government/industry/university proposals for science and technology had been made and rejected.

The main reason for a lack of results was the resistance by top decision makers to the need for, and benefits of a coordinated Science and Technology resource mobilization. The net effect of this absence of commitment has been a grossly under developed public Science and Technology infrastructure, which has acted as a constraint on process improvement, new product development, and overall competitive positioning of local industries.

Limited technical work force preparation, and a lack of flexibility and market responsiveness in the entire education/training system has also constrained local production. Up until the present time, this system has not been geared to instilling the specific skills in the work force that the Island's rapid economic evolution has required, creating often serious mismatches between labour's skill profile and the technological needs of industry. Until quite recently, the primary education system has not adequately emphasized science and mathematics education; even today, the total pool of current and newly graduated teachers in science and math is still 35 per cent below the levels presently needed in these subjects.[100]

Deficient preparatory education has resulted in inadequate core skills in the work force. Recent Economic Development Administration surveys of industrial employers revealed huge gaps in work force educational/technical competencies:

- Of the 539 firms surveyed (including 237 local firms), 56 per cent stated that their work force required immediate training/re-training, particularly in areas such as basic manufacturing processes, computers, and communications.
- In the pharmaceutical sector alone, 80 per cent of the firms requested the government provide training assistance in areas such as basics of automation, statistical quality control, good manufacturing practices, and written and oral English.[101]

In our case study of the pharmaceutical industry, we highlighted the active programmes of 'continuous work force retraining' that 936 firms have had to undertake in order to support modernization initiatives. Backed by the extensive capital and technology resources of their corporate parents, they have launched ambitious efforts in this direction. Local firms, on the hand, are far more limited in what they can initiate in the way of retraining work force. Given the lack of adequate publicly supported technical training resources directed at industry needs, local firms are obviously at a disadvantage vis-a-vis 936 firms. This has certainly contributed to the overall widening of the productivity gap between externally owned and local companies.

Finally, a more indirect way in which the uneven development of technological support infrastructure by government has put local firms at a disadvantage is highlighted by the example of waste treatment.

The promotion by Fomento of high-tech companies, and in particular the pharmaceutical industry, has generated high levels of industrial waste. This has severely strained the inadequate treatment resources of the Aqueduct and Sewer Authority, and has forced a federal ban on further industrial hookups to the local sewerage system. While 936 companies have sufficient financial and technological means to install expensive new point-of-production treatment systems, such alternatives are beyond the means of most local firms. A further constraint on local productive capital development has therefore resulted.

As Dr. José Villamil has noted:

> 'One branch of government is promoting technologically sophisticated industrial activities, while the rest of government is not geared to dealing with these high-tech operations. This is not a concern to 936 firms because they have their own support structures and markets. It is a major stumbling block, however, for the development of local industries.'[102]

In all these ways, the lack of a public technological support infrastructure has served to inhibit local productive forces and to reinforce a dualism in the economy.

9 The historical lack of public investment infrastructure to support entrepreneurial development

Yet another critical long term failure of government policy has been in the area of recycling capital surpluses into local productive investment. If successful, a development strategy centred on promoting technology based industries will generate intense capital formation activity, and create large profits and operating surpluses for reinvestment. A critical weakness of Puerto Rico's development strategy has been its historic lack of targeted policies and instruments designed to channel investment surpluses into local, productive enterprises.

Unlike Singapore, for example, Puerto Rico has not had effective policies and instruments in place to mobilize the surplus arising from the operations of externally owned high-tech industries, and to channel it into the local productive sectors. In fact, until very recently, the mechanisms that have been operating have only served to further distort the economy, and to widen the gap between the high technology enclave and local sectors.

Earlier we described how, as a secondary effect of Section 936, a redistributive mechanism was created to try to recycle more 936 company profits back into the island's industrial development. In 1976, Tollgate Tax on a company's total repatriated profits was imposed by the Commonwealth Government in order to capture additional benefits from the presence of a large US corporate production sector. To offset the effects of this tax, a US company could elect another option: compliance with Regulation 3087, which allowed the company to place profits in local banks and brokerage houses at attractive interest rates. For each year the corporate profit pool was left deposited in local banks, the company would benefit from a one per cent reduction in its Tollgate Tax. The intention, of course, was to create a large capital pool that could be used to help establish a portfolio of productive investment projects on the Island. In reality the execution and effects of this Regulation were quite different. The reality was of free flowing loans for consumers from the banking system. The reality was a consumption frenzy that wildly expanded consumer purchases of items such as autos, and gave the total economy 'a false sense of security.' According to the Planning Board, between 1972 and 1982, the outstanding balance on bank credit cards leapt from $70 million to $187.3 million.

It is a common observation among economists in Puerto Rico that this wholesale diversion of 936 funds into expanding the consumption sector was an attempt by the newly elected PNP Governor, Carlos Romero Barceló, to 'pumpprime' the economy and to build a broader constituency for his statehood party. Easy consumer credit became the touchstone of his constituency development strategy, and the regulations developed by his Office of Financial Institutions encouraged banks and lending institutions to utilize 936 funds on deposit to support this strategy.

In Romero's first year in office, his policies on recycling 936 funds-on-deposit into easy consumer credit produced a rise in total consumer debt from $221.2 million (1976), to $522 million (1977). During his full eight years in office, consumer debt rose 453 per cent to over $1 billion.[103]

It is therefore ironic, indeed tragic, that in the midst of a consumption frenzy fed by a glut of 936 funds-on-deposit in the banking system, a 1978 survey of 400 small and medium scale local manufacturers could report that 47 per cent of the firms were having 'great difficulties' in finding capital for upgrading operations.[104]

The Office of Financial Institutions under Governor Hernández Colón has radically changed the regulations regarding the use of 936 funds-on-deposit in local banks. In 1987, Regulation 3582 replaced 3087, and it is now required that 936 corporate profits deposited in local banks, a sum reaching $9.5 billion (1988) be used only for eligible productive activities within local manufacturing and services sectors. All uses of 936 funds for subsidizing consumer loan interest rates or credit card interest rates were disallowed.

By re-targeting the pool of 936 banking system funds for local production upgrading and expansion, this reform could represent a real turning point. The change in legislation is intended to signal a shift in government policy - a new and serious drive to help close the gap between the externally owned high-tech sectors of the economy and the local lagging sectors. This is part of a larger strategy shift we shall now discuss in more detail.

10 Towards the next stage of technological transformation

In the present period, Puerto Rico appears to be moving toward the next stage of development that is being propelled forward by external and internal driving forces, and that is generating a new set of government policy instruments and practices. This next stage might well represent a further transition to a knowledge intensive society, where *innovation, entrepreneurial skills, and local capital formation are emphasized.*

The external driving forces of such a transition are the following:

(1) A *global technological revolution,* which is transforming methods of production and generating waves of new processes and products in sectors as diverse as agriculture and electronics; which is creating new methods of processing and communicating information; and which is causing a *fundamental transition from a 'capital intensive physical resource based economy to a knowledge intensive human resource based economy'.*

This trend to increasing knowledge intensity in the economy is an important determinant of the shape of Puerto Rico's future, especially since the local information sector already constitutes 53.6 per cent of GNP (1987).

(2) Another external driving factor is a *new international economic competitive environment,* with US intermediate and high-technology products facing heightened competition from other OECD countries and from the Four Tigers of the Asian/Pacific Rim. This heightened competition is, in turn, triggering an extremely aggressive response from US state governments. These governments are investing heavily in business and technology development. In 1986 alone, 42 states spent $500 million on Science and Technology initiatives to bolster local competiteveness.[105] Thus, Puerto Rico will be facing intense competition both from abroad and from the US itself in the development and exploitation of new industrial opportunities.

The *internal driving forces* of the next stage of development appear to be the following set of factors:

(1) *Economic imbalances* created by over-dependence on US corporate capital inflows in manufacturing, as evidenced by the current situation where less than two per cent of the profits in manufacturing go to local owners, and only 20 per cent of employment is in local industry.

216

(2) *Unemployment and a need to better utilize the work force*, and to train and retain the work force for occupations currently in high demand or with dynamic growth potential.

(3) *Severe pressures on the Island's ecological carrying capacity.* By the end of the century, Puerto Rico is projected to have 1,240 persons per square mile versus the current 936 persons. These population pressures, as well as the pressures caused by economic activity, will severely strain the limited natural resources of the island and promote the use of factor saving technologies.

In his speech to the Annual Convention of the Chamber of Commerce on June 5, 1987, Governor Rafael Hernández Colón provided a strategic overview on these driving forces, and the role of innovation, entrepreneurial skills, and local capital formation in a next phase of economic advancement:

'Our agenda for the future requires the successful revision of the development strategy for all principal economic sectors. This revision has begun. We are examining our competitive position in each of these sectors. By next year, the Governor's Economic Advisory Council and the Advisory Council on Science and Technology will prepare a strategy and plan of action to increase economic activity and employment.

This strategy will aim to stimulate local business and Puerto Rican capital, and will provide new public and private incentives for these businesses. This strategy will help us confront the future with the most advanced technologies in the process of production, in the development of new products, and in the building of competitiveness in our current products. Our strategy will aim at stimulating excellence and quality in all phases of production, operations, and marketing. The strategy we are preparing will promote innovation, risk taking, and the mobilization of our human resources, and will expand our trade horizons to the Caribbean, Latin America, and Europe.'

Thus, a major rethinking of the development strategy is currently underway, and a new vision of Puerto Rico in the year 2000 is being articulated.

In Science and Technology, a policy thrust is being mobilized that aims to increase the Island's capacity to generate, transfer and utilize technology. To remain competitive in international markets, Puerto Rico will have to develop coordinated policy actions that will promote continuous innovation in its more advanced industries, and expand the range of products and processes based on quality, new technology, and exclusive design. Simultaneously, Puerto Rico must focus on more targeted technology transfer, on acquiring and diffusing technology and management systems that will upgrade its relatively small and unsophisticated local manufacturing industry. This two track approach: commercial innovation in

advanced industrial sectors, and technology transfer to lagging sectors can increase the flexibility, diversity, and
productivity of the whole production base.[106]

A *new generation of instruments and public management practices* has already been put into place to facilitate the implementation of this strategy. They are described below:

a Technology policy instruments

i Governor's Advisory Council on Science and Technology Executive Order 4939 of May 12, 1987, created an Advisory Council on Science and Technology within the Governor's Economic Advisory Council, with the purpose of recommending specific programmes and policies for the new Special Fund, for research and development, and for the transfer of technology. As a result of its recommendations, two new quasi public technology corporations - TROPICO and CTT - were approved by the governor and legislature in 1988. These new corporations were charged with taking a leadership role in technology development in Puerto Rico, and are being allocated $25 million over a five year period.

ii The Corporation for The Technological Development of Tropical Resources (TROPICO) TROPICO's fundamental goal is the deployment and development of new technologies utilizing tropical resources. TROPICO is designed as a worldwide technology search and transfer agent in the area of tropical biotechnology, and has already funded commercial projects in aquaculture, animal embryo transfer, and resource management software systems. In addition to sponsoring commercial demonstration projects, TROPICO also funds near term applied research and has projects underway in animal transgenics and bioinsecticides. TROPICO has an initial funding of 3.2 million dollars per annum; and a Board of Directors composed of the President of the University of Puerto Rico, the Secretaries of Agriculture and Natural Resources, and four members of the private sector with experience in manufacturing and finance.

iii The Corporation for Technological Transformation (CTT) CTT is designed to assist small and medium scale technology oriented businesses through operating both a network of Incubators and an Extension Service for Applications Engineering and Manufacturing Planning. Its Board of Directors is made up of the Economic Development Administration Director and four private sector members with experience in the manufacturing and service industries. CTT has an initial budget of $6 million.

b Technology related financing and tax mechanisms

i Regulation 3582 In 1987, Regulation 3582 was implemented and it is now required that 936 corporate profits deposited in local banks, a sum reaching $9.5 billion (1988) be used only for eligible productive activities within local manufacturing and services sectors. All uses of 936 funds for subsidizing consumer loan interest rates or credit card interest rates were disallowed.

ii The Special Fund for Research and Development The Commonwealth Tax incentives Act of January, 1987 created a Special Fund, based on a surtax of .00075 of sales volume of exempted businesses that derive industrial development income of more than one million dollars. Two thirds of the receipts of this Special Fund are to be used for scientific and technical investigations, and the development of new products and industrial processes.

iii The Capital Investment Fund The Capital Investment Fund Law of October 6, 1987, allows for the creation of independent, privately managed venture capital funds to promote investment in technology based enterprises. The government will allow these venture funds to raise a cumulative total of $50 million a year; and will grant tax credits to individual investors equal to 25 per cent of their investments up to a maximum of $250,000 in the year the investment was made. If the investment fund completely fails or if the investment is lost, the investor will be able to fully deduct the amount of his loss over a five year period. Any gain on the investment receives preferential tax treatment, with the capital gains tax fixed at 10 per cent.

iv R and D tax incentives R and D Tollgate Tax Credits This credit, contained within the revised Tax Incentives Act of 1987, allows corporations holding grants of tax exemption to take tax credits against tollgate taxes of up to 25 per cent of the amount by which R and D expenses incurred by the corporation during the taxable year exceed the annual average of those incurred during the prior three years. The R and D Tax Credit can be used to offset up to five per cent of the tollgate tax.
Industrial R and D Tax Exemptions and Export Service Exemption Section 2 (d) (7) of the Tax Incentive Act of 1987 authorized the governor to issue grants of industrial tax exemption to 'scientific or industrial R and D laboratories', providing exemption from 90 per cent of income and property taxes, and from 60 per cent of the cost of municipal licenses for a term of 10 to 25 years. It is also possible under this section to obtain a 'service industry tax exemption', covering the performance of 'scientific consultation services' for markets outside Puerto Rico.

c University based R and D and training centres

A variety of newly established university based research centres are currently operating. Among them are:

The National Science Foundation's Experimental Programme to Stimulate Competitive Research (EPSCOR) awarded in 1985. Provides $6 million of combined UPR/NSF funds over a five year period to enhance nationally competitive basic research capabilities of 24 researchers in targeted areas, such as genetic engineering and earthquake warning systems. This programme has a management committee composed of local members of the academic, scientific, and industrial community.

The Resource Centre for Science and Engineering Provides funds, research facilities, and instrumentation to faculty members from two and four year colleges in Puerto Rico; and stimulates continuing science and math education for teachers.

The Centre for Advanced Pharmaceutical Manufacturing Technician Training Funded by the Commonwealth Right-to-Work Administration, utilizing over $400,000 in Federal Job Partnership Training Act (JPTA) funds. Administered by a board composed of university and industry representatives, this centre has recently been established to provide cooperative training to pharmaceutical industry work force in areas such as automation technology, statistical quality control, and good manufacturing practices. Through this new generation of policy instruments, an alliance for technological transformation, uniting government, industry, and education, is being forged to meet the challenges that lie ahead. As the global competitive environment intensifies, the leadership of the Island will be under relentless pressure to more efficiently manage its combined portfolio of capital, technology, and skill assets; and to maximize linkage effects within the economy.

In addition to collective challenges, each of the partners in this new alliance will also have to confront and overcome special individual challenges.

Industry faces an ongoing challenge in shifting to a new production and service delivery paradigm, based on quick response to fast changing markets, radical telematics innovations and new, more flexible work practices. The Education/Training System faces the challenge of re-focusing its research and training agendas based on local need, and becoming a more effective catalyst for new products and processes in industry and for heights-skills creation in the economy. Government is required to streamline its operations, and to restructure an archaic patchwork of subsidies, so as to marshal a critical mass of resources for the further development of a new techno-industrial infrastructure.

Only by meeting these individual and collective challenges can Puerto Rico sustain its economic and technological transformation well into the next century.

VII Appendix

TABLE 7.1

CHANGES IN VALUE ADDED PER EMPLOYEE IN MANUFACTURING INDUSTRY; 1952-87
(IN CURRENT PRICES)

			1952				
			Participation of manufacturing in value added (millions	Total employment (thousands	Participation of manufacturing in value added per employee		Change
Branch	ISIC code	SIC code	of dollars)	of persons)	(thousands)	(per cent)	(per cent)
Consumer goods	31-34, 39	-	-	-	-	-	-
Food, beverages and tobacco	31	20-21	94.2	24,930	3,771	2.8	-
Textiles, wearing apparel, leather	32	22-23 Y 31	25.5	20,251	1,284	1.0	-
Wood products and furniture	33	24 Y 25	5.8	3,031	1,980	1.5	-
Paper, printing and publishing	35	26 Y 27	5.2	1,578	3,169	2.4	-
Other a)	39	20,30, 32 Y 39	825.4	7,168	115,095	85.8	-
Intermediate goods	35-36	-	-	-	-	-	-
Chemicals, petro-chemical	35	28	6.3	989	6,067	4.5	-
Non-metallic mineral products	36	-	-	-	-	-	-
Capital goods	37-38	-	-	-	-	-	-
Basic metals	37	-	-	-	-	-	-
Metal products and machinery	38	33,34,35 36,37 Y 38	5.8	2,109	2,845	2.1	
Total manufacturing	3	-	968.2	60,056	134,209	100.0	

			1961				
Consumer goods	31-34, 39	-	-	-	-	-	-
Food, beverages and tobacco	31	20-21	156.4	22,263	7,007	18.7	15.9
Textiles, wearing apparel, leather	32	22-23 Y 31	85.6	33,576	2,561	6.8	5.9
Wood products and furniture	33	24 Y 25	10.0	3,747	2,669	7.1	5.6
Paper, printing and publishing	35	26 Y 27	18.5	2,813	6,754	18	15.7
Other	39	20,30, 32 Y 39	66.7	11,176	5,995	16	-69.8
Intermediate goods	35-36	-	-	-	-	-	-
Chemicals, petro-chemicals	35	28	23.4	4,248	5,414	14.4	9.9
Non-metallic mineral products	36	-	-	-	-	-	-
Capital goods	37-38	-	-	-	-	-	-
Basic metals	37	-	-	-	-	-	-
Metal products and machinery	38	33,34,35 36,37 Y 38	63.8	9,018	7,097	18.9	16.8
Total manufacturing	3		424.4	86,841	37,497	100.0	

table continues ...

TABLE 7.1 (CONTINUED)

			1970				
			Participation of manufacturing in value added (millions of dollars)	Total employment (thousands of persons)	Participation of manufacturing in value added per employee (thousands) (per cent)		Change (per cent)
Branch	ISIC code	SIC code					
Consumer goods	31-34, 39	-	-	-	-	-	-
Food, beverages and tobacco	31	20-21 22-23	372.5	26,700	13,970	21.5	2.8
Textiles, wearing apparel, leather	32	Y 31	256.1	54,032	4,738	7.3	0.5
Wood products and furniture	33	24 Y 25	27.2	5,089	5,306	8.2	1.0
Paper, printing and publishing	35	26 Y 27	36.6	3,950	9,367	14.4	-3.6
Other	39	20,30, 32 Y 39	173.5	16,393	10,614	16.3	0.3
Intermediate goods	35-36	-	-	-	-	-	-
Chemicals, petro-chemical	35	28	121.0	11,854	10,208	15.7	1.3
Non-metallic mineral products	36	-	-	-	-	-	-
Capital goods	37-38	-	-	-	-	-	-
Basic metals	37	-	-	-	-	-	-
Metal products and machinery	38	33,34,35 36,37 Y 38	203.1	18,719	10,845	16.7	-2.3
Total manufacturing	3		1,190.0	136,737	65,047	100.0	

			1980				
Consumer goods	31-34, 39	-	-	-	-	-	-
Food, beverages and tobacco	31	20-21 22-23	934.1	25,472	36,668	16.4	-5.0
Textiles, wearing apparel, leather	32	Y 31	469.4	43,573	10,764	4.8	-2.5
Wood products and furniture	33	24 Y 25	31.9	3,573	8,956	4.0	-4.1
Paper, printing and publishing	35	26 Y 27	92.0	4,701	19,570	8.8	-5.6
Other	39	20,30, 32 Y 39	649.6	22,688	28,650	12.8	-3.5
Intermediate goods	35-36	-	-	-	-	-	-
Chemicals, petro-chemical	35	28	1,647.4	23,332	70,590	31.6	16.0
Non-metallic mineral products	36	-	-	-	-	-	-
Capital goods	37-38	-	-	-	-	-	-
Basic metals	37	-	-	-	-	-	-
Metal products and machinery	38	33,34,35 36,37 Y 38	1,498.1	31,304	47,853	21.5	4.8
Total manufacturing	3		5,322.5	154,643	223,050	100.0	

table continues ...

TABLE 7.1 (CONTINUED)

Branch	ISIC code	SIC code	1987 Participation of manufacturing in value added (millions of dollars)	Total employment (thousands of persons)	Participation of manufacturing in value added per employee (thousands)	(per cent)	Change (per cent)
Consumer goods	31-34, 39	-	-	-	-	-	-
Food, beverages and tobacco	31	20-21 22-23	1,420.7	24,817	57,259	14.9	-1.6
Textiles, wearing apparel, leather	32	Y 31	582.6	37,768	15,436	4.0	-0.8
Wood products and furniture	33	24 Y 25	41.9	3,585	11,715	3.0	-1.0
Paper, printing and publishing	35	26 Y 27	165.7	5,453	30,442	7.9	-0.9
Other	39	20,30, 32 Y 39	543.2	21,544	25,204	6.5	-6.3
Intermediate goods	35-36	-	-	-	-	-	-
Chemicals, petrochemical	35	28	3,899.2	24,751	157,529	40.9	9.3
Non-metallic mineral products	36	-	-	-	-	-	-
Capital goods	37-38	-	-	-	-	-	-
Basic metals	37	-	-	-	-	-	-
Metal products and machinery	38	33, 34, 35 36,37 Y 38	2,735.2	31,261	87,489	22.7	1.3
Total manufacturing	3		9,388.5	149,179	385,075	100.0	

Source: Puerto Rico Planning Board, Area of Economic and Social Planning, Census of Manufacturing Industries, Puerto Rico. Department of Labour, Bureau of Labour Statistics, Employment Statistics Division.

Notes: a)   Other include:

[1] Stone, glass, clay and concrete products.

[2] Other manufacturing: a) Petroleum refining and related products.

b) Rubber and plastic products and miscellaneous manufacture.

TABLE 7.2

CHANGES IN VALUE ADDED PER EMPLOYEE IN SERVICES INDUSTRY: 1952-87
(IN CURRENT PRICES)

Branch	ISIC code	SIC code	Participation of services in value added (millions of dollars)	Total employment (thousands of persons)	Participation of services in value added per employee (thousands)	(per cent)	Change (per cent)
1952							
Trade		50-59	172.1	94.0	1,830	35.4	-
Finance, insurance and real estate		60-67	92.1	4.0	979	18.9	-
Transportation, communication, and other public utilities		40-49	71.5	25.0	766	14.8	-
Services		70-89	57.0	79.0	606	11.7	-
Public administration		91-97	93.2	51.0	989	19.1	-
Total services			485.9	253.0	5,170	100.0	-
1961							
Trade		50-59	354.2	95.0	3,726	31.6	-3.8
Finance, insurance and real estate		60-67	219.8	8.0	2,316	19.6	0.7
Transportation, communication, and other public utilities		40-49	176.8	40.0	1,863	15.8	1.0
Services		70-89	157.9	79.0	1,663	14.1	2.4
Public administration		91-97	211.0	67.0	2,221	18.8	-0.3
Total services			1,119.7	289.0	11,789	100.0	
1970							
Trade		50-59	898.3	128.0	7,016	29.2	-2.4
Finance, insurance and real estate		60-67	613.8	14.0	4,797	20.0	0.3
Transportation, communication, and other public utilities		40-49	439.3	45.0	3,430	14.3	-1.5
Services		70-89	512.2	116.0	4,000	16.7	2.6
Public administration		91-97	609.9	106.0	4,766	19.9	1.0
Total services			3,074.0	409.0	24,008	100.0	

table continues ...

TABLE 7.2 (CONTINUED)

Branch	ISIC code	SIC code	1980 Participation of services in value added (millions of dollars)	Total employment (thousands of persons)	Participation of services in value added per employee (thousands)	(per cent)	Change (per cent)
Trade		50-59	2,277.3	114.0	19,974	27.4	-1.9
Finance, insurance and real estate		60-67	1,598.9	27.0	14,026	19.2	-0.8
Transportation, communication, and other public utilities		40-49	1,234.8	17.0	10,833	14.8	0.6
Services		70-89	1,316.1	84.0	11,544	15.8	-0.8
Public administration		91-97	1,896.3	250.0	16,632	22.8	2.9
Total services			8,323.0	492.0	73,009	100.0	

Branch	ISIC code	SIC code	1987 Participation of services in value added (millions of dollars)	Total employment (thousands of persons)	Participation of services in value added per employee (thousands)	(per cent)	Change (per cent)
Trade		50-59	3,503.0	123.0	28,480	26.4	-0.9
Finance, insurance and real estate		60-67	3,090.6	32.0	25,130	23.3	4.1
Transportation, communication, and other public utilities		40-49	1,872.4	16.0	15,220	14.1	-0.7
Services		70-89	2,154.7	96.0	17,520	16.3	0.5
Public administration		91-97	2,629.4	260.0	21,374	19.8	-2.9
Total services			13,250.0	527.0	107,724	100.0	

Source: Puerto Rico Planning Board, Area of Economic and Social Planning, Bureau of Economic Analyis. Census of Manufacturing Industries, Puerto Rico. Department of Labour, Bureau of Labour Statistics, Employment Statistics Division.

FIGURE 7.1

IMPORTANCE OF SECTION 936 AT THE INTERNATIONAL LEVEL

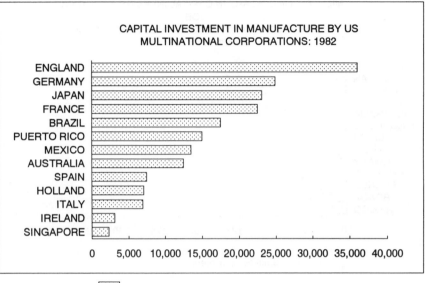

CAPITAL INVESTMENT IN MANUFACTURE BY US
MULTINATIONAL CORPORATIONS: 1982

Millions of dollars in investment.

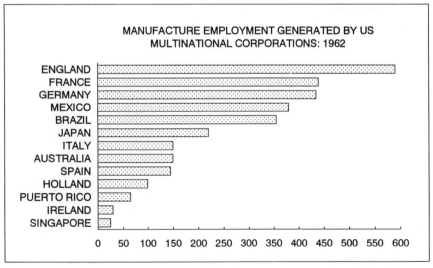

MANUFACTURE EMPLOYMENT GENERATED BY US
MULTINATIONAL CORPORATIONS: 1962

Thousands of jobs.

figure 7.1 continues...

FIGURE 7.1 (CONTINUED)

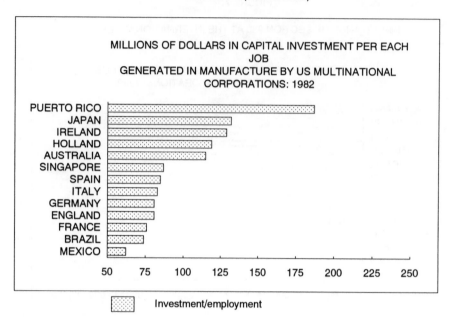

MILLIONS OF DOLLARS IN CAPITAL INVESTMENT PER EACH JOB
GENERATED IN MANUFACTURE BY US MULTINATIONAL
CORPORATIONS: 1982

Investment/employment

Source: Department of Commerce, EUA, Survey of Current Business, December 1985;
Department of Treasurer, EUA, Fifth Annual Report, Possessions Corporations System
of Taxation, 1986.

FIGURE 7.2

EMPLOYMENT OF PRODUCTION WORKERS: 1971-86

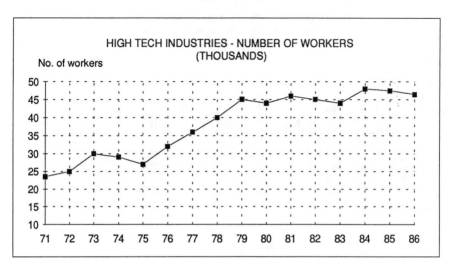

HIGH TECH INDUSTRIES - NUMBER OF WORKERS (THOUSANDS)

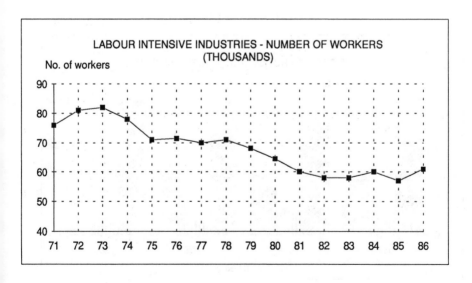

LABOUR INTENSIVE INDUSTRIES - NUMBER OF WORKERS (THOUSANDS)

Source: Puerto Rico Planning Board, 1987.

FIGURE 7.3

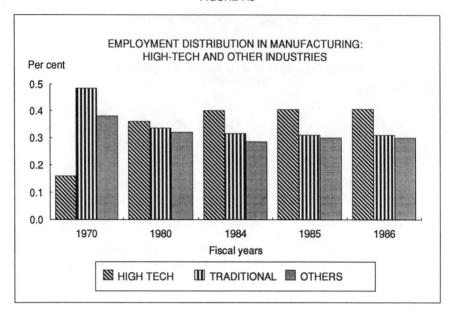

EMPLOYMENT DISTRIBUTION IN MANUFACTURING:
HIGH-TECH AND OTHER INDUSTRIES

FIGURE 7.4

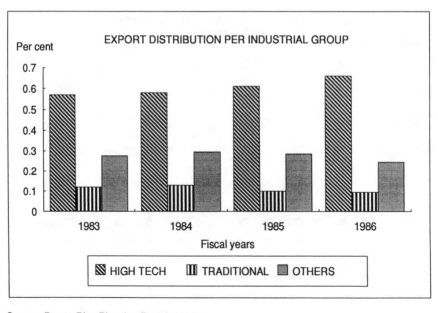

EXPORT DISTRIBUTION PER INDUSTRIAL GROUP

Source: Puerto Rico Planning Board, 1987.

230

FIGURE 7.5

RELATIVE IMPORTANCE OF HIGH-TECH INDUSTRIES
IN NATIONAL INCOME - PUERTO RICO AND UNITED STATES

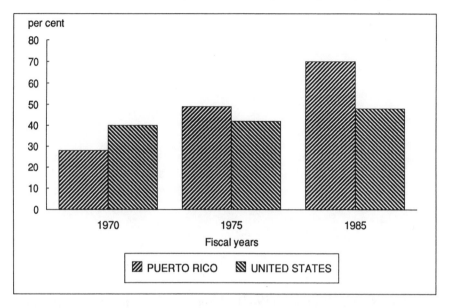

Source: Puerto Rico Planning Board, 1987.

Notes and references

1. Lockwood, William (1987), *Building Dynamic Competitiveness Through Industry: Singapore and Puerto Rico*, Institute of Development Studies, UK, (unpublished dissertation).
2. Government Development Bank (1988), *Puerto Rico's Economic Outlook.*
3. Patel, Surendra (1988), *A Report to the Governor's Economic Advisory Council of Puerto Rico.*
4. IBRD cited by Lockwood, op. cit.
5. Government Development Bank, (1987).
6. Curet, Eliezer (1986), *Puerto Rico: Development by Integration to the US*, Editorial Cultural Press, Río Piedras, Puerto Rico, p. 20.
7. Dietz, James (1986), *Economic History of Puerto Rico*, Princeton University, p. 260.
8. Patel, Surendra, op. cit.
9. Dietz, op. cit. pp. 51-77.
10. Dietz, ibid.
11. Gunther, John (1967), *Inside South America*, Harper and Row, New York, p. 177.
12. Dietz, op. cit.
13. Perloff, Harvey (1950), *Puerto Rico's Economic Future*, University of Chicago Press, pp. 10-40.
14. Perloff, ibid.

15. Dietz, op. cit.
16. School of Public Health, Demographics Section, University of Puerto Rico, 1988.
17. Muñoz Marín, Luis (1929), from his collected writings.
18. Perloff, op. cit.
19. Ross, David (1977), *Island On The Run*, Fomento, p. 20.
20. Ross, ibid. p. 71.
21. Moscoso, Teodoro, from an interview with the author, 1988.
22. Moscoso, ibid.
23. Moscoso (January 1953), *Industrial Development in Puerto Rico*, American Academy of Political and Social Sciences.
24. Perloff, op. cit.
25. Government Development Bank (1987).
26. Moscoso, T. *Industrial Development in Puerto Rico*, op. cit.
27. Muñoz Marín, Luis (1953), Address of the Governor on the occasion of the Puerto Rico Conference sponsored by Gilbert McKay Associates.
28. Muñoz Marín, Luis, from his collected writings.
29. Ross, David op. cit. p. 73.
30. Strassman, Paul (1968), *Technological Change and Economic Development: The Manufacturing Experience of Mexico and Puerto Rico*, Cornell University Press, New York, p. 40.
31. Perloff, op. cit.
32. Puerto Rico Planning Board (1950), *A Master Plan for Industrial Development*.
33. Lockwood, op. cit.
34. Barton, Hugh (1959), *Puerto Rico's Industrialization Program*, Fomento Office of Economic Studies.
35. Patel, S., from discussions with the author.
36. O'Connors, William (23 March 1988), Admiral of the US Navy Command in the Caribbean, quoted in 'Roosevelt Roads: Goliath in the Caribbean', *El Mundo*, p. 4.
37. Lockett, Edward (1964), *The Puerto Rico Problem*, Exposition Press, N.Y.
38. Lockwood, William (1987), *Building Dynamic Competitiveness Through Industry: Singapore and Puerto Rico*, Institute of Development Studies, (unpublished dissertation), p. 31.
39. From an article in a mainland newspaper in the early 1950s. Reported by Taylor, Milton (1957), 'Industrial Tax Exemption in Puerto Rico', University of Wisconsin Press, p. 144.
40. Moscoso, Teodoro (May 1989), Notes from an Interview; and General Accounting Office, *Information for Status Deliberations*, Washington D.C., p. 9b-15.
41. Hernández Colón, Rafael (31 May 1974), 'Section 931 and 232 of the US Internal Revenue Code', a speech to Ways and Means Committee of the US House of Representatives.

42. US Department of Commerce (October 1978), *Economic Study of Puerto Rico's Industrial Sector*, p. 1.12.
43. Ibid., pp. 1-12.
44. Casellas, op. cit., p. 1.
45. *Caribbean Business*, 10 March 1988.
46. Steward, John (1987), *An Analysis of the President's Tax Proposal*, Office of Economic Research, Fomento, p. 3.
47. Steward, ibid., p. 20.
48. Moscoso, T. (1954), Notes from an Interview, and *A Report On the Drug and Pharmaceutical Industry in Puerto Rico*, Office of Economic Studies, Fomento.
49. Fomento (1987), *Database on Companies 1947-1963*.
50. Comanor, William (23 April 1988), *Profitability of the US Pharmaceutical Industry*, a speech to a Fomento Conference on Research and Development.
51. Fomento, (1987), *Database on Companies 1947-1963*.
52. P.R. Treasury Department, 1987.
53. Presentation by Stewart Rose, (April 1988), General Manager of Lederle/Puerto Rico, *R and D in the Pharmaceutical Sector*, Fomento Conference, San Juan.
54. Comanor, W., op. cit.
55. Hill, W. (7 August 1964), Internal Memorandum, Fomento.
56. *Caribbean Business*, (13 August 1987), 'Pharmaceutical Industry Nears Self-Sufficiency.'
57. Ignacio, Rafael (March 1988), 'PRIDCO: Recent Achievements and Projections', *Puerto Rico Business Review*.
58. *Economist*, (6 August 1988), 'Survey of the Caribbean', and 'Annual Report on the Impact of the Caribbean Basin Economic Recovery Act, Second and Third Reports', US International Trade Commission.
59. Westinghouse, Puerto Rico, 1988.
60. *Wall Street Journal*, 29 June 1989, p. 1.
61. Cyert, Richard (ed.) (1987), *Technology and Employment*, National Academy Press, Washington, D.C. p. 44.
62. Chappuis, Bertil (1989), *The Organization of Pharmaceutical Innovation*, MIT thesis (unpublished), p. 52.
63. Machlup, Fritz (1962), *The Production and Distribution of Knowledge In The United States*, Princeton University Press.
64. Rubin Rogers, Michael and Huber Taylor, Mary (1986), *The Knowledge Industry In The United States, 1960-80*, Princeton University Press.
65. Patel, Surendra (1988) *The Future work of Science and Technology in Puerto Rico*, a commissioned report for the Governor's Economic Advisory Council.
66. Accounting Section, UPR Central Administration, Offices of External Resources: Inter-American, Catholic University and Anna Mendez.

67. National Governor's Association (1985), *Programmes for Innovative Technology Research.*
68. 1983-84 United Nations Statistical Yearbook and OECD Science and Technology Indicators no. 2.
69. *Caribbean Business to Business Guide, 1989.*
70. Ibid.
71. Fomento Profile of The Computer and Related Products Industry, 1988.
72. Jussawalla, Meheroo, *The Cost of Thinking: Information Economies of Ten Pacific Counties*, Ablex Publishing Corporation, Norwood, New Jersey, Foreward, p. x.
73. Beniger, James (1986), *The Control Revolution: Technological and Economic Origins of the Information Society*, Harvard University Press, Cambridge, Massachusetts, Preface, p. vii.
74. Perez, Carlotta (1986), 'The New Technologies: An Integrated View', in *La Tercera Revolucion Industrial*, edited by Ominami, C., Grupo Editor Latino-Americano, Buenos Aires, p. 8, and Freeman, Christopher and Perez, Carlotta (1988), 'Structural Crises of Adjustment, Business Cycles, and Investment Behaviour', in *Technical Change and Economic Theory*, edited by G. Dorsi, Pinter Press, London. p. 51-7.
75. Fishlow, Albert (March 1965), 'Empty Economic Stages?', *Economic Journal*, vol. 75, no. 297, pp. 112-6 and 120-5; reprinted in Meier, Gerald (1976), *Leading Issues in Economic Development*, Oxford University Press, pp. 82-9.
76. Perloff, Harvey (January 1952), *Form and Function of Master Planning in Puerto Rico*, a Report to the Governor of Puerto Rico, pp. 17-9.
77. Arthur D. Little Inc. (17 January 1961), *Opportunities in the Chemical Industry in Puerto Rico*, Report to Fomento, pp. 30-5.
78. Chappuis, Bertil (1989), *The Organization of Pharmaceutical Innovations: Implications for Technology Policies in Puerto Rico*, (unpublished dissertation), MSC, MIT, pp. 16-7.
79. International Monetary Fund (1988), cited by Stewart, John, 'Puerto Rico's Options in the Development of Science and Technology', *Puerto Rico Business Review*, vol. 13, no. 4, p. 12.
80. Patel, Surendra, *The Future Work of Science and Technology in Puerto Rico*, op. cit. p. 17.
81. Governor's Economic Advisory Council (1989).
82. North Carolina University, (1987), *CNC Project*, Dept. of Engineering.
83. Governor's Economic Advisory Council (June 1988), *Industry R and D Survey*.
84. Lipp, Joseph (1986), *Implementation Of CNC Technology in Small Businesses*, a study for the National Wood Working Association.
85. Internal documents, Bobbins International, South Carolina.

86. Institute for Scientific Information (ISI), Sci Search Database, 1987, Author's compilation.
87. National Science Foundation (1987), *Annual Report on the SBIR Programme*, Washington, D.C.
88. ISI, op. cit.
89. Author's compilation from Sci Search Database, ISI, ibid.
90. Perloff, Harvey, *The Economic Future of Puerto Rico*, op. cit.
91. Patel, Surendra, *The Future Work of Science and Technology in Puerto Rico*, op. cit.
92. Meier, Richard (1965), *Development Planning*, McGraw Hill, New York, pp. 28-9.
93. Herrera, Reynolds and Gregory cited by W. Morera, Puerto Rico Planning Board.
94. Perloff, op. cit. p. 241.
95. Notes from an interview with Teodoro Moscoso.
96. Ross, David (1973), *Island on the Run*, (unpublished document), p. 228.
97. Moscoso (1988), notes from an interview.
98. Office of Industrial Tax Exemptions, Fomento, 1988.
99. Patel, Surendra (May 1987), *India's Search for Technological Self-Reliance*, IDS.
100. Commonwealth Department of Education, (June 1986), *Assessment of Math, Science, Foreign Languages, and Computer Learning*, p. 27.
101. Fomento (July 1986), *Training Needs of Manufacturing Industries*.
102. Villamil, José, in discussions with the author.
103. Dietz, James op. cit., p. 261.
104. Clapp and Mayne (1978), *A Business Survey for Fomento*.
105. Minnesota Commission on Science and Technology (1987), *A Survey of State Spending on Science and Technology Programes*.
106. Boyson, Sandor (1986), *The Role of Science and Technology in Puerto Rico's Development*, a commissioned report for the Governor's Economic Advisory Council.

Venezuela

Alfonso Cordido J.
Luis Raúl Matos A.

Assisted by
Pedro González, Viviane Millán and
Gabriel Rodríguez

I   Introduction

The study of the technological transformation of a country linked to the analysis of the economy's key variables, as proposed by WIDER methodology, constitutes an excellent platform for any attempted plans in the future. In the case of Venezuela, it was necessary to make several special adjustments. It is a country where, on the one hand, the transformation dynamic has not been linked to the innovation-productivity-economic expansion ratio, but rather to a process through which an income - oil - has determined the dynamics of the goods and services demand; and where, on the other hand, an overvalued money ratio has oriented such a widely diversified demand to the exterior.

From this point of view, it is understandable how the technological capacity procurement takes place in a slow and costly 'learn-by-doing' process at the enterprise level, while state policy is not oriented to change the technological behaviour of enterprises but to promote science and establish institutions unrelated to the productive activity.

As demonstrated in this paper, these attitudes have changed over recent years, while there exists an increasing recognition of the need for planned action if technology favouring the development process is to be mastered.

This work has been subdivided in chapters as indicated by the United Nations University methodology. However, an attempt has been made in each chapter to examine the articulation: scientific base-economy-technology, since we consider that those who emphasize one or another approach fail to see an essential aspect: science and technology represent the qualitative component of economic development, self-evident under the new demands for future development.

Also, in Chapter IV we have stressed the point dealing with the establishment of the 'Gran Mariscal de Ayacucho' Foundation as a financial base for the accelerated formation of human resources. This represents an effort to respond, although lagging behind the times, to the pressure exerted upon the human resources - pressure which emerged in 1974 as a result of the new stage of industrial growth - and upon the capacity of our higher educational centres to give an immediate answer to those demands.

The final consideration put forward in our paper is that today Venezuela has the new structure to make the accelerated breakthrough like Korea or Brazil. But to achieve such a goal, it is necessary to pursue policies capable of provoking change in the technological behaviour of enterprises as well as the expansion of the bases of high-level human resources involved in industry-related problems.

Lastly, we believe that this first attempt at a comprehensive vision must be deepened by examining possible scenarios in case present tendencies remain, so that we could make the corrections in good time.

II   Socio-economic change and technological transformation

1 The socio-political factors

The 'technological transformation' concept implicitly conveys the idea of change from an old technological pattern to a new or modern one which would correspond with the new conditions experienced by a society.

Therefore, in addition to registering a number of indicators as to whether there is a process of technological transformation, it would be convenient to find out the causes - economic, social, political, and others, external and domestic - which condition and determine such a process in a country.

In the case of Venezuela, there is no doubt that the technological transformation process experienced by the society will be a direct effect of the country's entrance into the framework of the world capitalist system division of labour. Such a transformation, which implies a rupture with the ancient rural, simple production patterns, took place during the 1940s; but it has continued as a subordinated transformation in recent years.

Changes started in the middle of this century's second decade, when oil prospecting and exploitation, boosted by international oil capital, provoked a shift from an agro-exporting economy into a mineral-exporting one.

Already by the end of the 1920s, oil had surpassed agricultural production - primarily coffee and cocoa - in the country's export income and in its contribution to the total fiscal income. This became a decisive factor for the promotion of a lengthy but sustained process of changes and transformations to take place later on (see Figures nos. 7.1, 7.2 and 7.3).

The colonial legacy inherited by Venezuela from Spain contained legislation related to state property of mines and subsoil. Thus oil companies came to negotiate oil exploitation concessions with the Venezuelan state, which at that time was embodied in dictator Juan Vicente Gomez, who ruled from 1908 to 1935. Oil companies found their best, most reliable internal ally in the dictator, who enabled them to obtain unparalleled advantages during negotiations at the expense of the Venezuelan nation's interests. Figure no. 7.4 shows the amount of capital investments by oil companies in the years 1912-29, which indicate the extent of profit margins from their activities in this country.

So it was only in the year 1936 that a new economic and socio-political trend began to emerge and to have its first impact on Venezuela's existing technological pattern.

Following the fall of the Gomez dictatorship, the country began a slow process of organizational and popular mobilization: the original nuclei of many of today's political parties were established; the number of guilds and trade unions increased and the first oil-workers' strike took place; a broad sanitary policy was implemented to eradicate endemic diseases which decimated Venezuela's population; a process of greater exchanges and communication among the regions was initiated, which generated over-population around a few urban centres; the first factories emerged - modest in capital, technology, production and hired manpower; the armed forces unified and consolidated to move subsequently towards the professional training of its ranks. All in all, it was the beginning of concern in the accumulation of key human resources for technological development.

Overlying these modifications was always the shadow of oil exploitation, which was practically the only source of revenue necessary for the implementation of such transformations (see Figure no. 7.5). This income, which used to be significant, and increasing sums at the beginning of the oil exploitation, experienced a decrease in growth by the end of the 1920s and during the first half of the 1930s as a consequence of the US economic crisis starting in 1929. The fact is that the United States was the country receiving the largest volume of Venezuela's oil exports. Starting in 1935, the growth rates began to increase, a tendency boosted in 1939 by the start of World War II.

Due to the halt in international trade - excepting trade linked to the war itself - during World War II (1939-45), the vulnerability of Venezuela's economy became apparent; since beyond oil and some mineral ore exports, Venezuela had no other external links. Meanwhile, most manufactured goods - machinery, electric household items, food, clothes and others - which circulated internally, were foreign imports. This situation was encouraged by the high purchasing power of Venezuela's currency, stemming from its overvalued parity vis-à-vis the US dollar (see Figures nos. 7.3, 7.6 and 7.7).

It is essential to stress this historical period in order to understand

Venezuela's backwardness (practically the most backward country in Latin America) at the time of the modernization drive. This gained momentum during the brief three-year period following the fall of General Isais Medina Angarita's government.

The three-year Democratic Action Government (1945-48) gave a clear and unequivocal illustration of the country's transformation and modernization process, which became the predominant feature in the ruling political leadership: democratization of political and civic life; urgency of deep social reforms featuring agrarian reform, health care, struggle against illiteracy and access to education by peasantry and popular sectors, a policy of decent and low-cost housing proportionate to the income level of the population's majority; adoption of a clear, firm and nationalist oil policy aimed at protecting this main export, while designing a plan to invest the oil revenues in an industrialization strategy which would make use of the huge potential of available natural and labour resources, a task assigned to the recently founded 'Corporación Venezolana de Fomento' (1946).

During this constitutional period, the political projects had a clear modernization component permeated by a social content: integration of the peasantry into urban markets, education and health services; likewise, an alliance with small groups of entrepreneurs (essentially in commerce) in order to start a plan for the final assembly of consumer goods with little demand on local technology. This policy orientation defined a certain style of technological development, pursued until 1970, in which the procurement of technological capacity took place mainly in the branch of construction of smaller operations engineering. This stems from the emphasis laid on a policy of public works (access roads, schools and electrification). Both the incipient process of import substitution and the public works policy during this three-year period helped to create the basis for a rapid growth of gross fixed investment all through the 1950s (see Figures nos. 7.8 and 7.9).

The rupture of this incipient democratic experience (1948) plunged Venezuela into a decade of military dictatorship. The nation experienced an enormous regression in political development with the banning of political parties and trade unions, censorship of the press, audio-visual and radio media, the closing down of universities, the prohibition of meetings and freedom of movement, etc. Also, the nationalist policy in the oil sector was discarded, while new concessions in oil exploration and exploitation were granted to foreign companies under conditions which undermined the gains achieved by Venezuela after long conflictive negotiation with international oil capital.

The Perez-Jimenez dictatorship meant a break with the model of political management of Venezuelan society. However, this is not valid in the case of the industrialization process already under way, although admittedly still unfinished and slow in motion. Furthermore, the dictatorship, permeated with a strict modernizing vision, undertook the task of designing new projects, and moved towards the implementation of works aimed at providing the infrastructure without which industrialization was impossible. In addition it undertook the development of some basic industries (steel and petrochemicals).

For the purpose of the present study, we may summarize this first stage by emphasizing that the advent of oil revenues marked the commencement of rapid modernization. This process, although not specifically characterized by industrialization, created the fundamental basis for the subsequent technical-economical transformations started in 1958. This first part of the study can be examined with the socio-historical evolution of the country divided into the following time periods:

First period - Pre-oil producing Venezuela. A brief description of the nature and validity of the agro-exporting economy (coffee and cocoa), the country's social reality and the dominant technological structure.

Second period (1920-58 approx.) - Crisis and rupture of agro-exporting model, and the emergence of oil-based economy. Socio-political crisis and restructuring of Venezuela's society. Technological transformation transition, with emphasis on construction and assembly technology.

2 Scientific-technological factors

The socio-political process described in earlier paragraphs evolved in conjunction with an incipient, non-articulate, scientific-technological context. For this reason, it is considered necessary to emphasize its growth and self-integration with the production system in order to detect or realize its momentum as an influential factor in industrial expansion.

Notwithstanding the predominantly basic university research activity, we may speak of a real interest in the development of science by the ruling groups only when decisions were taken to set up the Venezuelan Scientific Research Institute (IVIC) in 1959, the Councils for Development of Sciences and Humanities at the university levels in 1958, and later the National Council for Technological and Scientific Research (CONICIT) in 1967.

As shown by the facts, this activity was essentially addressed to promote postgraduate research and studies related to medicine and basic sciences.[1] The Institute of Medical Research was established in 1952, and IVNIC (predecessor of IVIC) in 1954. A poll carried out in 1964 showed that 42.9 per cent of researchers devoted themselves to biological sciences, 33.1 per cent to physical sciences and 15.6 per cent to social sciences.

Neither the establishment of such high level centres nor the educational profile predominant within the managerial circles may be considered as a solid basis for a future industrial take-off. This is why, as we shall see later on, when priority was given to basic industrialization starting in 1970, Venezuela was obliged to import qualified manpower, engineering know-how (excepting construction engineering), capital goods and processing technology.

III   Structural changes

1 Period starting 1970

In terms of implementation of a new stage of substitutive industrialization measures and, therefore, reformulation of Venezuela's development model, the year 1974 could perhaps be considered as a proper point of reference bearing in mind the new strategy based on the development of basic industries and on the nationalization of iron and oil.

However, we decided to take 1970 as the starting point of the new substitutive industrialization period because between 1970 and 1974 several important events took place which were essential to the materialization of the subsequent 1974 strategy.

In the first place, it should be said that several officers of the new administration (1969-73), specifically including the Minister of Economic Development, soon declared that it would be necessary to deepen the substitutive industrialization process initiated in 1945-48 and then resumed in the sixties. It was asserted that the simple assembling stage was exhausted and that production of intermediate goods and capital goods would need to be encouraged. For proportionate reasons, the new industrial policy advocated export diversification as a precondition and as a way of obtaining alternative sources of revenue (other than oil). Likewise, it was deemed necessary to regulate foreign investment and the transfer of technology.[2]

This concern appears clearly in the 4th National Plan (IV Plan de la Nación) 1970-74:

'The new development strategy seeks to replace the growth pattern traditionally applied in most Latin American countries with a model which intensifies the relationship with foreign countries and calls for unprecedented efforts in the International Trade sector.'[3]

The industrial strategy adopted by the 4th Plan is even clearer:

'The late sixties marked the beginning of the first stage in the development of Venezuelan industry, and consequently the beginning of a new stage requiring considerable volumes of capital, more comprehensive technologies, skilled manpower, broader markets and further substitution of selected imports. Special emphasis will be placed in the coming years on creating conditions for our concurrence into foreign markets. In effect, steel plants, refineries and energy projects will receive special support as they will be the basis of our future exports.'

Concomitant with the official strategy, there also appeared a strategy of Latin American integration which likewise restated international economic relations.

As a result of this new overall view of the industrialization process, in 1972 the government withdrew from the Tratado de Reciprocidad Comercial (Commercial Reciprocity Treaty), signed with the United States in the late 1930s, and which had restricted most of the country's foreign trade to this bilateral treaty.

Another expression of the diversification of commercial relationships was Venezuela's subscription to the Cartagena Agreement in February, 1973, under which it became a member of the Andean Pact. Among other things, participation in the Andean Pact implied coordinated industrial programming with the other member countries, as well as the lifting of intercontinental duties, establishment of a common external duty and compliance with paragraph 24 of the Cartagena Agreement (December 1970) which provided for 'Common Policies for the Treatment of Foreign Capital regarding Trademarks, Patents, Licenses and Royalties'.[4]

These new policies were not applied as had been planned: on the one hand, the overprotection of local industrial activity (custom duties, import permits) brought about such inefficiency that penetration into foreign markets was precluded. In addition, an overvalued Bolivar (Bs. 4.30/1 U$S) greatly encouraged the importation of goods, technology and capital assets.

Notwithstanding, during this period there were some changes in the sectorial composition of the national gross product: in 1972 the secondary sector took the leading position. Besides, this sector underwent a qualitative recomposition towards the production of consumer durables. This reflected the growth rate of the intermediate industries: chemical, metal mechanics and tools (see Tables 7.10 and 7.11).

In all the attempts to start a new phase in the substitutive industrialization process, it has become apparent that science and technology must be politically dealt with by the state in order to encourage, control and develop the technological and institutional changes necessary for a more autonomous industrialization process and for the development of science and technology.

In addition, this hypothesis is enhanced by the inclusion of a chapter devoted to scientific and technological planning in the 4th National Plan (1970-74); by the creation of the CONICIT in 1969; by the introduction of changes in the higher educational system giving privileges to technological institutes and colleges over universities which, apart from being overcrowded and suffering financial problems, have become divorced from the productive system; etc.

In other words, after 1970 more explicit measures were taken in favour of scientific and technological development as compared to the preceding period. However, these measures were not enough to reverse the secondary effects of the economic policies with respect to the structural nature of the prevailing model of technological development.

During the 1970-74 period, gross fixed investment pursued an upward trend and the manufacturing sector grew accordingly. However, its expansion was based on the massive import of technologies: 12,000 million Bolivars were paid every year on account of royalties and capital goods.

The quinquennium 1974-78 marked a shift in emphasis and rhythm of the industrialization policies (see Table 7.14). This coincided with the coupling of a new socio-political environment to an 'oil boom' which boosted the national income considerably, reaching a 50 per cent increase between 1973 and 1974.

In this way the strategy proposed by the new administration, and clearly expressed in the 5th National Plan (1976-80), appeared at a time when the internal conditions had ripened. The first phase being exhausted, a step forward towards substitutive industrialization could be taken. Other favourable factors included the rise of international oil prices and the stagflation phenomenon in the central economies.

The development strategy was now based on investment in basic industries: refineries, steel, aluminium, metal mechanics, etc. (see Tables 7.15 and 7.17, Gross Fixed Investment Plans and Public Investment provided by the 5th Plan). This step into the second phase of substitution of intermediate and capital goods industries implied large investments in newer, more modern and more complex technologies than those of the previous period, as foreseen in the 5th Plan's balance of payment estimations.

The high level and the high rate of investment, in both the private and the public sector, generated a shortage of specialized labour. In addition, the local scientific and technological communities proved not to be prepared to solve problems posed by design engineering, process adaptation, product innovation and other aspects of the new projects. As a result, the government implemented policies favouring the immigration of specialized workers and professionals.

A careful survey carried out by CONICIT investigated the results of the 5th National Plan:

> 'In terms of the creation and propagation of technological knowledge, the country is not prepared to satisfy the requirements of the plan. The only activity reserved for our scientific and technical system will be the evaluation and selection of the techniques to be imported, but even the agencies in charge of this task lack the necessary technical capacity to handle the volume of imports.'[5]

However, it is undeniable that the impact of new public investments brought about a rapid increase in private investment aimed at satisfying the new demands. Consequently, there was a transformation of the industrial structure (intermediate and capital goods) and an improvement in the country's technological capacity:

a Further development of the metal mechanics sector;

b Development of engineering capacity and accelerated training - by the 'learn while doing it' method - of skilled labour;

c Launching of a special programme to train 30,000 technicians (PGMA: Gran Mariscal de Ayacucho Scholarship Program); and

d In the scientific and technological sector a break was made with the liberal concept of science that still prevailed in the document, *Politica Nacional Relativa A La Investigacion Cientifica Y Tecnologica* (National Policy for Scientific and Technological Research). This document was the basis for the scientific strategy of the 4th National Plan whose underlying concept placed priority on research for its own sake but failed to clearly and explicitly include the technological variable.

The 1st Scientific and Technological Plan also belongs to the 1975-80 period. This first plan clearly favours a two-way relationship between the productive sector and scientific and technological development as the only way of narrowing the gap produced during the first phase of substitutive industrialization, which threatened to become deeper in the second substitution phase of intermediate and capital goods.

Despite some implementation problems, this first plan acted as a factor of convergency between the scientific and technological system and the productive system.

After this 1st Scientific and Technological Plan, it became usual practice to include scientific and technological policies in national plans, in documents such as *Estrategia para el Desarrollo Científico y Tecnológico* (1980) (Strategy for Scientific and Technological Development) and *Versión Preliminar del Segundo Plan de Ciencia y Tecnología* (1981) (Preliminary Version of the Second Scientific and Technological Plan).

To get a complete picture of the deep structural modifications which took place during the 1970s, we should mention the public financing of industries. The number of financial operations and the total amounts

involved increased in the mid-1970s, after the oil boom. We should likewise analyze the role played at that time by institutions such as:[6]
- Corporacion Venezolana de Fomento (1946), which provided funds for the industrial sector during the 1975-79 period, amounting to 971 million Bolivars, excluding endorsements.
- Fondo de Credito Industrial (Foncrei, 1974): during the 1975-79 period, it granted 1,782 million Bolivars in long term credits to grantees within its priority sectors (agricultural food products, capital goods and intermediate industries).
- Corpoindustria (1974) devoted to the promotion and development of small and medium-sized industries, granting loans for 1,785 million Bolivars in the 1975-79 period.
- Fondo de Inversiones de Venezuela (FIV, 1974). By 1980, its net worth amounted to 41,418 million Bolivars, with accumulated earnings of about 13,494.7 million Bolivars. During 1975-79, the FIV invested 12,258 million Bolivars in the industrial sector (aluminium, steel, shipyards, bauxite, aircraft, etc.).
- Banco Industrial de Venezuela (BIV, 1974). In 1982 the bank's net worth was 1,251 million Bolivars.
- Sociedad Financiera Industrial de Venezuela (FIVCA, 1976).
- Fondo de Financiamiento a las Exportaciones (FINEXPO), etc.

During the 1975-79 period, public financing of the industrial sector amounted to 21,442.5 million Bolivars, of which 57.2 per cent were lent by the FIV (mainly to the steel and aluminium industries).

We should also analyze the response of private banks and finance companies to the growth of the industrial sector and its impact on technological development:

In 1980 the commercial banks received deposits of 101,125 million Bolivars, with placements and investments of 69,162 Bolivars. Twenty per cent of its credits benefited the industrial sector.

For their part, the financial companies received about 13,964 million Bolivars and their credit and investment holding amounted to 17,856 million Bolivars, of which 30 per cent were directed towards the industrial sector.

In view of the above we can conclude that there was an important amount of funds directed towards industrial development, particularly from the public sector. Consequently, the fixed net worth of the sector - excluding refinancing - increased from 6,000 million Bolivars in 1971 to 40,000 million Bolivars in 1981.[7]

2 The 1980s

Separation into periods is essential if we want to understand not only the quantitative, but also the qualitative aspects of technological development in Venezuela.

From 1979 on, and at times when once again oil revenues became important and produced a surplus of $19,000 million, the country's fixed gross investment fell drastically from 32,610 million Bolivars in 1978 to 13,105 million Bolivars in 1985, which marks the beginning of a recessive period that has lasted eight years (see Table 7.18).

However, it was necessary to make two adjustments in the rate of exchange (40 per cent and 90 per cent), and this gave new perspectives to three important factors of the whole process of technological development: reorientation of technological demand towards local offer, development of capital goods industries and real prospects for the diversification of non-traditional exports.

The modification of the first factor was evident in the behaviour of some companies, which now sought technologies of local origin. The reduction of imports from $14,000 million to $7,000 million without causing a great shock in the productive process (see Tables 7.19 and 7.20) illustrates the considerable degree of integration of industrial structure achieved by the country.

Capital goods industries were given the most systematic support. Helped by a specific UN-backed project, local offer was set to satisfy a demand of about $100,000 million in the following five year period. Concomitant with this demand, state owned companies, and particularly those in the oil sector, offered a significant technical assistance programme carried out by their technical research centre.

As for exports, in spite of the rise in the export figures of the last few years (see Tables 7.21 and 7.22), we cannot speak of accelerated progress. Furthermore, the value of many of these exports was based on occasional price advantages and not on competitive advantages resulting from technological capacity. However, the actual opening to external markets stimulated the companies to become concerned with productivity and technological development.

According to surveys carried out under the UNIDO-Development Ministry 84 Project, the annual productivity rate of the industrial sector grew 11 per cent between 1971 and 1980 and 4 per cent between 1981 and 1984, especially as a result of the decreased number of workers hired by the sector.

All these elements constitute a sufficiently broad background on which we can analyze the technological transformations that took place after 1980.

During this period the basic industries such as aluminium, iron and steel, as well as refineries, suffered severe financial problems. This led them to give priority to aspects related to managerial productivity and technological capacity. The Consejo Nacional para el Desarrollo de la Industria de Bienes de Capital (CONDIBIECA, Decree 621, 05/22/80) was created to promote the development of capital goods industries, and its main target is the integration of the sector.

IV   Procurement of technological capacity

1 The capital formation process

One of the most important indicators of a country's technological transformation is its capital formation process. In the specific case of Venezuela, this process took place during the last 15 years with numerous fluctuations, but in any case the level was sometimes so high that many authors consider Venezuelan industry to be the most modern in Latin America.

Table 7.23 shows the fluctuation of capital between 1950 and 1985: there is a sharp rise between 1974 and 1978, and after the 1978 peak there is a decline that reaches its lowest point in 1983.

A more detailed analysis of these figures reveals a strong presence of the public sector as compared with the private sector. This public prevalence was the result of a deliberate policy by which the oil surplus was used to steer industrial expansion towards the development of basic industries.

In this way, between 1969 and 1984 the number of companies with state owned interests rose from 52 to 367[8] and, in the particular case of the oil industry which was nationalized in 1974, a Technological Research Institute was immediately created for the sector.

Regardless of the fact that most of these projects were acquired as part of aggregate packages, they contributed to the creation of a considerable local technological capacity, not only by training the engineers and technicians on plant, but also due to the impact created as a result of the generation of small companies closely related to primary investment.

Unfortunately, two essential aspects for any explicit technological policy were left aside: (a) the projects were carried out outside the local scientific and technological infrastructure, and (b) there was no early policy for the promotion of capital goods industries, and so a gap was produced between basic and final consumer goods industries.

An important effect of the change of industrialization model started in 1974 is seen in the composition of export revenues, which has begun to show slow changes (see Table 7.22). This model was based on the development of industries of the basic sector: steel, refineries, aluminium, etc, and the quality of the goods produced by these local industries improved, with the consequent effect on technological capacity.

2 Investments in research, promotion and related activities

The level of investment in science and technology in Venezuela is practically marginal as compared with the country's GNP (see Table 7.24) or with other countries. For example, in 1963 they represented only 0.16 per cent of the GNP, and 0.40 per cent in 1986. However, it is important to make a careful analysis of these figures and of the target of investments in order to detect changes that contribute - even if to a limited extent - to the acquisition of technological capacity.

In the first place, it should be remarked that the most important source of funds is the state. Although only 0.4 per cent of the national budget is allocated to scientific and technical investigation, the funds assigned by the private sector are almost insignificant in terms of their investments. However, over the last few years some big corporations (SIVENSA group, POLAR, CORIMON) have created their own research centres and the Industrial Corporation of Venezuela has created FUNDEI, a foundation, which is intended to encourage a closer relationship between the industrial sector and research (see Table 7.25).

From the point of view of the targets for investment, a rapid growth can be seen in technological development research as compared to basic research.

However, these investments in technological development are scattered and diluted: the average investment per project is 400,000 Bolivars and there is less than one (0.95) investigator per project. This shows that they are mostly individual activities and not comprehensive programmes.

The problem of integration of research with the productive sector is being dealt with by the FINTEC (Fund for Technological Innovations). Although its aid is mostly directed towards high technology projects, e.g. electronics, its availability of funds is so limited that its activities could be considered almost experimental.

Other research centres have been created in the last ten years. Some of them are wholly devoted to industrial and agro-industrial problems (INTEVEP, CIEPE, CICASI, Centro de Investigacion de Ingenieria). Besides, although it cannot be said that there are official policies designed to influence the technological behaviour of the private sector, the ministry in charge of industrial matters has created a Technology Office.

We can conclude that investments in technology have increased over the last 15 years and that there are noticeable efforts to implement specific technological policies, which shows that there is an integration process going on as well as a slow growth of technological infrastructure which could be the basis for the country's technological take-off.

3 Capital investments in human resources

In 1958 Venezuela entered into an accelerated process of technological modernization and transformation, but the country lacked the necessary human resources. It also lacked academic and research institutions capable of training them in suitable numbers and with suitable qualifications.

This meant that the country depended on foreign sources not only for the supply of equipment and machines, but also regarding the technicians, professionals and managers who worked with them.

The economic pattern that had prevailed in Venezuela during the period of agricultural exports implied very low demand for qualified labour by the productive sector. Besides, as the illiteracy of the low-income classes favoured the political predominance of the big land owners, the efforts to eliminate it were limited. Furthermore, the demand of the oil industry's new economic power was for non-specialized workers.

In this way, before 1958 the socio-educational pattern of Venezuela was characterized by high illiteracy, lack of teachers and professors in appropriate numbers and subjects, insufficient physical infrastructure, very reduced funds for research work, a marked elitism in the admission to the existing institutions which were mainly devoted to traditional studies and professions and therefore gave little response to the new demand resulting from technological development.

a The dynamics of education and human resources

Table 7.26 presents the number of students enrolled for each educational level, showing a clear majority of students under primary education: in 1948-54 primary schooling represented 92 per cent of total enrolment, with 9 per cent for secondary schools and only 1 per cent for higher education.

Between 1955 and 1958 the absolute enrolment figures kept their growth rates while moderate changes became apparent in the distribution by levels: primary education made up 88.8 per cent of total enrolment, and there was an increased share of secondary and higher education.

Although these figures are obviously influenced by the country's age structure (with high percentages of the younger age groups), the absolute and relative distribution figures by educational level reflect the short average permanence of primary school children.

Table 7.27 shows secondary school enrolment figures. As can be seen, in 1948-58 the academic branch of secondary education (which prepares students for university) constituted 69 per cent of enrolment at that level, while the remaining 31 per cent was distributed among teachers' training schools and technical schools. However, as compared to the enrolment figures for universities, we can conclude that many secondary students either do not complete their studies and/or do not manage to enter the higher education system.

For example, the distribution of total enrolment for the school year 1958-59 was the following:

	Absolute	%
Primary education	917,000	87.7
Secondary education	111,000	10.6
Higher education	17,000	1.6
Total	1,445,000	100.0

In the same school period, the secondary education figures were:

	Absolute	%
High school	71,000	64.2
Teacher training	14,000	12.9
Technical school	25,000	22.9
Total	110,000	100.0

During the 1936-50 period the average expenditure in education was 6.7 per cent of total national expenditures, with budgets of 29, 72, 89, 126 and 127 million Bolivars respectively.

On the other hand, the average share of education in total national expenditure for the period 1950-58 was only 5.4 per cent.

The following table shows the distribution of resources and the enrolment figures of the educational system during the process of technological transformation produced by substitutive industrialization.

There was an obvious need to produce rapid changes in the training of human resources, and this was reflected in increased budgets for education from 1958 on.

Years	Expended on education: (million Bolivars)	% of the total fiscal expenditure
1957-58	196	3.6
1958-59	389	6.2
1959-60	456	7.0
1960-61	532	7.9
1961 (Jul.-Dec.)	289	8.5
1962	576	9.2
1963	674	10.2
1964	745	10.5
1965	878	11.9
1966	966	12.2
1967	1,096	12.7
1968	1,190	12.0
1969	1,350	12.7
1970	1,653	15.4
1971	1,875	15.7
1972	2,250	17.5
1973	2,805	18.7
1974	3,540	8.8
1975	4,694	11.6
1976	5,407	13.7
1977	7,068	13.6
1978	7,448	14.9

Source: B.C.V. and Memorias Min. Hacienda.

These growing amounts allocated to education will be reflected not only in the total number of enroled students but also in a change in the distribution among the different educational levels. For example, the relative share of primary education shows a reduction as a consequence of a longer permanence at school encouraged by the creation of new secondary schools, colleges and universities (see Tables 7.26 and 7.27).

In the case of secondary education, although schools that prepare students for universities still prevail, it is worth mentioning that technical education is undergoing a slow but steady growth, having reached an average 30 per cent of the total number of students enrolled during 1963-72.

The creation and reopening of a large number of higher education institutions account, to a large extent, for the larger share of higher education in total enrolment figures.

In 1958 there were six higher education institutions in Venezuela: four of them were national or state owned (one of which was closed), and two were private. Out of this total, three were located in Caracas and the rest in different parts of the country. The Instituto Pedagógico de Caracas (teacher training) should be added.

The University of Carabobo was opened in 1958 (21 March) and the University of Oriente was created in the same year with a new experimental design and an organizational structure supported by regional institutions; the Instituto Pedagógico de Barquisimeto was created the same year (6 November).

Three new universities were founded during the sixties, two of them state universities: Centro-Occidental Lisandro Alvarado University on 22 September 1962, and Simón Bolívar University on 18 June 1967; and one private university: the Metropolitan University, on 24 February 1965; the Instituto Politécnico was opened on 22 September 1962 in Barquisimeto.

However, the demand raised by an expanding productive structure outnumbered the students who graduated from technical institutes and universities. This fact, along with the high level and diversity of the demand, led the companies, many of them foreign, to import qualified labour.

It should be stated that in 1961, when the process of substitutive industrialization had just started, the percentage of foreign professionals and technicians, as compared to Venezuelan professionals, reached 54.6 per cent of engineers, 31.4 per cent of chemists, 13,5 per cent of teachers in general, 22.6 per cent of accountants, 36.1 per cent of economists and professionals in economics, 31.8 per cent of managers, etc.[9]

As the first stage of the process of substitutive industrialization became consolidated and the plants began to operate normally, the requirement for foreign technicians and professionals decreased. The growing number of graduates from universities and intermediate technical education centres was reflected in a reduced participation in the market of foreign professionals and technicians in 1971. However, even then, figures show that more than 30 per cent of professionals in the engineering field were foreign; 20 per cent was recorded as 'not nationalized foreigners' and their share in the administrative and management positions was also strong.[10]

Once the 'easy industrialization' stage had come to an end, Venezuela was faced with the necessity of progressing towards a substitution of intermediate and capital goods and once more it became necessary to import specialized human resources.

The immigration of professionals and technicians into the country during the period increased by 135 per cent in relative terms, i.e. twice as much as the relative number of immigrants entering the country during the same period. This determined a higher growth rate of foreign professionals and technicians than the growth rate of professionals graduated from Venezuelan universities, and the result was a hike from 1.5 per cent to 11.9 per cent of foreign participation in the total number of professionals entering the work market.

The shortage of professionals in 1970 was estimated by the above mentioned study at 1,200 to 2,000, the most critical areas being that of

256

engineers, estimated at 450 to 670, followed by managers, estimated at approximately 315 to 550 per year.

Similar investigations[11] concluded that the educational composition of the employed population for the period extending between 1971 and 1974 showed a high concentration of individuals at the lower levels of the educational profile.

Educational level	% of employment
No schooling/illiterate	23.0
Primary education	53.0
Secondary education	13.7
Commercial training	3.6
Higher education (G and non-G)	3.5
Technical and teachers' training	2.4

However, the trend of the market is to demand a work force with increasingly higher education levels, as is shown by the inter-annual growth rate of 10.3 per cent reached by the hiring of workers at professional level (the highest recorded during the period), followed by 6.9 per cent technical school graduates and teachers.

In view of the challenge posed by the necessity of training human resources to satisfy the demand for the diversity of skills required by the process of technological transformation, the government set a policy of creating new higher education and technological institutions in order to increase the number of local technicians and professionals.

Thus, the 1960s witnessed the foundation of 8 universities (6 state and 2 private), 5 university level teacher training institutes (4 state and 1 private), 3 polytechnic university institutes (all of them state), 27 technological and professional institutes (14 of which were state sponsored and 13 private).

The impact of this policy was soon reflected in student enrolment. For the school period 1969-70 the number of university students was 81,000 (3.5 per cent of total enrolment), whereas for the school period 1975-76 higher education enroled 222,000 students, almost three times as much as the previous figure, representing 6.8 per cent of the total number of students.

Between 1980 and 1985, 7 new universities were created - 3 national ones and 4 private, and 14 new university institutes - 5 of which were national. A new private university college was also established.

To summarize, at the beginning of the sixties there were only 8 higher education institutes - 6 of which were state owned and 2 private. By the end of 1985 there was a total of 90 higher education institutes, not including military academies. It is important to note that 42 per cent of the said institutions are private and 52 per cent of them are public.

b The 'Gran Mariscal de Ayacucho' Foundation

In 1973 the Arab countries agreed to establish an oil embargo in order to press the European countries, set a pro-Arab policy, and punish the United States for supporting Israel in the Arab-Israeli war. As a direct result of this measure, oil prices increased considerably and the national revenue in Venezuela rose from $1,406 million in 1970 to $10,000 million in 1975.

In view of the impossibility of the local economic and financial markets to absorb such a large amount of money productively and efficiently and in view of the menace of an inflationary outbreak, several financial policy strategies were designed to allocate such resources. These included the creation of the Fondo de Inversiones de Venezuela (Venezuelan Investment Fund), as well as strategies aimed at capital investment and training of human resources.

In the framework of the latter strategy, the Fundación Gran Mariscal de Ayacucho (Gran Mariscal de Ayacucho Foundation) was created by Decree no. 1000 on 1 July 1975 under the Oficina Central de Coordinación y Planificación de la Presidencia de la República (Central Coordination and Planning Department, CORDIPLAN) in order to institutionalize the Programa de Becas Gran Mariscal de Ayacucho (Gran Mariscal de Ayacucho Scholarship Program) created by Decree no. 132 of 4 June 1974.

The Decree provides in its first paragraph that

'the object of the Foundation will be to contribute to the training of human resources in those technical and scientific areas considered as priorities by the national economic development plans as well as to finance, direct and evaluate the training of human resources required for the implementation of the investment projects contained in the National Plan. In order to achieve this aim the Foundation will seek cooperation with the corresponding public administration agencies, the entities of decentralized administration and state owned companies in charge of the projects.'[12]

During the one year period between 1 July 1974 and 31 August 1975, the Scholarships Programme sponsored a total of 5,688 students in higher education courses, 3,747 (65.8 per cent) abroad and 1,941 (34.12 per cent) in Venezuela. Most of the students were enroled in American universities which received 2,286, or 40.19 per cent of the total.

With respect to the educational level of the grantees, 3.62 per cent were elementary technicians, 6.65 per cent intermediate technicians, 2.90 per cent advanced technicians, 76.93 per cent were college graduates and 9.90 per cent followed specialized studies.

As for the areas of study, grantees were distributed as follows:[13]

Areas of study	Total number of grantees
Hydrocarbons	1,124
Mining	482
Agriculture and farming	1,064
Teaching and investigation	106
Aeronautics	94
Naval	104
Supportive techniques	2,473
Administration	176
Sectorial programmes	65
Total	5,688

It should be pointed out that the first scholarships were granted by intuition and common sense rather than on the basis of any serious or accurate studies about the supply and demand in the labour market. The result of this was that many grantees returned to their country and could not find a position that matched their studies. In order to deal with this shortcoming, the Foundation decided to carry out a survey of the supply and demand of professionals and technicians in Venezuela which was conducted by the Centre for Policy Alternatives of the Massachusetts Institute of Technology between 1975 and 1977. This study led to the determination of priority areas of study and to the consequent financing by the Fundación Gran Mariscal de Ayacucho.

During the 1974-83 period (as of 30 September) the Foundation had granted a total of 32,833 scholarships classified as follows:

Academic level	Number of scholarships
Technical	7,185
Bachelor	17,350
Postgraduate	8,298

The fields of study were the following:

Fields of study	Number of scholarships
Elementary	1,872
Engineering and technology	16,757
Agriculture and maritime	3,376
Health	1,715
Education	2,307

It is worth noting that the above table shows that 51 per cent of the total number of scholarships granted between 1974 and 1983 were for studies in the engineering and technology field.

V Management of the technological transformation process

In this chapter we shall deal with the explicit and implicit technological policies sustained by the Venezuelan government as a basis for the process of technological transformation. We will make special reference to the industrial sector in order to try to understand the technological changes that took place in the country and to analyze the impact of this process on the scientific and technological sector as well as on society as a whole.

We should stress that it is possible to understand the accelerated process of technological transformation started in Venezuela in 1958 only if we bear in mind that such a process was determined by the growing fiscal revenue originated in oil exploitation.

Thus, the fact that the process of technological transformation in Venezuela was pushed ahead by a new reality makes it very specific. Apart from the historical context, it differs from the processes that took place in the leading European economies of the industrial revolution in the XVIII century in that the latter operated in a free market. In those countries, the industrialization process appeared as a necessary consequence of an evolution in their productive and social structures and a key element was the initiative and risk-assuming capacity of the incipient entrepreneurship.

The transformation process in Latin American countries has taken place at a time when international trade is highly monopolized. As a consequence of this monopolization, free competition is constrained and the new international distribution of work is based on scientific and technological advantages which destined some countries to be producers of raw materials while others produce manufactured goods. As can be seen in their balance of payments, the producers of raw materials are thus placed in a clearly disadvantageous position, precluding national saving and productive investment that might have made possible an autonomous industrial transformation.

What was the policy adopted by the government to manage this technological transformation? This question should be answered by dividing the industrialization process into two different periods as discussed above: (1) from 1958 to 1970, and (2) from 1970 onwards.

1 From 1958 to 1970

The first period coincides with the so called 'easy stage' characterized by the substitution of final product imports. There was great expectation regarding growth of the industrial product and creation of jobs as a consequence of the opening of many factories.

It should be added that 4,171 new factories were opened between 1961 and 1966 which represented 65.16 per cent of the 6,401 existing during 1961; similarly, another 2,197 new factories were created between 1967 and 1971 (which means that the factories opened between 1961 and 1971 amounted to 6,368, representing 74,1 per cent of the existing total of 8,598 that year).

Between 1950 and 1977 the non-oil GNP rate was about seven per cent. An important role was played by the behaviour of the industrial sector, accompanied by an inflation rate which averaged 1.7 per cent between 1950 and 1973.

Domestic consumption of imported goods per household was reduced from 34.7 per cent in 1957 to 12.9 per cent in 1964.

The abovementioned data prove the determination of the government in 1958 to permit the access of the industrial sector to the petro-dollars as a way of supporting and accelerating the substitution of imports and its impact on society.

Going beyond the decision to encourage substitutive industrialization and focusing on the problem of technological development, there is a hypothesis that the official policy was *laissez faire*. This hypothesis holds that no systematic efforts were made to provide the country with the technical and scientific capacity or the managerial resources required for relative control and an autonomous development in its industrialization process.

Private companies, encouraged by high protectionism and by the existence of a captive market purchased turn-key plants without making any efforts to improve their technological capacity. Moreover, the type of technology used by the substitutive industrial system, the conditions under which it is acquired, and the maintenance it requires are all part of the

261

'technological package' provided by the supplier. This reduces the demand for technicians and for the skilled labour needed to operate the system.

During the first stage of the substitutive industrialization process, the role played by the Instituto Nacional de Cooperación Educativa (INCE) (National Institute for Educational Cooperation) was remarkable. This Institute was created in 1959 with the object of training labour for the existing industrial demand. This implied training workers in certain skills necessary to work in the new factories and plants. Relatively speaking, the role played by the Institute was more important than that played by some universities or other higher education centres, such as secondary schools, which remained apart from the process of technological procurement.

Although the data and analysis provided so far have been very useful for understanding the framework of the different elements of our hypothesis, there is another set of data that goes straight into the matter.

In terms of management of the 'technological transformation process' we could speak of explicit and implicit actions.[14] Explicit actions are those instruments, mechanisms or policies designed for or directed toward the regulation of technological development, whereas implicit instruments, though not originally created for the said effect, exert an influence on the course of scientific and technological development.

The CONICIT investigation mentioned above proves how some implicit instruments have turned out to be more efficient than technological policies in orienting the technological behaviour of companies.

Among the so called 'implicit instruments' we could mention tariffs, export permits and duty free import permits as basic measures aimed at protecting local industry by precluding imports of goods produced locally and facilitating the importation of goods not produced locally which are necessary for the development of the national industry.

Given the flexibility of the instruments and their discretional application along with the fact that most of the fiscal revenue has historically come from oil and not from custom duties, together with the high purchase power of the overrated currency, these instruments played a decisive role in the expansion and diversification of industrial production, though their application in fact encouraged the massive importation of technologies and capital goods.

The facility with which companies could import technology in packages, added to the absence of political measures encouraging them to take advantage of the opportunity to develop local capacity, explains the inefficient technological progress of the country in the frame of massive investments in the industrial sector.

2 1970 onwards

The main conclusion in terms of a macroeconomic analysis of the management of the technological transformation process is that it was excessively based on the abundance of resources: the government did not establish sufficient qualitative conditions for subsidies and led a highly protectionist policy which, having created a captive market, did not force the private sector companies to make efforts to improve their productivity.

In view of the abundance of financial resources originating in the rising 1974 oil prices, it was rightfully decided to develop basic industries. However, the strong management requirements of such a programme were not carefully evaluated. In 1980, when fiscal revenue leapt ahead once again, the 1974 experience was not taken into consideration and no or very few resources were allocated to deal with the technological bottlenecks produced during the first oil boom.

To conclude, it could be said that in Venezuela neither the financial policy nor the fiscal policy or the so called exportation stimuli have focused on changing the technological behaviour of the industrial sector. Furthermore, the actions taken by the state in this field are of an institutional character - such as the creation of research centres - rather than measures designed to change the course of demand or to integrate technology into an industrial policy that could encourage industries to run the risks and make efforts towards technological innovation.

VI   Conclusion

From the above global analysis, it can be concluded that the technological capacity achieved by Venezuela as a result of sometimes spontaneous and sometimes managed efforts, is not sufficient to guarantee the competitive capacity required for entering foreign markets.

The new challenge in the present stage is to coordinate isolated efforts made by some sectors and thus create the synergy implied in the concept of technological capacity.

The main difficulty lies in the fact that these changes must be made at a time when financial resources are no longer abundant as was the case in the 1970s, and when one third of the annual revenues originated in the oil sector is allocated to the payment of the country's 35,000 million Bolivars debt. The country now faces the dilemma of whether to take advantage of the infrastructure investment made during times of prosperity and start a new process of industrial development or else miss the possibility of catching up with the future.

In any case, whichever option is decided upon, the technological question remains. On the other hand, it is essential to review the quantitative effort that has been made in the field of education: the new policies must lay further emphasis on qualitative aspects. The gap existing between the quality of public and private education, which has a higher level, must be reversed in order to reach a technological capacity in line with future needs. The poor correlation between economic and technological growth was due to the failure of technological policies to counteract the side effects of the economic policy.

The financial system has also failed to act in liaison between savers and investors, for which reason this aspect needs to be dealt with efficiently. Private banks must participate in the financing of the adjustment and generation of local technologies. If the banks are to play a new role, they have got to be modernized by changing applicable regulations, under which venture capital is difficult to obtain.

Four actions are of utmost importance in this matter:

a) Legislation providing for the establishment of companies capable of financing risk capital.

b) Large scale launching of the Fondo de la Innovación Tecnológica (Fund for Technology Innovation).

c) Increased investments in the adjustment of the educational system to the new qualitative demands.

d) Programmes for multinational cooperation.

As a result of the technological transformation undergone by the country, new and more complex problems have come about among which we should mention: on the one hand, the capacity to manage the process in a suitable manner and, on the other, the possibility to deal with the new social problems that have appeared, such as high urban concentration, marginality, housing shortage and malnutrition.

For example, it should be mentioned that five million housing units will be required in the next 15 years, six million children will suffer from malnutrition and disease, and seven million new jobs will have to be created at a time when the new technological pattern is characterized by reduced employment of manpower.

The challenge now is how to solve the false dilemma between accelerated industrialization and technological expertise. But the macroeconomic challenge is to redirect the production of goods and services towards the weakest sectors of the population under a new and efficient definition of priorities.

VII Tables and figures

TABLE 7.1

MAIN AGRICULTURAL EXPORTS: 1903/04-1927/28
(MILLIONS OF BOLIVARS)

	1903/04	1912/13	1918/19	1920/21	1927/28
Coffee	37.4	86.9	115.1	45.4	88.9
Cocoa	16.7	20.8	27.4	17.9	26.1
Sarapia (Dipteryx Odorata)	0.0	2.7	0.2	0.7	0.2
Rubber	0.2	2.3	0.4	0.1	-
Cattle	8.5	1.2	1.7	4.5	2.8
Hides	5.6	6.9	1.3	1.8	6.5
Sugar	-	-	5.0	7.3	3.9
Papelón	-	0.2	1.0	2.4	-
Balata	3.1	-	5.9	4.1	1.3
Total	71.5	121.0	158.0	84.2	129.7

Source: Velos, Ramon, 'Economía y Finanzas de Venezuela, desde 1830 hasta 1944', Impresores Unidos, Caracas, Venezuela.

TABLE 7.2

OIL EXPORT, VOLUME AND VALUE: 1920/21-1929/30

	Volume	Value
1920/21	101.0	5.0
1921/22	244.3	12.6
1922/23	377.8	18.9
1923/24	717.8	35.9
1924/25	2,015.3	101.0
1925/26	3,886.5	191.8
1926/27	6,126.8	259.1
1927/28	11,559.8	359.1
1928/29	17,520.2	545.7
1929/30	20,112.0	619.9

Source: Velos, Ramon, ibid.

TABLE 7.3

VENEZUELA'S IMPORTS AND EXPORTS: 1920-42
(THOUSANDS OF BOLIVARS)

Year	Imports	Exports	Oil exports
1920/21	194,002.0	117,724.0	5,000.0
1921/22	89,392.4	148,280.7	12,577.4
1922/23	125,636.1	144,497.7	18,945.4
1923/24	181,277.9	183,304.3	35,932.5
1924/25	266,409.5	275,907.8	101,020.4
1925/26	343,088.8	363,014.3	191,837.5
1926/27	433,258.3	411,092.8	259,147.4
1927/28	358,458.3	508,306.2	359,079.4
1928/29	457,354.3	732,382.8	545,652.4
1929/30	401,323.4	742,832.8	619,938.0
1930/31	290,508.4	722,379.5	588,004.3
1931/32	169,363.4	659,428.0	571,892.5
1932/33	150,540.0	584,890.5	504,747.1
1933/34	126,827.3	637,136.1	572,432.4
1934/35	225,344.3	636,323.0	630,696.2
1935/36	186,923.6	747,703.4	676,769.1
1936/37	277,745.5	788,276.6	684,221.4
1937/38	308,336.7	929,773.5	872,366.7
1938/39	331,339.8	938,609.1	888,326.4
1939/40	252,673.3	771,604.7	809,321.5
1940/41	299,194.2	936,773.9	867,009.5
1941/42	301,025.5	737,647.1	661,919.5

Source: Velos, Ramon, 'Economía y Finanzas de Venezuela, desde 1830 hasta 1944', Impresores Unidos, Caracas, Venezuela.

TABLE 7.4

DUTCH-BRITISH AND US CAPITAL INVESTMENT IN VENEZUELA:
1912 AND 1929

	US investment US $	Dutch-British investment US $	Total US $
1912	3,000,000	41,350,000	44,350,000
1929	161,565,000	92,141,000	253,706,000

Source: Figueroa, Federico Brito (1974), 'Historia Económica y Social de Venezuela' vol. 2, 2nd edition, p. 434, Edic. Biblioteca UCV, Caracas.

TABLE 7.5

OIL INCOME AND ITS SHARE IN THE REGULAR INCOME TOTALS

Year	Oil income tax (millions of Bolivars)	Fuel income (millions of Bolivars)	Total oil income (millions of Bolivars)	Total regular income (millions of Bolivars)	Oil/regular incomes Ratio
1944	19	250	269	369	72.9
1945	43	267	310	572	54.2
1946	143	273	416	843	49.3
1947	165	435	600	1,262	47.5
1948	297	720	1,017	1,776	57.3
1949	479	600	1,079	1,976	54.6
1950	273	603	876	1,907	45.9
1951	394	860	1,254	2,263	55.4
1952	525	813	1,338	2,399	55.8
1953	594	824	1,418	2,532	56.0
1954	507	901	1,408	2,632	53.5
1955	585	1,034	1,619	2,970	54.5
1956	712	1,219	1,931	3,397	56.8
1957	931	1,539	2,470	4,263	57.9
1958	1,198	1,361	2,559	4,705	54.4
1959	1,465	1,637	3,102	5,441	57.0
1960	1,260	1,631	2,891	4,967	58.2
1961	1,555	1,574	3,129	5,792	54.0
1962	1,500	1,603	3,103	5,910	52.5
1963	1,759	1,715	3,474	6,597	52.7
1964	2,155	2,499	4,654	7,133	65.2
1965	2,188	2,532	4,720	7,265	65.0
1966	2,355	2,557	4,912	7,751	63.4
1967	2,929	2,737	5,666	8,539	66.4
1968	3,046	2,745	5,791	8,775	66.0
1969	2,694	2,749	5,443	8,661	62.8
1970	2,844	2,864	5,708	9,498	60.1
1971	4,770	2,873	7,643	11,637	65.7
1972	5,090	2,794	7,884	12,192	64.7
1973	7,801	3,381	11,182	16,054	69.7
1974	26,820	9,628	36,448	42,558	85.6
1975	22,857	8,798	31,655	40,898	77.4
1976	21,264	6,760	28,024	38,130	73.5

Source: Ministry of Finance and Central Bank of Venezuela.

TABLE 7.6

COMPOSITION OF IMPORTS: 1913 AND 1926

Types of imports	1913		1936 a)	
	Total ($1,000)	Per cent	Total ($1,000)	Per cent
Capital goods	3,140	19.3	10,866 b)	20.0
Consumer goods	9,873	61.0	24,009	44.4
Food	2,378	14.8	8,147	15.1
Textiles	3,570	22.0	8,441	15.6
Others	3,925	24.3	7,421	13.7
Luxury goods	2,372	14.7	14,297	26.4
Raw materials	425	2.7	3,168	5.9
Fuels	378	2.3	1,720	3.2
	16,188	100.0	54,060	100.0

Source: Aranda, Sergio, 'La Economía Venezolana', Editorial Pomaire.

Notes: a)   Not including gold or postal cargo.
         b)   Not including oil company imports.

TABLE 7.7

SHARE OF NATIONAL PRODUCTION AND IMPORTS
IN THE TOTAL PRIVATE GOODS CONSUMPTION

| Year | Imports | Domestic production | | Total |
		Agriculture	Industry	
1950	47.4	18.4	34.2	100.0
1951	42.3	20.5	37.2	100.0
1952	36.3	20.1	43.6	100.0
1953	36.7	19.0	44.3	100.0
1954	35.2	16.1	48.7	100.0
1955	29.8	17.2	53.0	100.0
1956	26.0	17.4	56.6	100.0
1957	29.0	17.4	53.6	100.0
1958	31.9	15.0	53.1	100.0
1959	34.7	14.2	51.1	100.0
1960	22.0	19.0	59.0	100.0
1961	21.1	18.5	60.4	100.0
1962	17.5	19.8	62.7	100.0
1963	12.8	22.1	65.1	100.0
1964	12.9	20.9	66.2	100.0
1965	12.5	20.8	66.7	100.0
1966	11.5	21.1	67.4	100.0
1967	11.0	20.7	68.3	100.0
1968	11.9	19.8	68.3	100.0
1969	10.7	20.0	69.3	100.0
(AT CURRENT PRICES)				
1968	4.1	20.5	75.4	100.0
1969	4.7	20.9	74.4	100.0
1970	3.0	19.7	77.3	100.0
1971	1.9	19.4	78.7	100.0
1972	3.5	18.7	77.8	100.0
1973	3.1	17.5	79.4	100.0
1974	3.3	17.1	79.6	100.0
1975	2.6	17.8	79.6	100.0
1976	11.2	9.4	79.4	100.0

Source: Central Bank of Venezuela.

TABLE 7.8

INVESTMENT STRUCTURE: 1945-56
(MILLIONS OF BOLIVARS AT 1953 PRICES)

Year	Territorial investment	Oil sector	Other sectors	Public investment	Private investment in other sectors
1945	1,231	724	507	803	324
1946	1,351	980	371	350	21
1947	2,284	755	1,529	456	1,073
1948	2,667	1,230	1,437	627	310
1949	2,713	1,401	1,312	723	589

Source: Ministry of Development and CEPAL (ECLA), 'El desarrollo reciente de la Economía Venezolana' (Recent development of Venezuela's economy), October 1957, Celso Furtado Mimeograph, p. 48, Statistical Appendix. (The original contains a mistake in figure listings of "Other sectors" investments for the year 1948).
Taken from Sergio Aranda, op. cit. pp. 133-4.

TABLE 7.9

GROSS FIXED INVESTMENT PER CAPITAL STOCK TYPE

Year	Construction and improvements	Machines and equipment	Means of transportation	Cattle breeding	Total
(MILLIONS OF BOLIVARS AT 1957 PRICES)					
1950	1,946	927	316	75	3,264
1951	2,412	819	163	77	3,471
1952	2,658	1,099	519	82	4,359
1953	2,854	1,125	717	89	4,785
1954	3,186	1,308	875	97	5,466
1955	3,176	1,201	676	107	5,161
1956	3,688	1,574	213	119	5,595
1957	3,658	1,786	371	132	5,947
1958	3,553	1,864	331	148	5,896
1959	3,511	1,573	817	165	6,066
1960	3,067	932	543	183	4,725
1961	2,514	789	528	188	4,019
1962	2,440	877	688	191	4,196
1963	2,630	847	633	197	4,307
1964	3,269	1,075	634	200	5,178
1965	3,616	1,070	670	202	5,558
1966	3,732	1,019	721	205	5,677
1967	4,033	950	677	207	5,867
1968	4,644	1,074	779	210	6,707
1969	4,576	1,089	783	212	6,660
(MILLIONS OF BOLIVARS AT 1968 PRICE)					
1968	5,918	3,155	1,038	123	10,234
1969	6,138	3,395	1,116	113	10,762
1970	6,282	3,258	1,109	106	10,755
1971	7,056	4,025	1,094	51	12,226
1972	8,170	4,638	1,231	33	14,072
1973	8,921	5,103	1,423	44	15,491
1974	8,320	4,819	1,877	110	15,126
1975	9,843	6,443	2,573	135	18,994
1976	11,759	7,988	3,760	150	23,657
1977	12,423	8,289	3,468	145	24,325

Source: Central Bank of Venezuela.

273

TABLE 7.10

SECTORIAL SHARE OF GNP: 1950-76

Year	GNP a)	Sectors		
		Primary	Secondary	Tertiary
(AT 1957 PRICES)				
1950	100.0	38.0	17.0	45.0
1951	100.0	38.9	17.4	43.7
1952	100.0	38.7	18.5	42.8
1953	100.0	36.2	19.2	44.6
1954	100.0	35.4	19.9	44.7
1955	100.0	36.7	19.6	43.7
1956	100.0	37.6	20.0	42.4
1957	100.0	37.8	19.2	43.0
1958	100.0	35.8	20.2	44.0
1959	100.0	35.4	20.9	43.7
1960	100.0	36.0	19.8	44.2
1961	100.0	34.6	19.1	46.3
1962	100.0	34.2	18.6	47.2
1963	100.0	32.5	18.3	49.2
1964	100.0	31.5	18.8	49.7
1965	100.0	30.7	19.0	50.3
1966	100.0	29.6	19.2	51.2
1967	100.0	29.8	19.4	50.8
1968	100.0	28.9	20.3	50.8
1969	100.0	28.4	20.2	51.4
(AT 1968 PRICES)				
1968	100.0	28.9	22.4	48.7
1969	100.0	28.3	21.8	49.9
1970	100.0	27.6	22.2	50.2
1971	100.0	25.5	22.9	51.6
1972	100.0	23.1	24.1	52.8
1973	100.0	23.1	24.6	52.3
1974	100.0	20.6	24.5	54.9
1975	100.0	17.5	25.4	57.1
1976	100.0	15.7	26.7	57.6

Source: Central Bank of Venezuela.

Note: a) The period 1968-76 does not include import taxation in the calculation.

TABLE 7.11

SECTORIAL SHARE OF THE INDUSTRIAL PRODUCT
(PERCENTAGE)

Year	Durable goods a)	Non durable goods	Others	Total
(AT 1957 PRICES)				
1948	20.5	79.2	0.3	100.0
1949	21.5	78.1	0.4	100.0
1950	22.7	77.0	0.3	100.0
1951	21.9	77.7	0.4	100.0
1952	22.4	77.2	0.4	100.0
1953	23.2	76.3	0.5	100.0
1954	24.7	74.7	0.6	100.0
1955	24.4	75.0	0.6	100.0
1956	25.0	74.2	0.8	100.0
1957	26.7	72.4	0.9	100.0
1958	25.6	73.5	0.9	100.0
1959	26.0	72.9	1.1	100.0
1960	23.1	75.8	1.1	100.0
1961	22.6	76.0	1.4	100.0
1962	24.0	74.4	1.6	100.0
1963	24.4	73.9	1.7	100.0
1964	25.9	72.3	1.8	100.0
1965	27.9	70.3	1.8	100.0
1966	27.7	70.3	2.0	100.0
1967	27.9	70.2	1.9	100.0
1968	28.5	69.6	1.9	100.0
1969	28.5	69.6	1.9	100.0
(AT 1968 PRICES)				
1968	23.2	76.2	0.6	100.0
1969	24.1	75.2	0.7	100.0
1970	24.2	75.3	0.5	100.0
1971	23.6	75.7	0.7	100.0
1972	24.7	74.6	0.7	100.0
1973	25.4	74.1	0.5	100.0
1974	26.1	73.4	0.5	100.0
1975	29.3	70.2	0.5	100.0
1976	31.0	68.5	0.5	100.0

Source: Central Bank of Venezuela.
United Nations, Series F, no. 2, Rev. 2 and Rev. 3.

Note: a) The structure valued at 1957 prices includes "jewellery".

TABLE 7.12A

PUBLIC AND PRIVATE GROSS FIXED INVESTMENT
(MILLIONS OF BOLIVARS PER YEAR)

Year	Total	Public	Private	GNP	GFI / GNP
1972	15,842	6,001	9,841	61,797	25.6
1973	18,616	6,589	12,027	73,447	25.3
1974	21,004	6,828	14,176	112,506	18.7
1975	30,598	12,533	18,065	118,280	25.9
1976	42,770	17,597	25,173	135,317	31.6
1977	60,488	23,666	36,822	155,884	38.8
1978	71,010	29,371	41,639	170,956	41.5
1979	65,553	27,900	37,653	207,737	31.6
1980	64,145	31,162	32,983	254,201	25.2
1981	69,783	41,832	27,951	285,208	24.5
1982	70,163	47,869	22,294	291,268	24.1
1983	53,735	37,575	16,160	185,263	29.0

Source: Central Bank of Venezuela, Economic Reports, 1979; and 1983 Statistical Series Yearbook.

TABLE 7.12B

FIXED GROSS INVESTMENT
(MILLIONS OF BOLIVARS AT 1968 PRICE)

Year	Total	Public	Private	GNP	GFI / GNP
1972	12,209	3,559	8,650	54,173	22.5
1973	15,491	5,483	10,008	57,471	27.0
1974	15,126	4,907	10,219	60,978	24.8
1975	19,652	6,805	12,847	54,590	30.5
1976	21,170	7,036	14,134	70,015	30.2
1977	27,998	9,084	18,914	74,796	37.4
1978	28,331	9,547	18,784	77,161	36.7
1979	26,074	11,097	14,977	77,396	33.7
1980	22,090	10,628	11,462	78,857	28.0
1981	22,959	13,763	9,196	75,628	30.4
1982	22,093	15,070	7,023	76,144	29.0
1983	15,323	10,785	4,538	72,494	21.1

Source: Central Bank of Venezuela, Economic Report for 1972-78; 1983 Statistical Series Yearbook for 1979-83.

TABLE 7.13

IMPORT OF CAPITAL GOODS: 1973-75
(MILLIONS OF BOLIVARS)

	1973	1974	1975 a)
Machinery, accessories and tools for:	2,560.2	3,306.2	6,944.9
Industry (except power)	1,962.2	3,307.1	5,140.3
Agriculture and cattle breeding	272.4	259.4	600.6
Mining and fuels	9.7	-	-
Electric power	315.9	239.7	304.0
Transport material	1,623.3	2,429.8	3,900.5

Source: Ministry of Development, Statistical and National Census Office.

Note: a) Preliminary figures.

TABLE 7.14

INVESTMENT IN CONCRETE PROJECTS BY DEVELOPING AGENCIES

	Investment period 1970-74	1970	1971	1972	1973	1974
Corporacion Venezolana de Guayana	556.4	13.5	118.7	173.5	161.7	89.0
Aluminum enlargement	143.4	7.4	52.6	34.9	20.7	27.8
Metal-mechanic development	333.5	6.1	58.2	112.7	106.5	50.0
Forestry development	64.5	-	7.9	25.9	24.5	6.2
Chemical	15.0	-	-	-	10.0	5.0
Sidenurgica del Orinoco	1,522.4	108.8	411.8	502.5	373.7	125.8
Flat product plant	783.6	61.0	282.7	274.2	165.9	-
Steel making	348.0	-	69.6	139.2	139.2	-
Continuous casting	67.5	-	-	27.0	40.5	-
Docks and facilities	60.0	-	30.0	30.0	-	-
Oxygen plant	6.0	6.0	-	-	-	-
Pit furnaces	1.6	1.6	-	-	-	-
Modernization of piping factories	25.6	5.1	5.1	5.1	5.1	5.2
Improvement and building facilities	114.5	19.5	24.4	27.0	23.0	20.6
Centrifugal piping	11.9	11.9	-	-	-	-
Reaming machine	3.7	3.7	-	-	-	-
Expansion to 10 million t.	100.0	-	-	-	-	100.0
Instituto Venezolano de Petroquimica	2,229.4	465.3	922.5	624.0	142.5	75.1
El Tablazo Complex	821.0	52.6	359.1	389.3	-	20.0
Olefine	125.6	-	75.4	50.2	-	-
Sodium-chloride	43.4	31.2	11.3	0.9	-	-
Technical services/1st stage	453.4	-	181.4	272.0	-	-
Water supply	175.2	20.0	90.0	65.0	-	-
Preliminary works	3.4	1.4	1.0	1.0	-	-
Technical services/2nd stage	20.0	-	-	-	-	20.0

TABLE 7.14 (CONTINUED)

	Investment period 1970-74	1970	1971	1972	1973	1974
Moron Complex	190.2	100.9	89.3	-	-	-
Sulfuric acid	11.0	-	11.0	-	-	-
Urea	26.5	21.8	4.7	-	-	-
Ammoniac	6.7	6.7	-	-	-	-
Phosphoric acid and Grindine	23.2	16.2	7.0	-	-	-
Complex N.P.K.	22.1	15.2	6.9	-	-	-
Material management and service	100.7	41.0	59.7	-	-	-
Mixed enterprises	1,218.2	311.8	474.1	234.7	142.5	55.1
Corporacion Venezolana de Petroleo	262.0	6.0	24.0	32.0	100.0	100.0
Present refinery/equipment and services	4.0	2.0	2.0	-	-	-
Multiple pipeline El Palito/Puerto Cabello	4.0	4.0	-	-	-	-
Refineries	254.0	-	22.0	32.0	100.0	100.0
Corporacion Venezolana de Fomento	246.6	44.3	69.2	69.1	35.4	28.6
Basic metallic	5.7	2.8	2.9	-	-	-
Metallic products	9.3	2.4	2.9	1.3	0.7	3.0
Machinery	54.4	9.6	9.5	15.6	11.2	8.5
Electrical equipment	54.2	4.9	14.0	15.7	6.5	11.1
Transporting material	13.0	2.0	5.5	5.0	0.5	-
Chemical products	111.0	22.6	34.4	31.5	16.5	6.0
Comision Nacional de Financiamiento de la Pequeñay Mediana Industria	31.5	0.0	7.5	8.0	8.0	8.0
Industrial areas	31.5	-	7.5	8.0	8.0	8.0
Dry docks and shipyards	80.0	-	10.0	20.0	20.0	30.0
Total	4,929.3	637.9	1,563.7	1,428.9	843.3	455.5

Source: CORDIPLAN; Departamento de Promoción Industrial (Industrial Development Department).

TABLE 7.15

TOTAL GROSS FIXED INVESTMENT: 1970-80

	Absolute values			Percentage distribution		
	Public	Private	Total	Public	Private	Total
Traditional exports:	19,232	418	19,650	97.9	2.1	100.0
Oil	18,372	-	18,372	100.0	-	100.0
Mining	860	418	1,278	67.3	32.7	100.0
Domestic activities	71,386	79,656	151,042	47.3	52.7	100.0
Agriculture	6,478	8,608	15,086	42.9	57.1	100.0
Manufacturing	18,970	19,164	38,134	49.8	50.2	100.0
Electricity	11,725	418	12,143	89.2	10.8	100.0
Construction	-	2,060	2,060	-	100.0	100.0
Commerce, restaurants and hotels	-	7,440	7,440	-	100.0	100.0
Transport, storage and communications	13,478	6,617	20,095	67.1	32.9	100.0
Finance and insurance	-	1,153	1,153	-	100.0	100.0
Housing and city planning	7,606	15,803	23,409	32.5	67.5	100.0
Tourism	-	938	938	-	100.0	100.0
Equipment:	13,129	-	13,129	100.0	-	100.0
Education	2,456	-	2,456	100.0	-	100.0
Health	1,837	-	1,837	100.0	-	100.0
Sports and recreation	389	-	389	100.0	-	100.0
Justice	316	-	316	100.0	-	100.0
Sewage works	4,608	-	4,608	100.0	-	100.0
Institutions	357	-	357	100.0	-	100.0
Marginal areas	1,943	-	1,943	100.0	-	100.0
Other works	1,223	-	1,223	100.0	-	100.0
Other services	-	16,455	16,455	-	100.0	100.0
Total	90,618	80,074	170,692	53.1	46.9	100.0

Source: CORDIPLAN; Including administrative investments, furniture and ground preparations.

TABLE 7.16

PUBLIC INVESTMENT: 1976-80
(MILLIONS OF BOLIVARS AT CURRENT PRICES)

Sectors	Total 1976-80	1976	1977	1978	1979	1980
Oil and petrochemical industry	26,520	2,464	4,391	5,720	7,437	6,508
Oil	23,520	2,464	4,291	5,620	6,137	5,008
Petrochemical industry	3,000	-	100	100	1,300	1,500
Mining	1,030	420	285	155	110	60
Iron	220	120	70	30	-	-
Coal 'Zulia'	300	100	100	50	50	-
'Maricual'	250	50	60	30	50	60
Gold	140	100	25	15	-	-
Salt mines	120	50	30	30	10	-
Agriculture	8,205	1,428	1,537	1,695	1,885	1,660
Rural roads	2,640	700	450	450	520	520
Hydraulic resources	900	216	135	181	218	150
Well-drilling	305	12	60	68	80	85
Lagoon construction	200	35	45	50	35	35
Ground preparation	400	38	56	75	99	132
Maintenance and repair of works	300	75	75	75	75	-
Comprehensive development programmes	700	88	124	141	159	188
Construction and maintenance of infrastructure	260	43	49	52	56	60
Comprehensive development programmes	2,500	221	543	603	643	490
Apure modules	340	25	66	73	86	90
Maracaibo Lake Southern Zone	256	40	54	54	54	54
Guanare-Masperro	550	48	130	143	158	71
Unare-Naveri hydraulic usage	250	17	58	63	69	43
Yacambe-Quibor	405	40	91	110	114	50
Turen	184	16	36	41	45	46
Uribanto-Arauca	125	-	24	29	33	39
El Cenizo irrigation system	120	6	35	38	21	20
Basin maintenance	70	9	12	14	15	20
Reforestation and tree-planting	200	20	37	38	48	57
Manufacturing	22,895	6,020	8,501	3,816	2,782	1,776
Steelworks	15,370	3,800	5,550	2,050	2,320	1,650
Orinoco Steelworks, 4th plan	15,170	3,800	5,500	2,000	2,270	1,600
Zulia's Steelworks Study & Project	200	-	50	50	50	50
Aluminum	5,560	1,610	2,317	1,319	314	-
Venalum	2,560	470	1,115	749	226	-
Aluminio del Caroni	600	335	265	-	-	-
Alumina & Associates	2,400	805	937	570	88	-
Automobile and metal mechanics	565	196	220	116	27	6
Tractors and engines	75	-	24	18	27	6
Metal mechanical and foundry complex	490	196	196	98	-	-
Marine industry	600	166	189	145	50	50
Industrial areas	300	100	100	50	25	25
Others	500	148	125	136	46	45

TABLE 7.16 (CONTINUED)

Sectors	Total 1976-80	1976	1977	1978	1979	1980
Electric energy	17,677	2,196	2,779	3,438	4,090	5,174
Electricifaction del Caroni	8,167	531	716	1,758	2,421	2,741
C.A.D.A.F.E.	9,510	1,665	2,063	1,680	1,669	2,433
Transport and communications	16,881	3,355	3,901	3,304	3,294	3,027
Post and telecommunications	200	82	26	28	34	30
Telecommunications	3,981	675	762	898	848	798
Telephone and related services	3,631	575	662	798	798	798
Social communications	350	100	100	100	50	-
Roads	8,500	1,665	1,730	1,615	1,690	1,800
Motorways and super highways	2,000	400	400	400	400	400
Other suburban road services	600	85	100	115	150	150
Caracas metro line	2,200	280	480	400	440	600
Urban road services	1,000	250	200	200	200	150
Maintenance	2,700	650	550	500	500	500
Motorway transit and transportation	200	52	45	35	31	37
Railways	1,000	90	210	300	200	200
Air traffic and transportation	1,500	389	490	228	291	102
Waterway transportation	1,500	402	638	200	200	60
Ports	700	80	160	200	200	60
Merchant navy	800	322	478	-	-	-
Housing	9,750	1,170	1,560	2,340	2,340	2,340
Education	3,000	800	800	800	300	300
Health care	2,250	600	600	500	300	250
Sports and recreational works	500	50	100	100	100	150
Institutional works	460	40	75	120	100	125
Justice works	400	70	70	90	100	70
Drinking water and sewage systems	5,750	1,246	1,246	1,246	1,006	1,006
Marginal areas	2,500	259	409	584	624	624
Service modules	400	30	60	100	100	110
Internal roads and urban planning	1,550	154	254	354	394	394
Housing improvement	450	55	75	110	110	100
Community development	100	20	20	20	20	20
Others	959	168	181	192	204	214
Administrative investment, furniture, equipment and maintenance	959	168	181	192	204	214
Total	118,777	20,286	26,435	24,100	24,672	23,284

Source: CORDIPLAN.

TABLE 7.17

BALANCE OF PAYMENTS IN CURRENT ACCOUNT
(MILLIONS OF BOLIVARS AT 1975 PRICES)

	1976	1977	1978	1979	1980	Total 1976-80	Variation 1975-80
Exports (fob)	9,113	9,114	9,141	9,187	9,322	45,877	1.4
Oil	8,354	8,250	8,144	8,027	7,921	40,696	0.5
Iron	359	344	321	281	258	1,563	-2.8
Others	400	520	676	879	1,143	3,618	30.4
Imports (fob)	-6,131	-6,756	-6,713	-6,872	-6,868	-33,340	5.0
Capital goods	-2,705	-3,141	-2,898	-2,845	-2,617	-14,206	3.5
Inputs	-2,488	-2,647	-2,816	-2,996	-3,187	-14,134	7.1
Consumer goods	-938	-968	-999	-1,031	-1,064	-5,000	3.2
Balance of trade	2,982	2,358	2,428	2,315	2,454	12,537	-14.4
Transport and insurance	-521	-540	-490	-446	-405	-2,402	-4.1
Travellers	-132	-125	-119	-112	-106	-594	-5.4
Investment revenues	487	485	439	377	376	2,164	-
Other services	-430	-473	-521	-577	-640	-2,641	18.4
Balance of services	-596	-653	-691	-758	-775	-3,473	-21.4
Balance of goods and services	2,386	1,705	1,737	1,557	1,679	9,064	-9.5
Unilateral transfers	-155	-163	-171	-180	-189	-858	5.0
Total of balance of payments in current account	2,231	1,542	1,566	1,377	1,490	8,206	-10.6

Source: CORDIPLAN.

TABLE 7.18

REAL GROSS FIXED INVESTMENT
(MILLIONS OF BOLIVARS)

Year	Public investment	Private investment	Total investment	% Variation total investment
1968	3,480	6,875	10,355	-
1969	3,275	7,872	11,147	7.6
1970	2,549	8,400	10,949	(1.8)
1971	2,861	9,422	12,283	12.2
1972	5,350	8,772	14,122	15.0
1973	5,468	9,980	15,448	9.4
1974	4,888	10,178	15,066	(2.5)
1975	6,630	12,299	18,929	25.6
1976	10,006	14,313	24,319	28.5
1977	12,269	19,092	31,361	29.0
1978	13,829	18,781	32,610	4.0
1979	11,097	14,977	26,074	(20.0)
1980	10,828	11,462	22,290	(14.5)
1981	13,763	9,196	22,959	3.0
1982	15,079	7,023	22,102	(3.7)
1983	12,140	4,140	16,280	(26.3)
1984	7,098	6,111	13,209	(18.9)
1985 a)	8,296	4,809	13,105	(0.8)
ANNUAL AVERAGE PER TERM				
1968-73	3,830	8,554	12,384	
1974-77	8,448	13,970	22,419	81.0
1978-80	11,918	15,073	26,991	20.4
1981-85	11,275	6,256	17,531	(35.0)

Source: Central Bank of Venezuela, 'Anuarios de Cuentas Nacionales e Informe
Económico de 1985'.

a)   Real investment in 1985 was estimated on the basis of partial information
contained in the above economic report.

TABLE 7.19

BALANCE OF PAYMENTS, GENERAL SUMMARY
(MILLIONS OF US$)

Year	Exports	Imports	Balance of trade	Balance of current accounts	Net flow of capitals a)	Net international reserves
1970	2,640	1,713	927	(104)	147	1,023
1971	3,152	1,896	1,256	(11)	434	1,479
1972	3,202	2,222	980	(101)	333	1,756
1973	4,803	2,626	2,177	877	(333)	2,412
1974	11,290	3,876	7,414	5,760	(1,593)	6,581
1975	8,982	5,462	3,520	2,171	496	9,243
1976	9,342	7,337	2,005	254	(259)	9,285
1977	9,661	10,194	(533)	(3,179)	3,004	9,129
1978	9,174	11,234	(2,060)	(5,735)	4,174	7,599
1979	14,360	10,004	4,356	350	760	8,819
1980	19,275	10,877	8,398	4,728	(4,735)	8,885
1981	20,181	12,123	8,058	4,000	(1,529)	11,409
1982	16,516	13,584	2,932	(4,246)	1,526	11,624
1983	14,759	6,409	8,350	4,427	(3,680)	12,181
1984	15,967	7,262	8,705	5,418	(3,540)	14,064
1985	14,178	7,388	6,790	2,923	(1,216)	15,821

Source: Central Bank of Venezuela, 'Anuarios de Cuentas Nacionales e Informes Económicos (Yearbooks of national economic reports and accounts.)

Note: a) Including errors and omissions.

TABLE 7.20A

ACCUMULATED FLOWS OF INTERNATIONAL TRANSACTIONS
NOMINAL FLOWS
(MILLIONS OF US$, ANNUAL AVERAGE)

Year	Exports	Imports	Balance of trade	Balance of current accounts	Net flow of capitals a)	Balance of current and capital transactions
1968-73	3,124	1,920	1,204	41	176	218
1974-77	9,819	6,717	3,102	1,252	412	1,664
1978-80	14,270	10,705	3,565	(219)	66	(153)
1981-85	16,320	9,353	6,967	2,504	(1,688)	817

TABLE 7.20B

ACCUMULATED FLOWS OF INTERNATIONAL TRANSACTIONS
REAL FLOWS
(MILLIONS OF US$ AT 1980 PRICES, ANNUAL AVERAGE)

Year	Exports	Imports	Balance of trade	Balance of current accounts	Net flow of capitals a)	Balance of current and capital transactions
1968-73	8,281	5,114	3,167	12	530	541
1974-77	15,254	10,175	5,079	2,247	489	2,736
1978-80	15,793	12,232	3,561	(755)	502	(253)
1981-85	15,842	9,073	6,769	2,436	(1,649)	787

Source: Central Bank of Venezuela, 'Anuarios de Cuentas Nacionales e Informes Económicos'.

Note: a) Including errors and omissions.

TABLE 7.21

MANUFACTURING ENTERPRISES OF THE PUBLIC SECTOR
NON-TRADITIONAL PRODUCTS
PRODUCTION, DOMESTIC SALES AND EXPORTS
(THOUSANDS OF METRIC TONS)

	1983			1984			1985		
Enterprise	Output	Do-mestic	External	Output	Do-mestic	External	Output	Do-mestic	External
Sidor	1,662	1,068	785	1,939	1,437	612	2,176	1,235	1,027
Venalum	231	23	224	257	54	130	276	66	244
Alcasa	107	48	67	116	62	49	130	75	52
Interalumina	594	341	51	1,142	769	371	1,110	776	359
Nitroven	614	4	406	669	-	434	509	63	310
Pequiven	796	494	52	1,080	773	80	1,065	810	11

Source: Central Bank of Venezuela, Annual Reports 1985 and 1986.

TABLE 7.22

EXPORTS PER SECTORS AND PRODUCTS
(US$ MILLIONS)

	1983 Structure		1984 Structure		1985 Structure a)	
		Structure %		Structure %		Structure %
FOB Exports	14,759	100.0	15,967	100.0	14,178	100.0
Public sector	14,394	97.5	15,464	96.8	13,646	96.2
Oil	13,667	92.6	14,794	92.6	12,862	90.7
Iron	80	0.5	81	0.5	108	0.8
Aluminum	439	3.0	370	2.3	411	2.9
Steel products	149	1.0	134	0.8	192	1.4
Others	59	0.4	85	0.5	73	0.5
Private sector	365	2.5	503	3.2	532	3.8

Source: Central Bank of Venezuela, Annual Reports 1984 and 1985.

Note: a) Preliminary.

TABLE 7.23

GROSS FIXED INVESTMENT PER SECTORS a)

Year	Total	Oil and mining	Sectors	
			Public	Private
1955	7,968	1,793	-	-
1956	8,638	2,496	-	-
1957	9,182	2,553	-	-
1958	9,102	2,512	-	-
1959	9,365	2,313	-	-
1960	7,294	1,568	-	-
1961	6,205	794	-	-
1962	6,478	738	-	-
1963	6,496	825	-	-
1964	7,994	903	2,285	4,806
1965	8,581	832	2,421	5,328
1966	8,764	622	2,842	5,300
1967	9,058	652	3,571	4,835
1968	10,355	1,212	3,319	5,824
1969	11,147	1,569	3,097	6,481
1970	10,949	1,402	2,407	7,140
1971	12,283	1,222	2,697	8,364
1972	14,122	983	5,125	8,014
1973	15,418	1,044	5,149	9,225
1974	13,266	1,426	4,617	7,223
1975	18,929	802	6,333	11,794
1976	24,319	750	9,298	14,271
1977	31,361	1,242	11,076	19,043
1978	32,610	1,860	11,989	18,761
1979	26,074	2,464	8,657	14,953
1980	22,290	3,168	7,681	11,441
1981	22,959	4,059	9,723	9,177
1982	22,102	4,928	10,166	7,008
1983	12,828	3,542	5,472	3,814
1984	11,412	2,553	3,075	5,784

Source: 1955-67, Central Bank of Venezuela, 'Le economía venezolana en los últimos veinticinco años', Caracas, 1966, p. 151; and 'Informe Económico 1964', Tables A-VII-1 and A-VIII-3 and 5. Original values at 1957 prices were converted to 1968 prices.
1968-84, Central Bank of Venezuela, 'Anuario de Cuentas Corrientes', Tables III-13, 14, and 15.

Note: a) Although oil and mining investment have been made alternatively by the public and private sectors, they are herewith presented separately regardless of the origin.

TABLE 7.24

SHARE OF FINANCIAL RESOURCES ASSIGNED TO
SCIENCE AND TECHNOLOGY ACTIVITIES WITHIN GDP: 1978-85
(MILLIONS OF BOLIVARS)

Year	A Financial resources assigned to science and technology a)	B Gross domestic product (GDP) b)	A/B x 100
1978	601.60	170,483	0.353
1979	633.99	207,737	0.305
1980	851.28	254,201	0.335
1981	1,004.60	285,208	0.352
1982	1,151.82	291,268	0.395
1983	1,196.50	290,492	0.412
1984	1,361.64	347,530	0.391
1985	1,411.72	373,832	0.377

Source: a) División de Estadísticas.
b) Central Bank of Venezuela, 'Informe Económico' for the years 1982, 1983, 1984 and 1985.

TABLE 7.25

EXPENDITURE ON RESEARCH AND DEVELOPMENT AS A PERCENTAGE SHARE OF WORLD GNP

Country	Reference year	% of GNP
The Americas		
USA	1982	2.7
Canada	1981	1.2
Brazil	1982	0.6
Cuba	1981	0.6
Peru	1980	0.6
Argentina	1980	0.5
Chile	1980	0.4
Ecuador	1979	0.3
Costa Rica	1979	0.2
Guatemala	1977	0.2
Panama	1975	0.2
Guyana	1982	0.2
Colombia	1978	0.1

Country	Reference year	% of GNP
Europe		
GDR	1981	4.4
Czechoslovakia	1982	4.0
Bulgaria	1982	2.8
Hungary	1982	2.6
FRG	1981	2.5
Poland	1982	2.2
United Kingdom	1978	2.1
Switzerland	1981	2.0
Netherlands	1981	1.9
Sweden	1979	1.9
France	1979	1.8
Belgium	1977	1.4
Norway	1982	1.4
Finland	1981	1.2
Italy	1981	1.0
Ireland	1982	0.8
Iceland	1979	0.8
Yugoslavia	1981	0.8
Austria	1978	0.6
Denmark	1981	0.5
Portugal	1980	0.4
Spain	1978	0.3
Greece	1979	0.2

Country	Reference year	% of GNP
Asia		
Israel	1978	2.5
Japan	1982	2.5
Korea	1982	0.9
India	1978	0.5
Indonesia	1982	0.5
Jordan	1976	0.4
Singapore	1981	0.3
Turkey	1982	0.3
Sri Lanka	1975	0.2
Philippines	1982	0.2
Pakistan	1979	0.2
Kuwait	1977	0.1

Source: UNESCO, 1984 Statistical Yearbook.

TABLE 7.26

STUDENTS ENROLLED ACCORDING TO EDUCATIONAL LEVELS: 1948-76
(THOUSANDS OF STUDENTS AND PERCENTAGE)

Years	Elementary level		Intermediate level		Higher level		Total
	Number	%	Number	%	Number	%	
1948/49	442	92.2	32	6.6	6	1.2	479
1949/50	497	92.5	34	6.4	6	1.2	537
1950/51	503	91.9	37	6.8	7	1.3	547
1951/52	536	92.6	41	7.0	2	0.3	579
1952/53	570	92.6	41	6.6	5	0.8	616
1953/54	596	91.5	48	7.4	7	1.1	652
1954/55	623	90.7	56	8.2	8	1.1	687
1955/56	647	89.7	66	9.2	8	1.1	721
1956/57	694	88.9	77	9.9	9	1.2	780
1957/58	752	88.9	83	9.8	11	1.3	845
1958/59	917	87.7	111	10.6	17	1.6	1,045
1959/60	1,095	86.5	148	11.7	23	1.8	1,265
1960/61	1,244	85.7	181	12.4	26	1.8	1,451
1961/62	1,298	84.5	206	13.4	32	2.1	1,536
1962/63	1,340	83.5	230	14.3	34	2.1	1,604
1963/64	1,371	82.7	248	15.0	38	2.3	1,657
1964/65	1,422	81.9	273	15.7	41	2.4	1,736
1965/66	1,481	81.2	295	16.2	47	2.6	1,823
1966/67	1,541	80.3	325	16.9	54	2.8	1,920
1967/68	1,584	79.2	357	17.9	59	2.9	2,000
1968/69	1,675	78.2	394	18.4	72	3.4	2,141
1969/70	1,756	76.9	448	19.6	81	3.5	2,285
1970/71	1,848	75.2	508	20.7	101	4.1	2,457
1971/72	1,919	73.6	565	21.7	123	4.7	2,607
1972/73	1,997	72.5	612	22.2	145	5.3	2,754
1973/74	2,024	70.6	682	23.8	159	5.6	2,865
1974/75	2,113	69.0	757	24.7	194	6.3	3,064
1975/76	2,228	68.0	827	25.2	222	6.8	3,277

Source: Ministry of Education.

TABLE 7.27

STUDENTS ENROLLED IN SECONDARY EDUCATION
ACCORDING TO BRANCHES: 1948-76
(THOUSANDS OF STUDENTS AND PERCENTAGE)

Years	Secondary level		Teacher training		Technical training	
	Number	%	Number	%	Number	%
1948/49	22	70.7	4	13.5	5	15.8
1949/50	23	68.3	4	12.3	7	19.3
1950/51	27	72.1	4	9.6	7	18.3
1951/52	28	68.4	3	7.4	10	24.1
1952/53	27	67.0	4	10.0	9	23.1
1953/54	33	69.6	4	9.1	10	21.4
1954/55	39	69.2	5	8.5	13	22.3
1955/56	44	66.9	6	9.5	15	23.6
1956/57	52	68.0	8	10.0	17	22.1
1957/58	55	66.7	8	10.0	19	23.4
1958/59	71	64.2	14	12.9	25	22.9
1959/60	88	59.6	26	17.3	34	23.1
1960/61	105	58.1	32	17.5	44	24.4
1961/62	122	59.2	32	15.7	52	25.0
1962/63	139	60.7	29	12.6	61	26.7
1963/64	155	62.7	22	9.0	70	28.4
1964/65	173	63.6	17	6.3	82	30.1
1965/66	190	64.2	13	4.4	93	31.4
1966/67	210	64.4	11	3.4	105	32.2
1967/68	230	64.4	11	3.1	116	32.5
1968/69	255	64.7	12	3.0	127	32.3
1969/70	288	64.3	14	3.1	146	32.6
1970/71	321	63.2	17	3.3	170	33.5
1971/72	389	68.8	16	2.8	160	28.4

	Basic level		Diversified level	
	Number	%	Number	%
1972/73	463	75.7	149	24.2
1973/74	616	75.7	166	24.3
1974/75	562	74.2	195	25.8
1975/76	610	73.8	217	26.2

Source: Ministry of Education.

TABLE 7.28

SECTORS HAVING STATE PARTICIPATION

Sector	Type of enterprise	Quantity	Main enterprises
Agriculture	Peasant enterprise	34	
	Agro-industry	12	
	Milk	5	Indulac
	Sugar	17	CENAZUCA
	Storage and services	15	CORPOMERCADEO ADAGRO
	Financing	9	BANDAGRO Bank
Wood, pulp and paper	Production and development	8	CONARE (National Reforestation C.A.)
Mining	Production	11	BAUXIVEN, CARBOZULIA, ENSAL and Ferrominera del Orinoco
	Financing	2	
Oil and gas	Production, refining, trading and development	13	PDVSA
Chemical and petrochemical	Production and trading	1	PEQUIVEN and branches
Industry	Basic metals	8	ALCASA, VENALUM, INTERALUMINA, SIDOR
	Metal products	9	CAVIM
	Cement	4	CASA
	Textiles	5	
	Trading and others	10	
	Financing	2	CORPOINDUSTRIA, FONCREI
Electricity	Production and distribution	5	CADAFE, EDELCA , and Energía Eléctric de Venezuela
Naval	Shipyards	4	ASTINAVE
	Transportation	3	CAVN, INP, INC
Transportation	Air transportation	3	VIASA
	Road transportation	5	Metro Caracas Ltd. IAAFE (State Railways)
	Related services	3	IAAIM (Maiquetía Airport Autonomous Inst.
Economic development	Regional	13	CVG (Guayana regional) CORPOZULIA
	Urban	13	CSB (Simón Bolívar Centre) FONDUR
	Industrial	19	

table continues ..../.

TABLE 7.28 (CONTINUED)

Sector	Type of enterprise	Quantity	Main enterprises
Real estate	Housing	10	INAVI
	Construction	3	
	Administration	3	
	Financing	2	BANAP
Tourism	Hotels	25	Intercontinental, Meliá, Hilton and Sheraton
	Development and services	6	CORPOTURISMO
Financing	Holdings	2	CVF (Development Corp.) FIV (Investment Fund)
	Banks	15	BIV (Industrial Bank) BND (Discount Bank) a)
	Financing societies	9	
	Social welfare	6	IVSS (Social Security Institute)
	Letting and others	11	
Public services	Telephone and telegraph	3	CANTV, IPOSTEL
	Water supply and waste collection	4	INOS, IMAU
	Social communications	2	VTV
	Others	13	Monte Avila Editors Co.

Source: This list was compiled from various official sources and revised in accordance with interviews and press articles within the paper by Janet Kelly and Julian Villalba (1984b) 'Informacíon y criterios para la toma de decisiones en el sector de empresas públicas' (Information and criteria for decision making in public enterprise). The list includes those institutions of decentralized administration having as an (achieved or not) goal to generate self-financing to cover most of their costs. 'Main' means that the enterprise is rather large (more than 50 million bolivars in salaries for workers and office workers) or such where the state (with or without share control) plays a decisive role in the given sector through its influence in the enterprise.

Note: a) Closed in June 1984.

TABLE 7.29

DEMOGRAPHIC INDICATORS GIVEN IN FIVE YEAR PERIODS:
1960/65-1975/80
(PERCENTAGE)

	1960-65	1965-70	1970-75	1975-80
Annual growth rate:				
Total population	3.9	3.6	3.6	3.5
Migration	3.6	3.0	5.0	4.2
Age group structure:				
0-14 years	46.6	46.5	44.9	43.0
15-64 years	50.9	51.0	52.5	54.3
65 onwards	2.5	2.5	2.6	2.7
Dependency index a)	96.6	96.1	90.5	84.1

Source: CELADE (January 1981), Demographic Bulletin no. 27.

Note: a) Number of people under 15 and over 64 years per 100 people between the ages of 15 and 64 years.

TABLE 7.30

STRUCTURE OF INDUSTRIAL PRODUCTION: 1970-79

	Millions of Bolivars at 1975 prices		% Share of the total		% Share of total excluding oil refining	
	1970	1979	1970	1979	1970	1979
Non-durable consumer goods	4,343.5	7,824.1	25.4	34.0	46.6	44.9
Durable consumer goods	1,108.0	1,801.6	6.5	7.8	11.9	10.3
Capital goods	368.1	777.9	2.2	3.4	4.0	4.5
Inputs and intermediate products	3,493.0	7,011.0	20.4	30.5	37.5	40.3
Subtotal (oil refining excluded)	9,312.6	17,414.6	54.4	75.7	100.0	100.0
Oil refining	7,800.9	5,603.8	45.6	24.3		
Total	17,113.5	23,018.4	100.0	100.0		

Source: Centro de Proyecciones Económicas (Economic Planning Centre), based on official data.

TABLE 7.31

EVOLUTION OF THE RATIO OF INVESTMENT
AND INVESTMENT COMPOSITION AND FINANCING a)

	1950-60	1960-70	1970-73	1960-80	1974-80
Total gross investment ratio b)	25.5	18.2	29.9	19.6	33.4
Gross fixed investment	100.0	100.0	100.0	100.0	100.0
Construction	44.6	48.0	54.0	50.0	54.1
Machinery and equipment	55.4	52.0	46.0	50.0	45.0
Investment financing	100.0	100.0	100.0	100.0	100.0
National savings	96.2	107.5	104.3	107.9	103.4
Net external financing	3.8	-7.5	-4.3	-7.9	-3.4

Source: Centro de Proyecciones Económicas, based on national data.

Notes: a) Original figures at 1975 prices.
  b) Related to the GDP.

TABLE 7.32

RATIO EVOLUTION OF THE IMPORT, EXPORT AND
PURCHASING POWER OF SERVICES AND GOODS EXPORTS
(PERCENTAGE OF THE GROSS DOMESTIC PRODUCT)

	1961-70	1971-80	1961-73	1974-80
Exports:				
at 1975 prices	61.2	36.3	58.7	30.6
at current prices	33.5	31.3	32.3	31.5
Imports:				
at 1975 prices	15.8	27.3	17.4	30.8
at current prices	22.2	27.8	21.4	29.1
Purchasing power of exports at 1975 prices	24.8	30.7	34.4	33.4

Source: Centro de Proyecciones Económicas, based on official data.

TABLE 7.33

GNP PER PERSON EMPLOYED IN EACH SECTOR: 1978 AND 1983
(BOLIVARS AT 1968 PRICES)

	1978	1983
Agriculture	7,200	7,600
Mining	36,700	19,800
Hydrocarbons	217,300	135,400
Hydrocarbons a)	633,700	467,000
Industry	17,000	18,300
Construction	16,800	8,800
Energy and water	38,500	52,400
Commerce	10,100	6,700
Transport and communications	37,400	28,300
Services and government	23,300	21,800
Total GNP	19,300	16,700
Total GNP a)	22,500	20,000

Source: Central Bank of Venezuela.

Note: a)   Oil exports at 1968 purchasing power realization prices.

TABLE 7.34

VOLUME OF AGRICULTURAL PRODUCTION: 1978 AND 1983
(THOUSANDS OF M.T.)

	1978	1983	% Variation 1978-83
Rice	544	509	-1.3
Maize	804	429	-11.8
Oranges	263	384	7.9
Onions	55	80 a)	7.9
Sesame	57	51	-2.2
Coffee	72	50	-7.0
Sugar cane	5,132	4,747	-1.5
Mutton, thousands of heads	1,590	1,196	-5.5
Eggs, millions of units	1,869	2,232	3.6
Milk, millions of litres	1,237	1,382	2.4

Source: Central Bank of Venezuela, 1979 and 1983 Economic Reports.

Note: a)   Figure for 1982.

TABLE 7.35

BEHAVIOUR OF GNP: 1957 AND 1973
(PERCENTAGE OF AVERAGE ANNUAL VARIATION)

	1957	1973	% Variation 1957-73	% Variation 1957-73 a)
At 1957 prices:				
Total GNP	23,848	55,055	5.4	5.5
Hydrocarbons GNP	7,472	9,892	1.8	2.2
Rest of economy GNP	16,376	45,163	6.5	6.5
Including oil export at 1957 purchasing power:				
Total GNP	25,365	55,616	5.0	5.2
Hydrocarbons GNP	8,989	10,453	0.9	1.4

Source: Central Bank of Venezuela.

Note: a) The 1957 value was estimated on the basis of the 1950-56 tendency.

TABLE 7.36

BEHAVIOUR OF GNP PER SECTOR: 1957 AND 1973
(MILLIONS OF BOLIVARS AT 1957 PRICES)

	1957	1973	% Variation 1957-73
Agriculture	1,507	3,586	5.6
Mining	383	714	4.0
Hydrocarbons	7,472	9,892	1.8
Hydrocarbons a)	8,989	10,453	0.9
Industry	2,429	7,289	7.1
Construction	1,581	3,029	4.1
Energy and water	238	1,079	9.9
Commerce	3,933	5,698	2.3
Transportation and communications	940	6,071	12.4
Housing, services and government	5,365	16,737	7.4
Import duties	-	960	
Total GNP	23,848	55,055	5.4
Total GNP a)	25,365	55,616	5.0

Source: Central Bank of Venezuela, 'Anuario de Cuentas Nacionales', 1984, p. 68, Caracas.

Note: a) Oil exports at 1957 purchasing power realization prices.

TABLE 7.37

SECTORIAL SHARE OF GNP: 1957 AND 1973
(PERCENTAGE)

	1957	1957 a)	1973	1973 a)
Agriculture	6.3	5.9	6.5	6.4
Mining	1.6	1.5	1.3	1.3
Hydrocarbons	31.3	35.4	18.0	18.8
Industry	10.2	9.6	13.2	13.1
Construction	6.6	6.3	5.5	5.4
Energy and water	1.0	0.9	2.0	1.9
Commerce	16.5	15.5	10.3	10.3
Transportation and communications	3.9	3.9	11.0	10.9
Housing, services and government	22.6	21.2	30.4	30.1
Import duties			1.8	1.7
Total GNP (Billions of bolivars at 1957 prices)	23,848	25,365	55,055	55,616

Source: Central Bank of Venezuela.

Note: a) GNP including oil exports at 1957 purchasing power realization prices.

TABLE 7.38

GNP PER PERSON EMPLOYED IN EACH SECTOR: 1957 AND 1973
(MILLIONS OF BOLIVARS AT 1957 PRICES)

	1957	1973
Agriculture	1,800	5,500
Mining	34,300	73,500
Hydrocarbons	150,700	436,200
Hydrocarbons a)	192,800	460,900
Industry	9,600	14,300
Construction	8,600	12,300
Energy and water	23,800	25,600
Commerce	17,600	7,900
Transportation and communications	12,000	33,500
Services and government	6,800	19,400
Total GNP	11,300	17,000
Total GNP a)	12,200	17,200

Source: BID (Inter-American Development Bank), July 1959, 'Economic Situation of Venezuela', p. 18, Washington, D.C.

Note: a) Oil exports at 1957 purchasing power realization prices.

TABLE 7.39

BEHAVIOUR OF GNP: 1973 AND 1978
(PERCENTAGE OF AVERAGE ANNUAL VARIATION)

	1973	1978	% Variation 1973-78
Total GNP	57,260	76,376	5.9
Hydrocarbons GNP	10,288	6,879	-7.7
Rest of Economy GNP	46,972	69,497	8.2
Including oil exports at 1968 purchasing power			
Total GNP	62,682	89,551	7.4
Hydrocarbons GNP	15,710	20,054	5.0

Source: Central Bank of Venezuela, 'Anuario de Cuentas Nacionales'.

TABLE 7.40

EXTERNAL SECTOR INDICATORS
(IN MILLIONS OF US$)

	1957	1973	% Variation 1957-73
Goods export	2,751 100%	4,803 100%	3.5
Oil exports	2,570 93.4%	4,450 92.7%	3.5
Goods imports	1,776	2,626	2.5
Commodity balance	975	2,177	5.1
Service balance	-1,558	-1,189	
Current account balance	-583	877	
Capital account balance	982	142	-11.4
International reserves	1,396	2,412	3.5
Yearly reserve variation	469	656	2.1

Source: Central Bank of Venezuela, 'Anuario de Cuentas Corrientes'.

TABLE 7.41

VOLUME OF AGRICULTURAL PRODUCTION: 1957 AND 1973
(THOUSANDS OF M.T.)

	1957	1973	% Variation 1957-73
Rice	22	302	17.8
Maize	340	454	1.8
Sesame	21	72	8.0
Onions	23	35	2.6
Coffee	51	66	1.6
Sugar cane	2,120	5,241	5.8
Mutton, number of heads	643	1,306	4.5
Eggs, millions of units	86	1,428	19.2
Milk, millions of litres	320	1,023	7.5

Source: Central Bank of Venezuela.

TABLE 7.42

VOLUME OF INDUSTRIAL PRODUCTION: 1957 AND 1973
(MILLIONS OF BOLIVARS AT 1957 PRICES)

	1957	1973	%Variation 1957-73
Foodstuffs	2,522	6,935	6.5
Beverages	502	1,577	7.4
Tobacco	188	691	8.5
Textiles	431	1,495	8.1
Garments	713	827	0.9
Paper	128	1,010	13.8
Chemicals	384	1,497	8.9
Rubber products	155	495	7.5
Transportation material	780	1,985	6.0
Total	7,790	23,346	7.1

Source: Central Bank of Venezuela, 'La economía venezolana en los últimos 35 años' (Venezuela's Economy in the Last 35 Years), Table IV-8, p. 110 and our own estimates.

TABLE 7.43

GNP COMPOSITION AT MARKET PRICES
(PERCENTAGES)

	1957	1973
Net national income	70.5	84.2
Depreciation of fixed capital	8.4	8.1
Net payments to external factors	13.6	4.0
Indirect taxes - subsidies	7.5	3.7
Gross national product	100.0	100.0

Source: Inter-Amercian Development Bank, Venezuela's Economic Situation, Washington, D.C.

FIGURE 7.1

BEHAVIOUR OF GNP: 1957 AND 1973

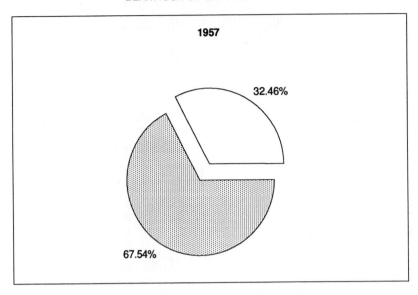

1957

32.46%

67.54%

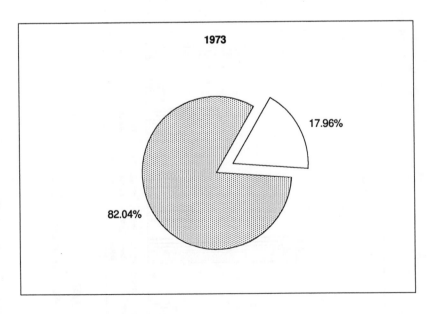

1973

17.96%

82.04%

Hydrocarbons GNP   GNP for rest of the economy

303

FIGURE 7.2

SECTORIAL SHARE OF GNP: 1957 AND 1973
(PERCENTAGE)

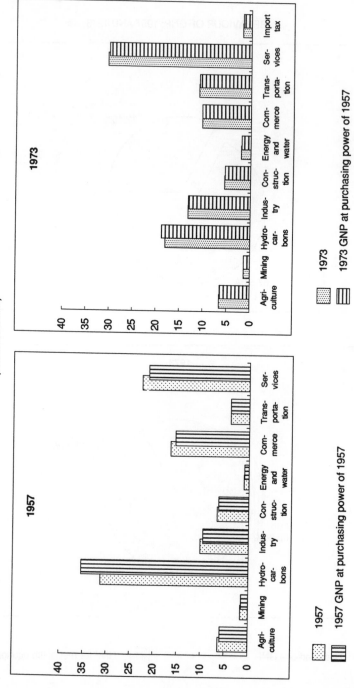

FIGURE 7.3

SECTORIAL BEHAVIOUR OF GNP: 1957 AND 1973
(BILLIONS OF BOLIVARS AT 1957 PRICES)

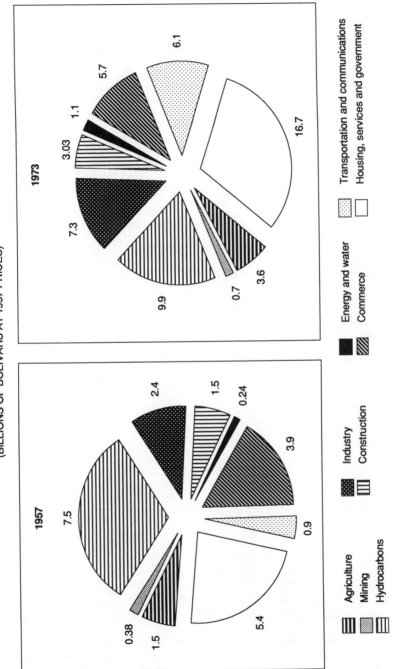

FIGURE 7.4

GNP PER PERSON EMPLOYED IN EACH SECTOR: 1957 AND 1973
(THOUSANDS OF BOLIVARS AT 1957 PRICES)

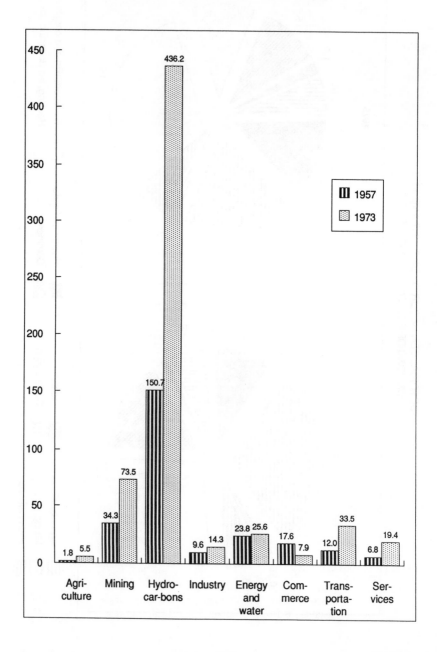

FIGURE 7.5

VOLUME OF AGRICULTURAL PRODUCTION: 1957 AND 1973
(MILLIONS OF M.T.)

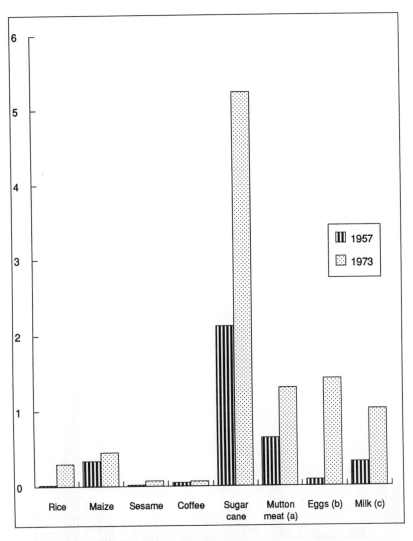

Note: (a) Millions of heads   (b) Millions of units   (c) Millions of litres

Variation rate:	Rice	17.8%	Sugar cane	5.8%	Mutton meat	4.5%
	Maize	1.8%	Onions	2.6%	Eggs	1.9%
	Sesame	8.0%	Coffee	1.6%	Milk	7.5%

FIGURE 7.6

VOLUME OF INDUSTRIAL PRODUCTION: 1957 AND 1973
(BILLIONS OF BOLIVARS AT 1957 PRICES)

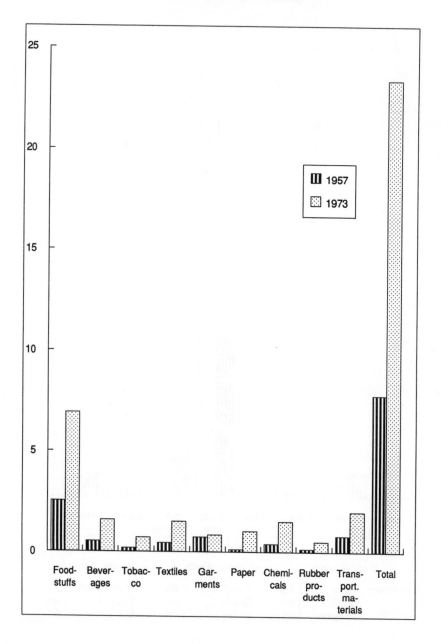

FIGURE 7.7

BEHAVIOUR OF GNP: 1973 AND 1978

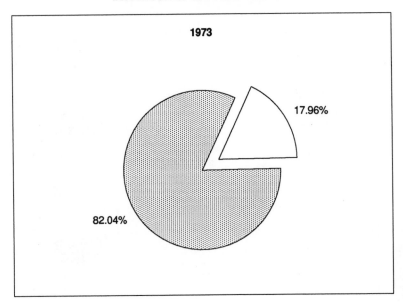

1973

17.96%

82.04%

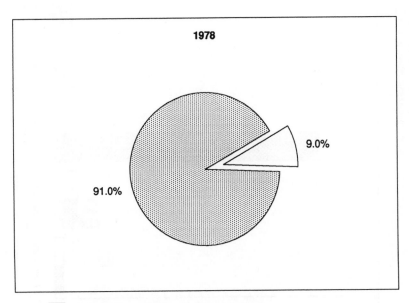

1978

9.0%

91.0%

Hydrocarbons GNP, variation rate: -7.7%

GNP for the rest of the economy, variation rate: 8.2%

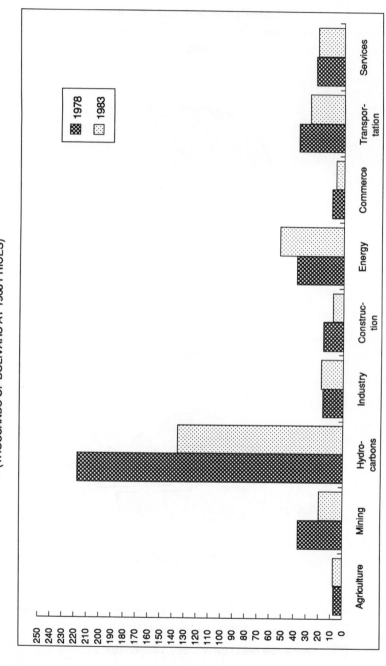

FIGURE 7.8

GNP PER PERSON EMPLOYED IN EACH SECTOR: 1978 AND 1983

(THOUSANDS OF BOLIVARS AT 1968 PRICES)

310

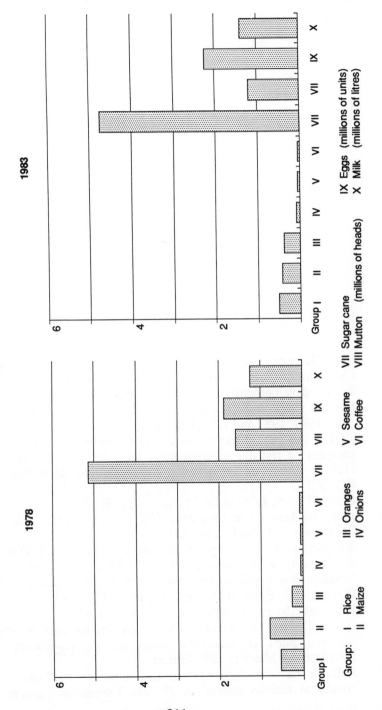

FIGURE 7.9

VOLUME OF AGRICULTURAL PRODUCTION: 1978 AND 1983
(MILLIONS OF M.T.)

Group:
I Rice
II Maize

III Oranges
IV Onions

V Sesame
VI Coffee

VII Sugar cane
VIII Mutton (millions of heads)

IX Eggs (millions of units)
X Milk (millions of litres)

Notes

1. See Gasparini, Olga (1976), *La investigación en Venezuela. Condiciones para su desarrollo* (Research in Venezuela, Conditions for its development), IVIC Publications, Caracas. Also CONICIT, *Ciencia y tecnología* (Science and technology), in Figures 1, 2 and 3, years 1981, 1983 and 1986, Caracas.
2. During this period there was a national debate on the problems of payment of transfer of technology fees. See Tirado, Getulio, et al (1981), *Costos de importación de tecnologia* (1976-80), Caracas, CONICIT.
3. CORDIPLAN, *IV Plan De La Nacion*, pp. 9-10.
4. Junta del Acuerdo de Cartagena, C.F., *Ordenamiento Juridico del ...*, Decisiones 1-90, book 1, pp. 59 and 85.
5. Study coordinated by Avalos, Ignacio, for CONICIT (1979), *Análisis de la política tecnológica nacional* (Final report of the project 'Instrumentos de política científica y tecnológica'), Caracas, pp. 7-8.
6. Blanco, C.F. Eglée Iturbe de (August 1982), *Política industrial de Venezuela durante la década de los setenta*, UNIDO.
7. Buvat, Daniel, *Lineamientos de estrategia, sinopsis de políticas y acciones para el desarrollo industrial de Venezuela*, UNIDO-Development Ministry 1984 Project.
8. Kelly de Escobar, Janet (1984), 'Las empresas del Estado: del lugar común al sentido común' in *El caso Venezuela*, Ediciones IESA,

Caracas. (See separate paragraph.) Also Kornblith and Maingon, *Acción estatal en Venezuela por el estudio de la dinámica institucional y el gasto fiscal. Período 1936-90*, CENDES-UCV.

9. Freeman, Richard B, and Naim, Moisés (February 1986), *Desarrollo de la fuerza laboral por sustitución de importaciones*, CPA/WP-76-1A, Center for Policy Alternatives, M.I.T., Cambridge, Mass., Table no. 2 pp. II-9 and II-10.

10. Ibid, Table no. 1 p. II-4.

11. Gutierrez, Arnoldo (March 1976), *Situación del mercado de trabajo de los profesionales en Venezuela*, CPA/WP-76-2A, Center for Policy, M.I.T.

12. C.F. Gaceta Oficial no. 30738 dated 09-07-75.

13. C.F. Fundación Gran Mariscal de Ayacucho, Memoria y Cuenta Año 1983 - Passim.

14. Avalos, Ignacio, op. cit.

References*

'Acta Final' XI Congreso Venezolano de Ingeniería, Arquitectura y Profesiones Afines. (11th Venezuelan congress on engineering, architecture and related professions), Caracas, 1986.

Aranda, Sergio (1984) *La economía venezolana* (The Venezuelan economy), Edit. Pomaire, Caracas.

Avalos G., Ignacio (1977) *Análisis de la política tecnológica nacional* (Analysis of national technological policy, final report of the project 'Scientific and technological policy instruments'), CONICIT.

Banco Central De Venezuela (1983) *Anuario de cuentas nacionales* (Yearbook of national accounts), Caracas.

Banco Central De Venezuela, *Boletín Mensual* (Monthly review), October 1986.

Banco Central De Venezuela (1965), *La economía venezolana en los últimos 25 años* (Venezuela's economy during the last 25 years), Caracas.

Banco Central De Venezuela (1978), *La economía venezolana en los últimos 35 años* (Venezuela's economy during the last 35 years), Caracas.

Barreto, Angel (1986) *Sidor en el desarrollo de la ingeniería venezolana* (Sidor and the development of Venezuela's engineering). 11th congress of engineering, architecture and related professions, Caracas.

---

* Unofficial translation of titles.

Buvat, Daniel (1984), *Lineamientos de estrategia, sinópsis de políticas y acciones para el desarrollo industrial de Venezuela* (Strategy guidelines, synopsis of policies and actions for Venezuela's industrial development). Project by UNIDO and Venezuelan Development Ministry.

Camara Industrial del Edo. Carabobo (Carabobo State Industry Chamber) (1984), *Productividad: Verdadera solución a la crisis económica venezolana* (Productivity: the real solution to Venezuela's economic crisis), Valencia.

CANTV (1986), *La CANTV y el desarrollo de la industria electrónica nacional* (CANTV and the development of the nation's electronic industry), 11th congress of engineering, architecture and related professions, Caracas.

Cardenas, Eduardo (1986*), La industria petroquímica bajo PDVESA: Estado actual y desarrollo futuro* (Petrochemical industry under PDVESA: present state and future development), 11th congress of engineering, architecture and related professions, Caracas.

Cardenas, Rodolfo (1970), *Ciencia y tecnología* (Science and technology), OCI, Caracas.

CENDES (1978), *Agricultura y agroindustria en Venezuela* (Agriculture and agro-industry in Venezuela), Caracas.

Center for Policy Alternatives (1977), 'M.I.T. Research on human resources and grants policy', Massachusetts.

CEPAL (ECLA) (1982), *Modelo económico y social: caso Venezuela.*

CONDIBIECA, *Estrategia de desarrollo del complejo de bienes* (Capital stock complex development strategy)

CONICIT, Bibliography of technological registers.

CONICIT, Collective catalogues of periodical publications.

CONICIT (1980), *Science and technology in figures*, Statistical report no.2, Caracas.

CONICIT (1983), *Science and technology in figures*, No.3, Caracas.

CONICIT (1985), *Researchers directory.*

CONICIT (1976), *Mechanisms and causes for importing capital goods in machinery, tools and agricultural machinery*, Caracas.

CONICIT, *Programa nacional de política y administración en ciencia y tecnología* (National policy and management programme for science and technology).

Consejo de Desarrollo Cientifico y Humanistico (Council for the Development of Sciences and Humanities) (1987), *Institutional Questionnaire*, School of Metallurgy and Material Science, Caracas.

Consejo Nacional de Ciencia y Tecnologia (National Council for Science and Technology) (1976*), Plan nacional indicativo de ciencia y tecnología* (National directive for science and technology), Mexico.

Consejo Nacional de Recursos Humanos (Human Resources National Council) (1983*), IV Informe sobre actividades* (4th Activity Report), Caracas.

CORDIPLAN, *Plan de acción de ciencia y tecnología. VII Plan de la nación 1985-1988* (Science and technology - plan of action. 7th National plan 1985-1988).

CORDIPLAN (1983), *Informe social 1982* (1982 Social report), Caracas.

CORPOINDUSTRIA (1983) 'Herramienta del Pacto Social', *Bulletin*, Maracay.

CORPOINDUSTRIA (1986), *Credits granted for economic perfomance. Years 1979-1985*, Maracay.

Cuadro resumen de inversiones en educacion superior (Summarized chart on investments in higher education)

De Paola, Sonia (1985), *Pronóstico de control de indicadores en la coyuntura* (Forecast control for conjuncture indicators), IVEPLAN, Caracas.

Fernandez-Moran, Humberto (1986), *Venezuela, ciencia y tecnología. preludio del futuro* (11th congress of engineering, architecture and related professions), Caracas.

F.I.V., General Assembly 1983.

Flores D., Max (1981), *La industrialización y desarrollo en América Latina* (Industrialization and development in Latin America), Instituto de Investigación en Ciencias Económicas y Sociales, UCV, Caracas.

Freeman B., Richard (1978), *Mercado de recursos humanos* (Human resources market), Center for Policy Alternatives, M.I.T., Mass.

Freeman B., Richard (1976), *Desarrollo laboral por sustitución de exportaciones* (Labour development by import substitution), Center for Policy Alternatives, M.I.T., Mass.

Fundacion Gran Mariscal de Ayacucho, 2nd, 3rd, 25th, 39th Meetings, Caracas, 1975-1976.

Fundacion Gran Mariscal de Ayacucho, Memoria y cuenta (Statements and accounts) 1983, 1984 and 1985.

Fung S., et al (1977), *Government action and the innovation process*, Center for Policy Alternatives, M.I.T., Mass.

Gasparini, Olga (1976), *La investigación en Venezuela* (Research in Venezuela), Publicaciones IVIC, Caracas.

Gasparini, Olga, *La institucionalización de la investigación en Venezuela* (Research institutionalization in Venezuela) (see Cárdenas, R.J., *Ciencia y tecnología*).

Gutierrez, Arnaldo and Stela, Pinto, *Análisis de la evolución de los empleadores sobre el mercado de profesionales y técnicos en Venezuela* (Employment evolution analysis on the technicians and professionals market in Venezuela).

Gutierrez, Arnaldo and Stela, Pinto (1976), *Situación del mercado de profesionales en Venezuela* (Situation of the professional's market in Venezuela), Caracas.

Hausman, Ricardo *(1985)*, *Empresas del estado. Problemas macroeconómicos a corto plazo* (State enterprises. Short-term macroeconomic problems), Caracas.

Iturbe de Blanco, Eglee (1982), *Estudio sobre cooperación regional en el sector industrial* (Study on regional cooperation in the industrial sector), UNIDO.

Katz, Jorge M. (1979), *Importación de tecnología, aprendizaje e industrialización* (Technology imports, learning and industrialization), Editorial Fondo de Cultura Económica, Mexico.

Kornblith, Miriam and Thais Maingon, *Acción estatal en Venezuela por el estudio de la dinámica institucional y el gasto fiscal. Período 1936-1980* (State activity in venezuela through the study of institutional dynamics and fiscal expenditures. 1936-1980), CENDES-UCV.

La Fontant, Jorge (1986), *Fuentes alternas renovables de energía. Estado actual y perspectivas* (Alternative renewable sources of energy: present state and prospects), 11th congress of engineering, architecture and related professions, Caracas.

Matos Azocar, Luis (1975), *Estudio sobre transferencia de tecnología a través de empresas transnacionales* (Study on transference of technology through the transnational enterprises), CONICIT.

Matos Azocar, Luis (1977), *Importancia de una estrategia de desarrollo científico-tecnológico para el sector metalúrgico, en función de objetivos económico-sociales* (Relevance of a scientific-technological development strategy at the service of social-economic objectives), CONICIT.

Matos Azocar, Luis (1977), *Investigación de recursos humanos y política de becas para la Fundación Gran Mariscal de Ayacucho*, CONICIT.

Mendez, N. (1987), *Factibilidad de las tecnologías alternativas. Jornada de enseñanza de la ingeniería* (Feasibility of alternative technologies. a day on teaching engineering), Caracas.

Ministerio de Energia y Minas (Energy and Mining Ministry), *Petróleo y otros datos estadísticos* (Oil and other statistical data), Caracas 1986, Pode 1984, Caracas 1985.

Ministerio de Fomento (Ministry of Development) (1986), *Boletin de propiedad industrial* (Industrial property bulletin), Caracas.

Ministerio de Hacienda (Ministry of Finance) (1986), *Memoria 1985* (1985 Statement), Caracas.

Monagas, Antonio J. (1986), *Pertinencia de la formación profesional del ingeniero en términos de la realidad social venezolana* (Relevance of professional training for engineers in terms of Venezuela's social reality), 11th congress of engineering, architecture and related professions, Caracas.

Naim, Moises and Piñango, R. (1984), *El caso Venezuela* (Case Venezuela), Publicaciones IESA, Caracas.

OCEI, *Comercio exterior en Venezuela 1984-85* (Foreign trade in Venezuela, 1984-85).

OCEI, *Encuesta cualitativa del sector industrial, 1986* (Industrial sector qualitative poll, 1986.

OCEI (1984), *Encuesta industrial* (Industrial poll).

317

OCEI (1981-84), *Principales indicadores de la industria manufacturera fabril* (The main indicators of manufacturing industries).

OCEI, *Venezuela: XI Censo general de población y vivienda 1985* (Venezuela: 1985 General population and housing census).

O.P.S.U. (1986), *Boletín estadístico No. 2* (Statistical bulletin No. 2), Caracas.

P.D.V.S.A., *Informe annual 1985* (1985 Annual report).

P.D.V.S.A. (1986), *Política de comercialización de la industria petrolera nacional - Folleto ENFOQUE 1986* (Commercialization policy of the national oil industry - ENFOQUE brochure).

P.D.V.S.A., *Situación financiera de la industria nacional a corto plazo 1983* (Short term financial state of the nation's industrial sector 1983).

Perez, Carlota (1980), *Pronóstico de ingreso fiscal petrolero de Venezuela 1980-2000. Análisis de cuatro alternativas* (Forecast of Venezuela's fiscal oil revenues for 1980-2000. analysis of four alternatives), Caracas.

Quintini, Cesar (1986), *Recursos humanos: estrategia para el desarrollo tecnológico* (Human resources: A strategy for technological development), 11th congress of engineering, architecture and related professions, Caracas.

Salas Capriles, Roberto (1983), *Educación-Industria (Experiencias, resultados y proyecciones). Fundación Educación e Industria. Consejo Venezolano de la Industria* (Education-industry - Experiences, outcomes and perspectives. Education & Industry Foundation. Venezuelan Industrial Council), Caracas.

Valecillos, Hector (1986), *Proceso y crisis de la inversión privada en Venezuela* (Process and crisis of private investment in Venezuela), Caracas.

World Bank (1984), Economic Memorandum on Venezuela, Washington.

Yanez B, Leopoldo (24-27 November 1986), *La economía venezolana: problemas y perspectivas* (Venezuela's economy: problems and perspectives), position paper presented at the Colloquium 'Venezuela hacia el año 2000, desafíos y opciones' (Venezuela by the year 2000 - Challenges and options), Caracas.